DICTATORS

Priya Narayanan is a designer, researcher, traveller and writer whose explorations are informed by a keen interest in philosophy, semantics, sociology, architectural psychology, art and design. An award-winning children's author, her poems and stories for older audiences have found home in various anthologies and literary journals. In a parallel universe, she is an interior architect straddling the professional and academic worlds of design with equal passion.

DICTATORS

THE WORLD'S MOST NOTORIOUS TYRANTS

PRIYA NARAYANAN

RUPA

Published by
Rupa Publications India Pvt. Ltd 2026
161-B/4, Gulmohar House,
Yusuf Sarai Community Centre,
New Delhi 110049

Sales centres:
Bengaluru Chennai
Hyderabad Kolkata Mumbai

P-ISBN: 978-93-5352-309-1
E-ISBN: 978-93-5352-836-2

First impression 2026

10 9 8 7 6 5 4 3 2 1

Printed in India

Contents

Introduction

One of the saddest lessons of history is this: If we've been bamboozled long enough, we tend to reject any evidence of the bamboozle. We're no longer interested in finding out the truth. The bamboozle has captured us. It's simply too painful to acknowledge, even to ourselves, that we've been taken. Once you give a charlatan power over you, you almost never get it back.

—Carl Sagan

Dictators is a topic that has been much exploited not only by biographers but also historians, journalists and researchers with interests in fields as varied as psychoanalysis, power, politics, economy, literature, art, food, fashion and sex-lives. The genres of these works have been varied too, with information about dictators being available in the form of biographies, hagiographies, academic research papers, newspaper articles, how-to handbooks and guides, satires and literary fiction, not to mention autobiographies by the men in question themselves.

With the Western media of our time having supplied the world with selective and many-a-times biased, stereotyped and over-sensationalized accounts of twentieth century dictators, and their actions, habits and mannerisms, there is also a proliferation of eyeball-grabbing tell-alls to be found. Not surprisingly, the task of finding a novel lens through which to scrutinize the lives of dictators was a daunting one. However, I did find one after reading tons of material about dictatorships in general and a selection of dictators in particular. This was the lens of ordinariness.

Ordinariness, dullness, perhaps even drabness...these were what typified the early lives of the eight dictators I have chosen to portray in this book: Joseph Stalin, Adolf Hitler, Ayatollah Khomeini, Francois Duvalier, Kim Il-sung, Nicolae Ceausescu, Pol Pot and Idi Amin. Hailing mostly from poor families with rural or small-town upbringings, they lived the most ordinary lives before stumbling upon power. They were also the most ordinary lookers, the most ordinary students and the most ordinary thinkers. The only exceptions, perhaps, were Khomeini, who was a scholar of Islam, and Idi Amin, whose height and build—not to mention colour—made people, especially the Western media, take note.

Despite this ordinariness, none of the dictators—save for Pol Pot, whose ordinariness was a cultivated one—wanted to be perceived as being ordinary. Indeed most of them went to extraordinary lengths to portray themselves as perfect humans and perfect leaders, not without some humorous outcomes. So while Duvalier often dressed up like Baron Samedi, the Voudou spirit of death, Kim Jong-il, Il-sung's son and heir to the dictatorship, let it be known to his people that he never had the need to defecate, the divine being that he was.

In being a politician who wanted it all for his wife, kids and extended family, Ceausescu was perhaps the most ordinary, yet he, as did several others, enjoyed bequeathing himself with extraordinary titles. And so, Ceausescu was the 'Genius of the Carpathians', Stalin, the 'Gardener of Human Happiness', Il-sung, the 'Heavenly One', and Duvalier, the 'Incorruptible Leader of the Great Majority of the Haitian People'.

Although the ordinariness of their upbringing was an

important part of their propaganda, deployed every now and then to emotionally connect with the masses, these dictators clearly loathed being ordinary. And even as they extolled themselves, they made good use of propaganda to condition the masses to perceive themselves as ordinary beings whose inadequacies and incompetency would be compensated for only by their extraordinary rulers. This feeling of indebtedness to the ruler, forced or otherwise, was important to the maintenance of many a dictatorship.

What was also ordinary—and here I use the word cynically to mean normalized—was the life of people under the rule of these dictators. Being under state surveillance was normal, news of torture and execution were normal, being sent to labour camps was normal, constantly looking over one's shoulder was normal, poverty and hunger were normal, being forced to participate in fake referendums was normal.

And while there was a normality to this terror, there was also an ominous ordinariness to those who perpetrated it, which prompted Jewish-German philosopher Hannah Arendt to write about the banality of evil. Recounting her experience at the 1961 trial of Nazi officer Otto Adolf Eichmann, one of the key organizers of the Holocaust, she wrote, 'I was struck by a manifest shallowness in the doer that made it impossible to trace the incontestable evil of his deeds to any deeper level of roots or motives.' In other words, Eichmann, the man credited with transporting tens of thousands of Jews to their deaths in extermination camps, was as ordinary a man as could be, with no monstrous looks or sinister behaviour to amplify his deeds. Being just another average student who job-hopped for a while before joining the Nazi Party on the advice of a family friend, there was also no root cause or deep reason—say hatred or vendetta—for his actions.

In his book *Modernity and the Holocaust,* Polish sociologist

Zygmunt Bauman makes a telling observation when he says that while a passionate mob might be able to kill a few hundred at most, one needs something much more lethal than passion to kill millions. This something, according to him, is a clinical bureaucracy where actors at all levels of the hierarchy have been picked and chosen carefully to execute, with obedience and indifference, the orders handed to them. In dictatorships, most people in the lower rungs of this hierarchy were ordinary men like Eichmann. Be they members of Duvalier's jeans and straw-hat clad Tonton Macoutes, Khomeini's Komiteh, Pol Pot's Khmer Rouge, Hitler's SA or Stalin's Red Army, it was the ordinary common man, lured, mesmerized, indoctrinated or radicalized, who became an instrument of intimidation and torture of fellow citizens.

Oversimplification, perhaps, is another manifestation of ordinariness in dictatorships. According to historian Jacob Burckhardt, 'The essence of tyranny is the denial of complexity.' Dictators have used several different strategies to deny this complexity of human life and living, forcing the ordinariness of uniformity and sameness down the throat of gullible masses. So while on the one hand you find Hitler and Duvalier simplifying the concept of nationalism to one race and one people, on another, you find Khomeini simplifying governance to Vilayate-e-faqih and a strict implementation of the Sharia (laws of God), and on yet another, you find Stalin, Il-sung and to an extent Ceausescu resorting to bureaucratization of the party to ensure that even terror was systematized. They were answerable not to the country but to a very small group of cronies or loyalists.

When Pol Pot forced professors, businessmen and engineers alike to shift to the villages, build their own huts and perform manual labour, when he banned all religion and obliterated racial classifications so that everyone in Cambodia was Kampuchean and spoke no language other than Kampuchean, his justification was the creation of an equal society. What he did though, was erase the vibrant and complex heritage of the entire nation in one clean sweep.

Finally, except for the dramatic suicide of Hitler and execution of Ceausescu, ordinariness also characterized the deaths of these dictators. They all lived well into their seventies and eighties and died of either old age or disease. Duvalier and Il-sung also managed to seamlessly pass the baton of their dictatorship to gen-next even as politicians of the Western world, who boast of being upholders of human rights, democracy and freedom, either aided and abetted or watched silently from the wings.

And so, in the coming pages, I have presented the lives of eight dictators whose ordinary early lives belie the ominousness of their extraordinary actions once they came into power. Irrespective of differences in their geographic locations and political ideologies, they systematically isolated their people from the rest of the world, censored communication internally and internationally, eliminated every last rival or dissident voice, sanctioned state-sponsored violence and intimidation at every opportunity, and repressed the masses without remorse.

When creating these mini-biographies of sorts, with equal focus on their lives before and after they became dictators, the recurring question plaguing me was, 'Why do the masses allow dictators to come into power?' An unsettling discovery has been that it was perhaps the ordinariness (and here I use the word to mean mediocrity) of these men that encouraged the masses to put their faith in them and vote them into power the first time.

Stalin's writings have been panned by scholars worldwide as being less than impressive, but he managed to connect with the masses like no intellectual could, not even Lenin. Ditto for Hitler to hear whose speeches, masses filled football stadia.

Khomeini captured the imagination of the masses and intellectuals alike as an ordinary Islamic scholar out to fight a debauched monarch, as did Ceausescu who donned the hat of an underdog daring to stand up to the Russians. Pol Pot, of course, fashioned himself to look like any other Kampuchean in black peasant clothing, red-and-white *krama* around the neck and car-tyre sandals on his feet, difficult to pick out from the rest of the masses. Il-sung posed for photographs with orphan children, positioning himself as a gentle father-figure, Idi Amin drank and joked with his subordinates and danced with the common man, and Duvalier endeared himself to the rural masses as an ordinary doctor on a mission to change their lives. And boy, did he change their lives!

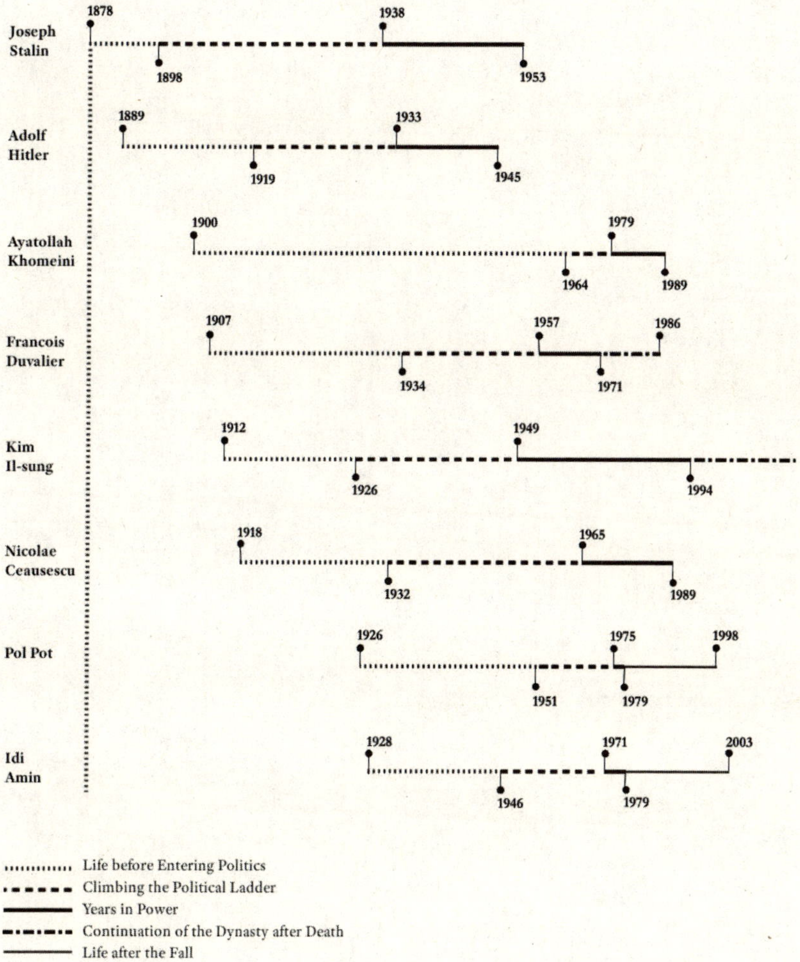
Joseph Stalin
1878
1898
1938
1953
Adolf Hitler
1889
1919
1933
1945
Ayatollah Khomeini
1900
1964
1979
1989
Francois Duvalier
1907
1934
1957
1971
1986
Kim Il-sung
1912
1926
1949
1994
Nicolae Ceausescu
1918
1932
1965
1989
Pol Pot
1926
1951
1975
1979
1998
Idi Amin
1928
1946
1971
1979
2003
Life before Entering Politics
Climbing the Political Ladder
Years in Power
Continuation of the Dynasty after Death
Life after the Fall

Joseph Stalin

Georgia became a part of the Russian Empire in the early nineteenth century, allegedly by the invitation of King George XII who sought protection against an imminent Persian invasion. A century later, following the overthrow of monarchy during the Russian Revolution, Georgia declared its independence in 1918. However, it was brought back into the fold of the United Soviet Socialist Republic (USSR) in 1922, when the Red Army captured Tbilisi (then Tiflis) in the aftermath of WWI. For the next 70 years, Georgia remained a key member of the USSR, even sending 700,000 of its soldiers to fight against Germany in WWII, only to once again declare independence just before the collapse of the USSR in 1991. Despite this historic dilly-dallying, Georgia's claim to fame or infamy, is perhaps that it was in this country, nearly 300 times smaller in area than its behemoth neighbour, that Russia's 'Man of Steel' was born.

In 862 CE, the warring tribes of Chuds, Merias, Ilmen Slavs, Veses and Krivichs inhabiting the cold subarctic East European plains invited the Varangian chieftain from eastern Scandinavia, Rurik, to establish order. Rurik obliged and arrived with his entourage to settle in Rus', the region between Lake Ilmen in the south and Lake Ladoga in the north. Following his death, his immediate descendent expanded the territory to Kiev along the Dnieper River in the south and established the state of Kievan Rus' that flourished under the Rurikid Dynasty until the invasion of Mongols in the thirteenth century. Soon, all the principalities the Rurikids had managed to unify during their four centuries of rule disintegrated, except for the Grand Duchy of Moscow. Despite being burnt down by the invaders, it regained importance owing to its proximity to the river Moskva, which allowed easy trade access to the Baltic Sea in the north and the Black Sea in the south.

With a string of powerful rulers at the helm, Moscow steadily grew through the years until it became the centre of political action in 1547 when its Grand Prince, Ivan IV (more popularly Ivan the Terrible), assumed the title of 'Tsar' and expanded the territories of the now rechristened Tsardom of Rus' or Russia towards the east and south. During the seventeenth century, Russia grew even larger under the Romanov Dynasty with the inclusion of Siberia, Crimea, large territories of modern-day Kazakhstan and Uzbekistan, several regions of Central Asia, parts of Chinese Manchuria, the Kuril Islands north of Japan, and Alaska.

The expansions came with substantial baggage for the Tsardom though. Protecting, administering and policing the vast territories demanded a management acumen that the Tsars lacked, leading to the birth of a feudal system where land was divided equally and handed over for governance to the nobility or landed gentry, in exchange for tributes in cash and kind. With agriculture being the mainstay of the economy, these nobles in turn employed farmers to till the land. However, with the land ultimately belonging to the state, the gentry lived in constant fear of their holdings being seized and transferred to someone else, lest they failed to serve the Tsardom well. This fear morphed the peasant-gentry relationship into one of slave and master, leading to the introduction of serfdom in the twelfth century that tied farmers to the land and made them a commodity that could be bought or sold along with the land they tilled.

Although serfdom existed in other areas as well, such as commerce, art and administration, the peasants were the worst affected, particularly after the introduction of the Charter to the Gentry in 1785 that exempted the gentry from compulsory service to the state and from paying taxes even as peasant serfs were forced to pay taxes, serve in the army, and perform any and every labour-intensive work demanded by the state. Further, the gentry now wielded extensive power over its serfs, with judicial authority to sentence them for most crimes and send them to penal servitude in Siberia if required.

When Russia transitioned into an imperial state in the eighteenth century, several emperors tried to abolish serfdom, but did not go the whole haul fearing backlash from the nobility. Then, Russia's defeat in the Crimean War of 1853–56 exposed the backwardness of its economy that had remained largely agrarian even as other European nations had embraced the industrial revolution. Perhaps sensing an opportunity to hit two birds with a single stone, Alexander II introduced the Emancipation Reform in 1861, freeing nearly 23 million serfs from their masters. However, the terms of their freedom forced peasants to choose between buying their land from the gentry (which most couldn't afford and were consequently sucked into debts) or abandoning their homes and migrating to cities in search of work. For the latter, Russia's plunge into industrialization only exacerbated their disillusionment. With cities ill-equipped to house the influx of migrant labour, they found themselves in ramshackle, unhygienic and freezing housing conditions with not much to eat. In the factories, they were forced to work long hours in bleak and dangerous conditions to meet the production goals of an expansionist monarchy.

The Emancipation Reform was thus instrumental in creating an as-yet non-existent working class or proletariat in Russia that was frustrated despite gaining the promised freedom. Amongst these was the family of a cobbler in Gori, a small town in the outskirts of Tiflis, Georgia.

Not a Seminarian

The son of peasant serfs, Besarion Jughashvili moved from rural Georgia to Tiflis after the reform to work at a shoe factory. Skilled, enterprising and fluent in Georgian, Russian, Armenian and Turkish, he moved to Gori in 1870 to set up his own shop where he made shoes for Russian soldiers stationed there. Soon after, he married 16-year-old Ekaterine Geladze, the deeply religious daughter of peasant serfs who too had moved to Gori after getting freed. Although Besarion's business flourished initially, it started to slow down when railway lines connecting Gori to Tiflis—and the ports of Poti and Baku—were laid, making it convenient for people to travel for shopping. Further, while these cities lured customers with their fancy shops and modern design sensibilities, Besarion, unable to adapt to modern tastes, continued making traditional footwear. With the Georgian custom of paying for goods in part with wine already having initiated him into drinking, the downturn in business pushed him into alcoholism. It did not help that the first two children born to him and Ekaterine died in infancy.

It was in these circumstances that the couple was blessed with another child, Ioseb (Joseph) Besarionis dze Jughashvili, on 6 December 1878. Although born weak and with a set of conjoined toes, Ioseb managed to survive infancy and grew up with his mother doting on him. When he turned five, Besarion left home to re-join the Tiflis shoe factory, hoping to improve the family's finances. Within a year, he ensured that his son too began apprenticing at the factory, much against Ekaterine's wishes. However, when Ioseb was stricken with smallpox at the age of seven, his mother took him back to Gori.

Nurturing him back to health, she admitted him to the local church school in the hope that he would grow up to become a priest at the seminary. The tug of war to decide Ioseb's future continued till he turned 11. That year, Ekaterine broke off with her husband and took charge of her own and her son's life. Working odd jobs at first, she found a place at a tailoring shop as a seamstress that she kept for the next 17 years.

Under his mother's care, Ioseb, or Soso as he was lovingly called, had a regular childhood albeit one filled with piety. In 1890, he joined the Gori Religious School where he learned religious subjects along with Georgian and Russian. Well-behaved, obedient and hard-working, he took part in prayer readings and sang in the church choir. He also performed well in exams, outshining his peers in Russian, catechism, penmanship, geography and liturgical chanting. Singing, in particular was something Ioseb both enjoyed and excelled at, with his teachers apparently referring to him as a *bulbuli* (nightingale). Outside school, Ioseb mingled with the multi-cultural crowd of boys, playing rough and cultivating friendships despite being bullied at times for his short stature and an arm that had been deformed in an accident.

During his last year at the Gori School, Ioseb frequented the reading room set up in town by a secret revolutionary group that stocked radical works by unknown authors alongside Russian and Georgian classics. He soon got sucked into the world of books that provided him an alternate view of the world.

In 1895, 15-year-old Ioseb earned a scholarship to study at the Theological Seminary in Tiflis. However, the regimental and monotonous routine at the seminary irked him, as did being under constant surveillance and the fear of being punished for every slip in conduct. The angst of Georgian students in particular was exacerbated by obvious attempts to Russify Georgian culture through language and literature. Not surprisingly, seeds of discontent and rebellion were sowed in the minds of students like Ioseb who took pride in their Georgian origin and histories. Much later, as leader of the USSR, he would tell his biographer that 'the humiliating and Jesuit methods' of the seminary were responsible for him becoming a revolutionary. In the same interview, he would ironically decry the Jesuit methods of snooping, spying, humiliating and 'prying into one's soul'—methods that he often used to his political advantage in later years.

With the seminary prohibiting the reading of secular literature, Ioseb initially found solace in writing poetry extolling Georgian nationalism and its peasants, endorsing the idea of service to the motherland. Five of these poems were published in leading Georgian newspapers under the pseudonym Soselo during his second year. However, a clamp down on Georgian language newspapers for alleged propaganda against Russian authority brought a premature end to his publishing journey. Despite the setback, the experience ensured that he would keep going back to writing as a tool to express his revolutionary ideas in the future. And in what was the first step towards that revolutionary future, Ioseb, in his third year, joined a group of seminarians that met secretly to read and discuss books forbidden by the Jesuits. Renting a small room outside the seminary, the group met every evening to read Victor Hugo, Lev Tolstoy, Charles Darwin, Ilia Chavchavadze, Akaki Tsereteli and Shota Rustaveli before moving on to Mikhail Tugan-Baranowskii, Szymon Diksztajn, Karl Marx and Friedrich Engels.

While Ioseb initially enjoyed reading and romanticizing Georgian literary heroes such as Koba, a peasant turned anti-Russian Robin Hood from Alexander Kazbegi's novel *The Patricide*, discussions around *The History of a Piece of Bread*, *The Russian Factory*, *The Communist Manifesto* and *The Development of Scientific Socialism* fired up his nascent radical ideas. Having become fascinated with Marxism, he lost interest first in religion and then in nationalism. Soon, he stopped attending religious classes, singing in the choir and romanticizing his Georgian heritage. While his peers watched him turn into a recluse, spending more and more time with books and hardly interested in play, his teachers were perplexed with the change that saw him being pulled up more often for misconduct and falling grades. Ioseb himself wasn't worried though. He had discovered his calling and, much to the disappointment of his mother, it was not that of a priest.

Not a Moderate

By the end of his third year at the seminary, the clandestine group discussions weren't enough to satiate Ioseb. So, at the age of 18, he engaged in grassroot propaganda for a covert group of social democrats. Listening to the discussions of the *mesame dasi*, the group's intellectual core, Ioseb was enchanted by the universal ideals of Marxism that revolved around humanity as represented by the working class, irrespective of religion, community and nationality. Soon after, he attended his first political meeting with railway workers. He was also assigned his own secret circle of six workers whom he met every Sunday to educate them on concepts of capitalism, the need for a labour movement and political struggle.

The deeper he delved into Marxist literature, the more defiant Ioseb became at the seminary. His acts of insubordination included laughing and talking during church service, arriving late for morning prayers and flaunting banned books in the classroom. As a result, he endured frequent surprise inspections at the dormitory, with punishments that ranged from being forced to burn his books to month-long confinement within the seminary grounds. Rather than causing him anxiety, the penalties made Ioseb rebel more and even question the authority of the seminary directors. Not surprisingly, he was amongst those expelled from the seminary in 1899 for participating in the secret reading groups.

Although Ioseb moved to Gori after the expulsion, the yearning for action brought him back to Tiflis where he rented a room with another expelled seminarian, Misha Davitashvili. With the help of friends, the duo got themselves jobs as meteorologists at the Tiflis Physical Observatory, which—despite being a low-paying job—allowed them to continue with propaganda activities. It was during this time that Ioseb formed a deep friendship with Vladimir Ketskhoveli, or simply, Lado, three years his senior at the Gori and Tiflis schools and who, like Ioseb, had been expelled from the seminary. The two like-minded friends would often talk into the night about their common misgivings with the moderate elements in the social democratic organization and Lado's plans of setting up an illegal printing press. For Ioseb, Lado was his first mentor and it was from him that he absorbed the ideas of radicalism.

His peasant serf ancestry, privileged education and radical Marxist leanings qualified Ioseb as what his future mentor, Vladimir Ilyich Ulyanov (more popularly Lenin), would call an *intelligent*—a person concerned with the fate of his people and the saving of Russia—as against the intelligentsia who were individualist in their quest to gain knowledge. Unaware of the label though, Ioseb, now a lean young man with long hair and a beard, took it upon himself to not only spread the social democratic ideology among peasants and workers but also educate the ignorant among his peers. However, just as he had dared to question the authority of the seminary directors, he now dared to question the strategies of those higher up in the hierarchy of social democrats.

Amongst those he was highly critical of was the man credited with being the 'father of Russian Marxism', Georgii Plekhanov. While Plekhanov called for exercising patience and moderation on the long road to socialism, Ioseb thought quite the opposite. Impatient to get on with the revolution, his defiant and rebellious nature drew him towards the radical wing of social democrats that believed not in legal and peaceful means to achieve their ends but in agitation, demonstrations and strikes. And so, at the turn of the century, he entered his twenty-second year with the conviction of a revolutionary.

Ioseb was not alone in seeking a radical approach for the impending revolution. With thousands of *intelligenty* like him emerging across the Russian Empire thanks to reading rooms and workers' circles, the young blood of the Marxist movement seemed to be gravitating towards agitation. And so, the period between 1899 and 1901 saw several strikes by workers' groups demanding higher wages, better working conditions and the removal of punitive work rules. The May Day strike in 1900 by horse-trolley-line workers in Tiflis, in particular, set the tone for things to come when the government that had initially arrested over 150 demonstrators eventually gave in to the workers' terms. The success of the strike sparked a series of others in printing presses, and leather, tobacco and textile factories. Some of them ended in victories, some did not.

The volatile atmosphere in Tiflis soon led to an increase in police crackdowns on workers and suspected social democrats. Following a search of his room at the observatory, Ioseb went into hiding in early 1901. Although he still conducted circle meetings and met covertly with his peers, his impatience with the moderates in the group was palpable.

It was around this time that Lenin printed his pamphlet *What is to be Done?* that propagated the idea of radical full-time revolutionaries who would not accommodate, negotiate or act in moderation but rather display an impatience for revolutionary action. The pamphlet also discussed the need for the creation of a Social Democratic Party comprising the intelligenty that would organize efforts to help the working class move away from piecemeal trade-unionism and generate in them a 'revolutionary consciousness'. Although the pamphlet hadn't yet reached Tiflis, its content was everything Ioseb would have rooted for. Much later, he would pen his own book *The Foundations of Leninism* that would expand upon Lenin's ideas and become the go-to book for aspiring communists. Now, however, his constant questioning and diatribes against the veteran moderates resulted in his expulsion from the Tiflis arm of the social democrats.

Not a Faint Heart

Ioseb saw in his ouster from Tiflis, the opportunity to move to a smaller centre—Batumi—where he could give wings to his vision. A port on the Black Sea, Batumi was a city of stark contrasts with its millionaire oil refinery owners inhabiting plush mansions, frequenting clubs and casinos while factory workers and their families lived bleak lives on streets that reeked with overflowing gutters. Moreover, if geography had rendered

Tiflis a small and remote province of the Russian Empire that the waves of Marxism had just about managed to wet, Batumi was even smaller, even more remote and had but a negligible presence of social democrats. To counter the local Marxists who viewed him as an unnecessary intellectual who knew nothing about the problems of the workers, Ioseb got himself a job at a refinery owned by the Rothschilds, and redefined himself as an intelligent worker who could both sympathize with the condition of the workers and guide them into revolution.

During his first few months at Batumi, Ioseb met covertly with representatives of workers from various factories to set up study circles and plan strikes, the latter reaping small victories initially. However, in his impatience to steer the revolution forward, he grossly misjudged the factory management's response to a strike in 1902, resulting in hundreds of workers being thrown behind bars and several others losing their lives. Ioseb wasn't perturbed by the outcome though. When fellow intelligenty blamed his erratic strategies for the lives lost, he retorted with 'you are not a revolutionary', and went on to explain how it was important for people to die for the revolution to gather momentum. After all, spilled blood only tightened emotional bonds and intensified feelings of vengeance that in turn fuelled revolutionary fervour.

Despite its failure, the strike had a domino effect on the political landscape of Batumi. Over the next two years, several workers would turn to political action, form their own Marxist committees, continue with protests and even attempt the assassination of a factory director. Now, however, Ioseb's role as the 'teacher' of the protestors made him a much sought after felon and in April 1902, betrayed by a disgruntled factory worker, he was arrested and imprisoned for the first time.

Ioseb initially tried every trick up his sleeve to get out of prison, be it getting his mother to write a pleading letter to the authorities regarding her failing health or trying to create a false alibi for himself for the day of the strike. However, he soon settled into prison routine and got back to what he did best—instigating political prisoners to protest. Much later, Stalin's propaganda would portray Ioseb as a dignified and disciplined prisoner who spent his time exercising, learning economics and German, and writing letters. What really transpired though was his transfer to the Kutaisi prison as punishment for organizing a protest during the inspection visit of the exarch of Georgia.

Although it had taken a betrayal to give Ioseb the first whiff of prison, his reputation as a radical revolutionary would see him in and out of prison for the next several years. Soon after completing his term at Kutaisi, Ioseb was tracked down by the Tiflis police and sentenced to three years of exile for his past involvement in underground activities in the city. In November 1903, having tried and failed to avoid exile by feigning tuberculosis, he found himself on a ship to the freezing, sub-zero climes of a village near Mount Kitkai in eastern Siberia. Ioseb had no intention of serving his time there though. Like many others before him, he managed to escape in early 1904 using a forged document, and persuaded a carter with vodka and money to take him to the nearest railroad.

Not a Pushover

During Ioseb's time in prison and exile, much had transpired in the Marxist world outside. Key among these was the arrival of Lenin's *What is to be Done?* in Russia in 1902, creating a flutter among the social democrats and polarizing its members. Soon, the Russian Social Democratic Labour Party (RSDLP) split into two factions: the Bolsheviks comprising the radicals led by Lenin and the Mensheviks comprising the moderates led by Lenin's former friend and ally, Iulii Martov. Even as debates raged and social democrats scrambled to choose ideological sides—Bolshevism or Menshevism—the choice was a no-brainer for Ioseb. In a letter to a friend, his idolization of Lenin was apparent in his reference to the Bolshevik leader as a 'mountain eagle'.

Upon his return to Georgia in 1904, Ioseb moved between Tiflis, Batumi and Kutaisi with caution, reviving old contacts and finding his way back into the revolution. In due time, he got elected to the Caucasian Union Committee that represented social democrats across the Caucasian regions of current-day Georgia, Azerbaijan and Armenia. To friends and revolutionary colleagues, he now became known as 'Koba' after his first literary idol from *The Patricide.*

Known for his passionate defence of Bolshevism, Koba was often chosen to present the case of faction across Caucasia. Travelling extensively during 1904–05, he established himself as a political intellectual who could quote not only Lenin but also Marx, Engles and Karl Kautsky. Selling Bolshevism was not easy though, especially after the first Russian Revolution of 1905 ended in a bloodbath, driving more people towards the moderate Mensheviks. Undeterred, he continued working to make himself an indispensable part of the Bolshevik faction by displaying an unparalleled passion for the revolution and deploying his unorthodox organizational skills to rally the Bolshevik cause. He also wrote perceptive articles decrying autocracy and defending Leninism in underground publications. With each piece he wrote, Koba got surer and bolder with the ideas he put forward to his audience. His inimitably forthright and defiant style of writing earned him both staunch admirers and bitter detractors. His violent call of 'blood for blood and death for death' in a pamphlet, for instance, was interpreted variously as being uncouth as well as self-assured.

In December 1905, as the revolution raged on, Koba

met Lenin for the first time at the Finland conference of representatives of Bolshevik organizations. Three distinct emotions defined this first meeting between the star-struck follower and his mentor—disappointment, awe and anger. Having expected to meet a tall man with a formidable personality, Koba was disappointed to find a short, stocky and prematurely balding Lenin who he later described as 'the most ordinary man, in no way different from ordinary mortals'. He was also disappointed that instead of making a celebrity entrance to the conference, Lenin was dot on time and mingled with representatives like 'any ordinary delegate'. When Lenin started his speech though, Koba was captivated by his ideas and the force of his logic. At the same time, never afraid of insubordination, his idolizing of Lenin did not stop him from questioning the Bolshevik leader's decisions. Consequently, their first meeting ended with a confrontation regarding the nature of elections to the Imperial Duma (lower house of the Russian Parliament), a confrontation in which Lenin yielded to the opinion of the majority put forth by his future protégé.

With time—although Koba would come to be known within the party as the 'Caucasian Lenin'—his interpretation of the culture of violent autocratic totalitarianism propagated by Leninism would not only become more flexible than that of his mentor's but also more unsavoury.

In 1906, Koba courted and married Yekaterina Svanidze, a seamstress and sister of fellow Bolshevik, Aleksandre Svanidze. The couple soon had a son Yakov. However, engulfed by the revolution, Koba did not have time for his new family. Two months after Yakov's birth in March 1907, he was back to representing the Caucasian Bolsheviks at the London Congress of the RSDLP. Later that year, in a move that seemed to be a conscious decision to leave the regional politics of his native Georgia and plunge into the mainstream of national politics, he shifted base to Baku, the key oil-producing centre of the empire. This new phase in the life of the now 30-year-old revolutionary was however marked by the death of Yekaterina, who succumbed to a sudden illness while she struggled alone to raise her new-born. The loss of his wife affected Koba deeply. Handing over his infant son to Yekaterina's mother for care, he returned to Baku and cocooned himself for months as he grieved, telling a friend that his 'last warm feelings for people' had died with his beloved wife.

It was only in March 1908 that Koba returned to active politics. Although he kept a low profile, he found himself in and out of prisons until, in October 1910, he was exiled to Siberia for 10 months despite feigning tuberculosis by trying to pass off phlegm from a genuine patient as his own. After completing his term, he left the Caucasus for good, moving to the hotbeds of the revolution in Moscow and Petrograd (modern-day St. Petersburg). Constantly under police surveillance, he worked underground for the next two years, setting up Bolshevik newspapers, writing articles and travelling abroad in disguise to meet with Lenin and other exiled colleagues.

Although he had had many ideological run-ins with his mentor during these meetings, with his brand of Leninism being more Leninist than Lenin's himself, the latter was astute enough to recognize the power of Koba's rhetoric—some arguments in his works such as *Notes of a Delegate* and *Letters from the Caucasus* impressing the moderate veteran Plekhanov himself. Koba was precisely the kind of party worker Lenin required as he contemplated the creation of a separate political party devoid of the Mensheviks. Consequently, Koba was elevated to the Central Committee of the Bolshevik Party in 1912, a membership he would retain until his death in 1953. He was also put in charge of *Pravda* (*Truth*), a newly established legal daily newspaper of the Bolsheviks. It was during his time writing for this paper that he adopted the pseudonym 'Stalin' or 'man of steel' that would define him for the rest of his life and after.

Not a Pacifist

Stalin's elevation to the Central Committee came at a time when the Russian Empire was coming down hard on revolutionaries following the assassination of Prime Minister Pyotr Stolypin. The Marxist underground was infiltrated by police spies, making it difficult to separate them from party workers. In February 1913, as soon as Stalin returned to Petrograd from Vienna where he had spent time deliberating on and writing one of his most important theoretical works, *Marxism and the National Question,* he was arrested and exiled, betrayed by Roman Malinovsky, a police spy within the party. However, with Malinovsky having been a close aide of Lenin's since years, no one in the party suspected him. Instead, he was made the party's only point of contact with Stalin during the first of the latter's three years of exile in Siberia.

This misplaced trust cost Stalin heavily. In early 1914, Malinovsky's tip off helped the police intercept the 100 roubles the Central Committee had sent to help him escape. As punishment, he was exiled to the harsher climes of Kureika, 20 kilometres to the north of the Arctic Circle. Even from this remote location, he continued corresponding with Malinovsky, addressing the latter as 'my friend' in letters where he described his deteriorating health and the horrible circumstances of his exile alongside political discussions. It was only when, unable to carry on as a double agent, Malinovsky resigned from his party post in April 1914 and left the country, did his treason become apparent. The defection of someone he had deeply trusted left an emotional scar on Stalin that made him chronically suspicious, a trait that would only grow exponentially with time.

The same year, Tsar Nicholas II dragged Russia into WWI. Even as Lenin used his political acumen to turn an imperialist war between nations into a class-based civil war for national liberation, all Stalin could do was cool his heels in exile. In 1917, the frustration of the Russian masses with inflation, breakdown of transportation and food shortages led to the February revolution and the subsequent abdication of the Tsar.

When Stalin, now on the cusp of his fortieth year, was finally released from exile, he returned to his role on the editorial board of the *Pravda* in Petrograd and was soon appointed member of the party's Russian Bureau of the Central Committee. With the Provisional Government formed after the fall of the monarchy largely seen as representing only the bourgeoisie, his articles and speeches called for an armed struggle by the worker's councils or 'soviets' across the erstwhile Empire to establish a government that represented the proletariat. In a testament to his growing influence in the organization, the Bureau soon ratified the formation of the revolutionary Red Guards or Red Army comprising volunteer factory workers supported by the armed military division of the Cheka (Bolshevik secret police).

In April 1917, Lenin returned to Petrograd from his decades-long exile to take charge of the final leg of the revolution. Impressed with Stalin's dedication and loyalty, he supported his candidacy for the Central Committee elections where, in what was perhaps a sign of things to come, Stalin managed to gather 97 votes despite several detractors, just a few votes short of Lenin's 104. Although no one paid heed to the gradual rise of the short, stocky radical with a pockmarked face and deformed arm then, it would only be a matter of time before he would assert a complete domination of the party, something even Lenin could not achieve despite his stature and long-standing goodwill as leader of the Bolsheviks.

With his mentor engaged in spurring an ideological

polarization within the party, Stalin took to writing for the *Soldatskaia Pravda* (*Soldiers' Truth*), a publication targeting over 200,000 soldiers of the Petrograd garrison whose support was deemed vital for a future armed struggle. Despite being branded as lacklustre, his writings managed to connect with the layman. Between then and October, he would write nearly 70 articles with provocative titles, such as 'The Truth about Our Defeat at the Front', 'The Conspiracy Continues', 'A Government of Bourgeois Dictatorship' and 'Who Is Torpedoing the Constituent Assembly?', and give several speeches to defend and propagate Leninism. Reflecting that the revolution could not satisfy everyone, Stalin reiterated the need to support the soviets at all costs saying, 'It would be a reactionary utopia to hold back this beneficial process of purging the revolution from unneeded elements...he who tries to stand still during the revolution will inevitably fall behind and he who falls behind will find no mercy.' Although not taken seriously then, the statement offered a rare peek into the extremist nature of his thoughts that would manifest in disturbing ways two decades down the line.

With several of his senior colleagues—including Lenin and Menshevik-turned Bolshevik Leon Trotsky—either in hiding or in prison, Stalin became the de facto leader of the party between July and October 1917. During this time, he worked tirelessly to help achieve Lenin's vision for a Bolshevik coup d'état to topple the Provisional Government and assume power at the centre through what is now famously known as the October Revolution. In the months that followed, a series of shrewd political manoeuvres executed by Lenin ensured that the new government would be a Bolshevik-led one, despite the party polling a meagre 24 per cent in the elections to the Constituent Assembly.

By early 1918, Lenin abandoned his revolutionary slogan of 'power to the soviets' and steered Russia into an oligarchy-based Bolshevik dictatorship where power was concentrated in the hands of an elite few who constituted the Council of Peoples' Commissars. Recognizing the need of the hour to keep non-Russian ethnic territories of the erstwhile Russian Empire under Bolshevik control, Stalin—given his years of experience working in Caucasia—was appointed 'People's Commissar for Nationalities' Affairs'.

Not an Ideal Protégé

Soon after, Lenin initiated the process of religious subversion in line with communist thinking even as non-Bolshevik publications were shut down and rival political parties outlawed. However, the irate Socialist Revolutionaries who were denied power despite polling 42 per cent votes in the elections, allied with the Mensheviks, monarchists, intellectuals and militarists to form the counter-revolutionary White Guards to challenge the government. Soon Russia descended into a bloody Civil War that pitted the Bolshevik Red Army against the White Guards.

In June 1918, the White Guards sabotaged railway lines across southern Russia's grain belt, triggering a country-wide food shortage. With the Red Army failing to contain the crisis, Stalin was dispatched to Tsaritsyn (the future Stalingrad) to restore order. Though instrumental in creating the Red Army, Stalin had grown to detest it when, under the reins of arch-rival Trotsky, his guerrilla army of peasants and workers was replaced with former Tsarist military officers. For him, the officers were mere 'pen-pushing specialists' and not true revolutionaries. Now, his first act as he consolidated control of the region's military operations was to dismiss the veteran commanders and reinstate his guerrilla fighters. However, the latter's lack of experience against a regular army worsened an already dire situation. When there were nothing but set-backs to show even after two months, Stalin manufactured the idea of a 'plot against the revolution' from within the party to save face and avoid blame. What followed was a mass purge of everyone deemed suspicious, with the Cheka executing over a 100 tsarist officials, businessmen and army men without trial.

Years later, an insider would reveal that while Stalin was complicit in these killings, the permission to purge all towns surrounding Tsaritsyn of 'counter-revolutionary elements' had come from Lenin himself. Clearly, the front runners of the Communist Party had developed a taste for blood in the name of 'saving the revolution', giving birth to the infamous Red Terror that prevailed through the Civil War. More importantly, the Tsaritsyn incident brought to the fore the impatience for radical action that Stalin had displayed in his youth—random arrests and executions of those plotting against the revolution would become his go-to response when confronted with difficult situations.

In 1919, Stalin married Nadezhda Alliluyeva, the 18-year-old daughter of a fellow revolutionary, whom he had known since she was a child. Soon after, he was elected to the five-member Politburo, the highest decision-making body of the Communist Party, and appointed political commissar to the Red Army and 'Commissar for State Control'. Then, in 1920–21, he was put in charge of the south-western command in the war against Poland that was seen as an extension to the Russian Civil War. If Poland was won, it would pave the way for the spread of the revolution into Germany and the rest of Western Europe. Although Stalin's campaigns started with wins, his decision to spread the Red Army thin to cover multiple bases at once, springing no doubt from overconfidence as was expressed in a letter rejecting Lenin's idea of signing a truce with the Polish army, resulted in a disastrous outcome. Not only was the war lost, it also led to Poland imposing humiliating peace terms on the Communist Party. As had become his style, Stalin placed the blame for the debacle on Trotsky and the military leadership's lack of 'effective fighting reserves'.

It was around this time that Nadezhda gave birth to the couple's first child, Vasily. As before, Stalin had no time for family, what with Russia being at the brink of a historic revolution.

In 1922, the Civil War finally ended with a Bolshevik victory when the Red Army entered Transcaucasia, Ukraine and the Byelorussian Republic and helped local communists take power through the soviets. In this moment of triumph though, Stalin found himself at odds with Lenin once again. While he wanted to merge the Republics of these and other smaller ethnic territories into the Russian Federative Socialist Soviet Republic (SFSR) with a centralized government, common legislation and limited autonomy, Lenin proposed a union of independent Soviet Republics that would unite with Russia on equal rights. Despite most party officials supporting Stalin, both in Russia and the ethnic territories, it was the veteran Bolshevik leader who prevailed, leading to the formation of the United Soviet Socialist Republics (USSR). It was a snub Stalin would not forget.

The years 1922–24 saw the implementation of Bolshevik ideals across sectors in the USSR, not only to change the economic and political landscape of the Republics but also to create a 'New Soviet Man'. With religion already having been made redundant, sweeping changes were implemented in the educational system—schools and universities were nationalized, access to higher education was made easy for all who desired to study, and subjects deemed subversive were replaced with those that promoted ideological indoctrination. To suppress political dissent, newspapers and publications considered hostile were shut down and strict censorship was instituted over both printed materials and performing arts. As a temporary measure to tide over the impact of WWI and the Civil War, Lenin also moved away from socialist principles to introduce a more liberal New Economic Policy (NEP) that reintroduced money and private ownership of small enterprises, both of which were banned during the wars.

Even as the masses struggled to adjust to the new socio-political and economic realities, Stalin found himself at the centre of constant conflicts within the Politburo, with his mentor not only questioning but also opposing his actions even when unwarranted. An alleged reason was Lenin's insecurity with the growing popularity of his protégé. This, however, did not stop Stalin, an adept organizer, from getting elected as the general secretary of the Central Committee. The new position gave him complete control over all appointments within the party and, realizing that he could control the party if he controlled the cadres, he soon ensured that everyone who mattered in the administration owed their position of power to him.

By mid-1923, when Lenin was left paralysed and unable to speak after a series of strokes, Stalin had created a strong political clique that would support him no matter what, so much so that he even controlled who could or could not meet the ailing leader. Consequently, when his mentor turned on him in his last year, writing a political testimony doubting Stalin's efficiency as general secretary and calling for his removal from the post, Stalin was able to discredit and supress the document to his advantage. With Lenin virtually under house arrest, Stalin formed an alliance with fellow Politburo members Lev Kamenev of the Russian SFSR and Grigory Zinoviev of the Ukrainian SSR to keep Trotsky from usurping the top post when the time came. So, when his now-estranged mentor died in early 1924, his path to the helm of the Russian Communist Party was nearer and clearer.

Not a Team Player

In 1924, the Soviet Politburo comprised largely gifted Marxist ideologues. However, while most of them were primarily men of theory, Stalin was a man of action. This meant that he could twist theory to his advantage when required, a trait that had served him well until now. After Lenin's death, Stalin used the same trait to manipulate circumstances when he agreed to the formation of the *troika* with Kamenev and Zinoviev. However, he had no intention of going through the inconvenient arrangement of collective rule that was, in fact, only a stepping stone towards an eventual power grab. And so, the next few years bore witness to Stalin's deft political manoeuvres as he presented himself as a loyal and committed member of the troika even while he plotted against it. In 1925, to the surprise of his colleagues and rivals alike, he effected a Machiavellian break in the troika by questioning the integrity of Kamenev and Zinoviev over a minor issue and citing the 'impossibility of an honest and sincere political collaboration with these comrades'. Soon after, he joined rivals Nikolay Bukharin and Aleksey Rykov to form a new coalition.

A year later, even as Nadezhda gave birth to their daughter Svetlana, Stalin used the Cheka, now disbanded and regrouped under the Joint State Political Directorate (OGPU), to fabricate evidence against his rivals of aligning with capitalist nations and acting as 'enemies of the people'. Of those arrested, a lucky few were exiled while others were summarily executed. A desperate Trotsky tried everything in his power to prevent Stalin's takeover of the party; but his nemesis brought down the entire strength of his loyalists in the administration to ensure his expulsion from the Politburo along with Kamenev and Zinoviev on charges of creating an illegal, anti-party 'Left Opposition'.

If Stalin's self-assuredness increased with the success of each of his political manoeuvres, so did his thirst for the blood of his rivals. He soon became accustomed to ordering the execution of those against him at the drop of a hat. In June 1927, for instance, he used the murder of the Soviet ambassador to Poland to recommend ruthless purges across the USSR. In a letter to the Politburo, he urged that they should 'immediately shoot five or ten monarchists and announce that with every assassination attempt, new groups of monarchists will be shot'. He went on to suggest that the OGPU be directed to conduct house-to-house searches for monarchists and counter-revolutionists so as to 'completely liquidate them'.

The same year, Stalin's manipulation of the Central Committee ensured that Trotsky was thrown out of the party and banished from the USSR. In 1940, Trotsky—living in Mexico City—would be assassinated with an ice pick on Stalin's orders. In a show of deep animosity towards his arch-rival, Stalin would confer the Order of Lenin and the Gold Star on the assassin, Ramon Mercader.

Having crushed his key opposition within the party, Stalin made a show of submission to Lenin's last testament when, at a plenary session in December 1927, he offered to step down from his position as general secretary now that the 'tough job' of weeding out the opposition was done. The Central Committee, which by now largely consisted of Stalin's staunch loyalists, interpreted his pretence as magnanimity and rejected the resignation, not only diminishing the importance of Lenin's opinion but also providing Stalin with enough affirmation of his own influence over the party to go the extra mile and dream of dominating the Politburo. His ambition was given a shot in its arm when Bukharin secretly met with Kamenev to discuss issues plaguing the Politburo in 1928. Although Bukharin wasn't a rival or threat, Stalin seized the opportunity to discredit his dumbfounded colleague. Similar attempts were made to sabotage

Rykov's credibility and by 1929 the duo was expelled from the Politburo for creating a 'Right Opposition' within the party.

Not an Economist

After consolidating his leadership of the party, Stalin dismantled the NEP and introduced the Great Leap policy, a Five-Year Plan to thrust the USSR into rapid socialist industrialization. Declaring that 'We are fifty to a hundred years behind the advanced countries... We must make good this distance in ten years', he set an unrealistic goal of a 300 per cent increase in industrial production in as little time as possible. Propaganda posters soon appeared with slogans such as 'We Smite the Lazy Workers', 'The Five-Year Plan in Four Years', '5-in-4', and '2+3=4'. To achieve these targets, workers were made to toil in gruelling shifts without breaks and were punished with arrest or exile for production shortfalls.

If this 'revolution from above' was hard on industrial workers, it came at a much greater cost to peasants who were virtually sent spiralling back to the days of serfdom. Soon, traditional strip-farming was abandoned in favour of the more efficient mechanized farming over large collectivized tracts of land.

Although radio announcements, rallies and posters constantly drummed up the role of collectivization in building socialism, the peasants were a difficult lot to motivate, with them having little to profit from this new system. Moreover, while mechanization in itself was a boon, its arbitrary implementation by inexperienced bureaucrats magnified the problems of peasants who were made scapegoats for shortages in productivity. Soon, the focus of collectivization shifted from creating well-structured, largescale largescale agrarian enterprises to hounding peasants who were allegedly 'out to sabotage socialist construction'.

Top on the list of Stalin's suspected saboteurs were the *kulaks*, or peasants owning more than eight acres of land who had prospered under the NEP. Accusing them of hoarding grain, he called for the decimation of their entire class. Although the party itself was willing to be lenient, giving the kulaks a chance to allow the peaceful takeover of their lands and livestock, Stalin insisted that they be either exiled, sent to *gulags* (forced labour camps), imprisoned or executed. To further demoralize the kulaks, their churches were shut down and desecrated, clergy arrested, and women threatened with rape if they did not give up their lands. The result was the deportation of over two million kulak households in 1930–32, with inexperienced city-workers being brought in to fill the yawning gap created in farm labour.

Stalin's demand for a hasty transition from an agrarian to industrial economy 'come what may' created devastating circumstances that led to the Great Famine of 1932–33. Even as peasants across the USSR starved, which in turn weakened them enough to impact production, Stalin refused to backtrack on his collectivization and *dekulakization* drives. Instead, in his now habitual tactic of shifting blame away from himself, he announced to the country that the peasants had 'declared war against the Soviet government'. With him ignoring suggestions to stop forced confiscation of grains and cease exports, the peak of the famine saw over 70 million Soviet citizens officially starve while several thousand others ate less than half their regular intake.

While an immediate fallout of the situation was an increase in crime, with people trying to steal and hoard food to keep themselves alive, the years that followed saw an unnatural number of deaths due to malnutrition, starvation and disease. The worst impacted were the peasants of Ukraine and North Caucasus, the two regions that usually produced more than half the grain required by the Soviet population. When productivity in these regions fell by 40 per cent owing to collectivization, Stalin suspected the peasants of plotting with foreign powers, especially Poland, to bring 'death by starvation' to the USSR.

To cover up the devastation wreaked by the famine, Stalin instituted a decree in 1932 under which artists were ordered to develop didactic artwork that portrayed a rosy picture of the socialist society and glorified party objectives. Soon, book covers, hoardings, paintings and posters depicted seas of smiling workers and collective farmers, happily participating in hard work and communal efforts.

The Last Man Standing

In late 1932, Nadezhda shot herself in the heart after a fallout with Stalin. The extreme step was not unexpected considering her frustration with his constant absence from family life, opposition to his extreme politics and their fights over his alleged affairs. Despite being devastated, Stalin ensured that neither his children nor the masses knew of the true circumstances of her death, with the official announcement attributing it to appendicitis. At the same time, he did not allow the event to impact his political exploits. In fact, it took the twin threats of the Japanese invasion of Manchuria and the Nazis coming to power in Germany in 1933 to shake him out of his destructive anti-peasant stance. Realizing that the famine had weakened the nation and made its defences vulnerable, he introduced much-needed measures to reverse the impact of his erratic Five-Year Plan. He grudgingly brought back the NEP, slowed down industrialization and abandoned the barter economy in favour of a cash economy.

In 1935, Stalin approved the Politburo's suggestion to allow voting through secret ballot and opened up voting rights to those previously labelled aliens within the Soviet Union. In an attempt to improve foreign relations, he also signed a pact for mutual assistance with France and Czechoslovakia. As the USSR tottered back to normalcy, with agricultural production and urban lifestyle vastly improving in 1935–36, Stalin famously declared to the nation that, 'Life has become better, life has become more cheerful!' Soon paintings titled 'Thank you beloved Stalin for our happy childhood!' and 'The captain of the land of the Soviets steers us from victory to victory!' started making appearances across the USSR.

The liberal honeymoon, however, did not last long. Using the December 1934 murder of Sergei Kirov, a close associate, and the unearthing of a 1935 plot to assassinate Stalin by Kremlin staff as pretexts to investigate anti-party elements, he slowly eased back into 'executioner' mode. While planted evidence led to the incrimination and execution of rivals Kamenev, Zinoviev, and 14 other prominent party officials in the former case, Stalin did not show mercy even to his old friend Avel Yenukidze who had been accused for the latter. During 1935–38, the USSR was plunged into what is famously known as the Great Terror or Great Purge, with hundreds of thousands of people being executed without trial for charges as varied as espionage, treason, sabotage and terrorism. While these included known names such as former colleagues Bukharin and Rykov, hundreds of lesser known party workers and army officers also lost their lives after spuriously conducted show trials. By the end of the Terror, 93 of the 139 members of the Central Committee had been killed as had 81 of the 100 odd army generals and admirals.

While the purges had initially remained within the party, their scope soon widened to include intellectuals, writers, clergy, musicians, actors, jurists, teachers, peasants, ordinary workers and even homemakers. People belonging to minority ethnicities such as Poles, Chinese, Bulgarians, Germans, Latvians, Estonians, Romanians, Finns, Iranians and Afghans were also targeted for executions and deportations, what with them being viewed as easy recruits against the communist leadership by hostile foreign powers. At the peak of the Terror in 1937–38, nearly 1,500 'enemies of the Soviet' were allegedly executed every day, taking the overall toll at the end of 1938 to over 700,000 summary executions and over three million deportations to gulags. As WWII loomed in 1939, Stalin suspected the counter-revolutionaries of trying to use the opportunity to start another Civil War, just as the Bolsheviks had during WWI. Consequently, he sought them out and had them executed.

The sheer scale of the executions prompted many in the Western world to speculate that Stalin had literally gone insane during the time, in all probability owing to extreme paranoia following the bid on his life. What was troubling, however, was that, perhaps fearing for their own lives, no one within the party ranks made an effort to question or oppose the mass murders, and none of the US or British journalists in Moscow sent detailed reports of the executions back home for the world to know. By the end of 1938, there was no opposition to Stalin within or outside the party. After having eliminated every person even remotely capable of thinking independently, including five of his Politburo colleagues, Stalin found himself, much as per his plans, the last man standing.

The *Vozhd*

With Europe at the cusp of WWII in 1939, Stalin signed a non-aggression pact with Adolf Hitler of Nazi Germany that allowed both parties to divide Polish territories between themselves and leave each other alone. Although the shocking deal earned him widespread international criticism and prompted British prime minister Winston Churchill to remark famously that Russia was 'a riddle, wrapped in a mystery, inside an enigma', Stalin valued the assurance of relative peace following the pact that gave him time to consolidate his position within the USSR. Well aware of the disrepute his purges had brought him, he turned to his trusted propaganda machinery to correct the situation.

During 1934–38, Stalin had appointed himself 'Commissar of Cultural Enlightenment' to oversee every aspect of state propaganda and had decreed that all works of art and literature had to portray what he called 'socialist realism'. According to this new concept, 'basic human truth' extracted from folklore and myth was to be combined with socialist ideals to create a new reality for the audience, facilitating the 'ideological remaking and education of working people in the spirit of socialism'. While at different times he had used propaganda to either motivate peasants and workers to increase productivity, induce communist pride amongst the masses or incite terror in them, he now used it, in 1939, to gloss over his alleged indiscretions, justify the purges and glorify himself as a true leader.

The same year, the Stalin Prize was instituted to commemorate his sixtieth birthday, with awards given out to outstanding works of socialist art and literature, most of which were flattering depictions of Stalin. Also published the same year was the 16-page publication, *In commemorating the sixtieth anniversary of J.V. Stalin: what to write about the life and activities of Comrade Stalin*, intended to help writers with birthday greetings to their leader. With industrial economy having bounced back by now, posters depicting the USSR as a socialist utopia also appeared across the Soviet Union, as did slogans and posters to induce patriotism in the background of WWII.

With propaganda taking care of crafting a people-friendly personality for their one and only leader, Stalin's next step was to create a bureaucratic hierarchy to manage the running of the USSR, with each step of the pyramid taking orders directly from him. Having eliminated most veteran Bolsheviks and immediate party colleagues, he now turned to younger figures such as Andrei Zhdanov and Nikita Khrushchev to occupy the now defanged Politburo. At the same time, he created a parallel power centre called 'the Five' comprising of himself and four loyalists including Vyacheslav Molotov, Kliment Voroshilov, Anastas Mikoyan and Lazar Kaganovich to monitor the workings of the party. Be it the Politburo or 'the Five', Stalin was the only one authorized to take decisions.

It was around this time that Khrushchev introduced the term *vozhd* or 'leader' to address Stalin, a term that stuck with the latter till the very end. Then, at the 18th Party Congress in May 1941, he was declared both the general secretary of the Central Committee of the Communist Party and chairman of the Council of People's Commissars of the USSR, signalling the official transition of the Soviet Union from oligarchy to dictatorship.

Having finally become the undisputed leader of the USSR, the vozhd turned his attention to WWII. Or rather, he was forced to. Until mid-1941, he had strongly believed that Hitler would honour the 1939 pact. But now, on 22 June 1941, there was no doubting his sources—Hitler, with his three-pronged attack on the Soviet Union under the codename Operation Barbarossa, had indeed breeched the pact, taking the grossly underprepared Red Army by surprise. Stalin's first reaction was one of shock and disbelief. Instead of tackling the situation head on, he withdrew into a cocoon of silence to emerge from which it took the dogged persuasion of 'the Five'.

Once back in office though, Stalin lost no time in looking for a scapegoat to pin his misjudgement on. He found one in the commander of the Western Front, General Dmitry Pavlov, who was soon tried and executed. Then, even as he ordered a large-scale evacuation of people and material from the frontline, he appointed himself 'People's Commissar for Defence' as well as 'Supreme Commander in Chief' and took charge of the war. However, with no past experience in the field, his orders were impulsive and erratic, causing the Red Army to fumble around at the front without a robust strategy to thwart the advancing enemy.

To add to the army's woes, the initial failures on the battlefield fed Stalin's paranoia, causing him to suspect someone 'on the inside' of aiding and paving the way for Hitler's forces. The next few months saw over 10,000 soldiers of the Red Army being executed on suspicion of treason. When German troops entered Kiev in Ukraine, he pronounced that surrendering the city would be construed as 'criminal, bordering on outright treason against the Motherland'. Further, declaring it a crime to be taken prisoner by the enemy, he issued a decree that those taken prisoner were to be killed by any means and their families arrested and deprived of government pensions. In line with the decree, he had the wife of his eldest son Yakov arrested when the latter was taken prisoner by the Germans in the early days of the war. Although Stalin subsequently arranged for her release, he is not known to have made any attempt to get back Yakov, who later died in a Nazi camp.

With the Germans making striking progress into Soviet territory during the first few months, Stalin recognized his shortcomings in the war department and soon corrected course by appointing fiercely capable commanders to steer military operations. He also abandoned the communist ideology of atheism in favour of a religious and patriotic one to motivate both the troops and masses. Propaganda was designed to focus on protecting 'mother Russia', creating heroes out of slayed army commanders and painting the Germans as villains. Despite the

Red Army's best efforts though, both Ukraine and Belarus were lost to the Germans, and by September that year Leningrad had been surrounded by the enemy. What followed was the Leningrad Blockade that would continue for 872 devastating days, with shelling, hunger and disease claiming nearly a million civilian and military lives.

Now though, Stalin was determined to defend Moscow on which Hitler had set his sights. Bringing together all possible military resources, he ordered the Red Army to launch a counteroffensive rather than continue with the defensive stance they had taken thus far. His risk paid off, frustrating the German army and forcing it to retreat in early 1942. Even as Soviet troops rejoiced their first big victory, a reinvigorated Stalin proclaimed, 'In just a few months, just a half year, perhaps a year, Hitler's Germany will collapse under the weight of its own crimes.'

It is not known whether Stalin's prediction was a result of his understanding of the way the war was headed or a random declaration to keep up the spirits of the troops. Nevertheless, the Germans did find their Russian nemesis in the Battle of Stalingrad the very next year. In February 1943, the Red Army trounced the Nazis, inflicting hundreds of thousands of fatalities and taking over 90,000 prisoners of war. It seemed befitting that Stalin had managed to defend his namesake city and if anyone had doubted it before, the victory sealed his position as the vozhd. He was soon being celebrated as 'the organizer of victories' and 'a great commander' and was promoted to 'Marshal of the Soviet Union'.

Although the war was far from over, the defence of Stalingrad raised the morale of the Soviet Union and gave Stalin more heft in his dealings with his British and US colleagues—Winston Churchill and Theodore Roosevelt—who had treated him as a minor ally until then. Consequently, he became part of the 'Big Three' that met thrice over the next two years—at

Tehran, Yalta and Potsdam—to decide the course of the war. In each instance, Stalin managed to eke out a favourable bargain for the USSR. Key amongst these was the right of the Soviet Union to retain its sphere of influence on all countries of Eastern Europe the Red Army had helped liberate from the German-led Axis powers, including Latvia, Lithuania and Estonia.

Even as he struck the right chords with his allies, Stalin's paranoia surfaced once again when his aircraft faced turbulence when flying from Baku to Tehran for the November 1943 conference. It was the first and last flight he ever took. His growing importance in the international scheme of things was made apparent when both Churchill and Roosevelt went out of the way to accommodate his fear of flying, with Churchill flying into Moscow for a 1944 meeting and an ailing Roosevelt making an arduous journey to reach Yalta in Crimea in 1945, which was only a short train-ride away for Stalin.

The 'Brilliant Genius of Humanity'

By the end of WWII in 1945, Stalin had become a hero. While his efforts made USSR an international superpower with a permanent seat in the United Nations Security Council, he was promoted to *generalissimo*, the highest military rank one could hold in the Red Army back home. Soon, larger than life statues of Stalin greeted visitors to every public building in the Soviet Union, even as his portraits graced every room in each of these buildings. While his busts, large and small, were installed in schoolrooms, universities, railroad stations, bus stations and airports, streets, squares and cities across the Soviet Union were named after him, making him omnipresent in the lives of the people. However, even as propaganda ensured the conferring of glorious titles on him such as 'Father of Nations', 'Brilliant Genius of Humanity', 'The Sun that Lights up the Whole

Country', 'Gardener of Human Happiness' and 'Great Architect of Communism', Stalin slowly returned to his pre-war self.

Determined to catapult the USSR to the top of the industrialized world and catch up with the US in the nuclear race despite extreme post-war misery, Stalin introduced stringent measures to bolster the economy. First amongst these was an overnight redenomination of currency, reducing the old rouble to one tenth its original value and rendering the savings of peasants—who had accumulated significant amounts of cash by selling food at wartime prices—worthless.

Next, Stalin revoked the limited wartime freedoms granted to the church and collective farmers and ordered the purging of the many who had become party members during the war, branding them as opportunists. When poverty and hunger drove Soviet citizens to steal food to feed themselves and their children during the famine of 1946–47, Stalin ordered even petty thieves to be sent to gulags, resulting in over two million people being added to the dreaded labour camps during the next five years. Finally, with rapid industrialization high on his wish list, he issued unrealistic production targets, demanding that coal, steel, cast iron and petroleum yields be immediately increased by three to five times. Consequently, there was no reprieve in sight for the exhausted workers, who had already been overworked for meagre salaries during the war years.

In 1947, ideological differences between the former Allied powers brought down the metaphorical iron curtain between Eastern and Western Europe, with countries of the Eastern Bloc, including Poland, East Germany, Yugoslavia, Hungary, Romania, Bulgaria, Albania and a re-established Czechoslovakia, becoming the USSR's satellite states. Soon, Stalin instituted the Communist Information Bureau (Cominform), an international body of communist leaders, to ensure that the satellite states conformed to Soviet ideology. When the then US president

Harry Truman issued the Truman Doctrine promising political, military and economic aid to democratic countries under the threat of communism, Stalin authorized the launch of a counter doctrine to establish the superiority of Soviet socialism over Western capitalism. Soon, any intellectual within the Eastern Bloc whose work showed Western capitalist influence was either arrested or deported.

Even as the misery of the masses continued, Stalin's propaganda worked overtime to ensure that he was perceived both nationally and internationally as a benevolent leader who promoted peace. This was evident in paintings and posters commissioned during 1948–53 with captions such as 'We stand for peace and we defend the cause of peace', 'Stalin is our great standard-bearer of peace!', 'Great Stalin is the banner of friendship of the people of the USSR!' and 'Great Stalin is the best friend of the Latvian people!' This last caption was particularly paradoxical considering Stalin had targeted over half a million soldiers and refugees from the newly acquired territories of Latvia, Estonia, Lithuania and western Ukraine, branding them as traitors and ordering them to exile or execution soon after WWII ended.

In August 1949, the Soviet Union successfully detonated its first atomic bomb, nicknamed Joe-1 in the West. In December that year Stalin turned 70. With the occasion calling for celebrations, party cadres from across the Soviet and its satellite states made grand announcements to please their leader. These included declarations of how miners in the USSR had voluntarily undertaken to produce 630,000 tons more coal than envisaged in the 1949 plan, how Bulgarian canal workers had voluntarily worked overtime to exceed targets by 242 per cent and how workers at tractor manufacturing units in Romania had pledged to produce 300 tractors more than planned 'out of great love for their leader and teacher'. The festivities held at

Moscow's famous Bolshoi Theatre also saw the newly appointed Chinese premiere Mao Tse-tung in attendance, what with China becoming only the second communist regime in Asia (after Outer Mongolia) with Soviet assistance in October that year. In his commemorative speech, Mao proclaimed that Comrade Stalin was 'a teacher and friend of the people of the world as well as a teacher and friend of the Chinese people'.

Not a Nice Man to Know

By 1950, Stalin started showing signs of aging. Although he became less involved in day-to-day administration, remaining absent from the Kremlin for long periods, his paranoia ensured that his subordinates were always on edge. During this period, he also became suspicious of Jews, probably as the result of a trickle-down effect of Nazi anti-Semite propaganda. Consequently, the USSR soon saw the shutting down of the Jewish Anti-Fascist Committee established during the war and the execution of several Jewish intellectuals. In 1952, he accused his close aides Molotov, whose wife was Jewish, and Mikoyan of spying for the US and Britain respectively. He then dissolved the Politburo and established a nine-member Central Committee Presidium Bureau sans the alleged traitors. In January 1953, Stalin ordered the arrest of Kremlin doctors, many of who were Jewish, charging them with plotting to murder top Soviet officials. Even as he prepared to unleash another round of purges, ostensibly targeting Soviet Jews, he died of a haemorrhagic stroke on 5 March.

At the time of Stalin's death in 1953, the USSR spread across 22,400,000 sq. km, accounting for nearly one sixth of all land available on earth—from Ukraine in the west to the shores of the Bering Sea in the east, from islands in the Arctic Ocean in the north to Tajikistan in the south—and covering eleven of the world's twenty-four time zones. It also boasted a population of 190 million that was both smitten by the charisma of and frightened by the terror of their vozhd.

During the 25 years of Stalin's rule, the Soviet Union had transformed from an archaic agrarian economy to the fastest growing industrial economy in the world and was on the brink of becoming a nuclear power, with the USSR testing its first fusion-based device in August 1953 and commissioning its first nuclear power plant in 1954. During the same 25 years, workers and peasants, the proletariat for whom the communist government had ostensibly been formed, consumed a daily diet meant for prisoners, lived in uninhabitable 'barracks' or slum dwellings, struggled to clothe themselves and their children decently and toiled away as slaves in factories and farms alike. Also during these years, 15 million of the same proletariat died due to starvation, 20 million, including soldiers, lost their lives during WW2 and hundreds of thousands of Soviet citizens were executed for various reasons of convenience irrespective of who they were. Perhaps, it would not be an exaggeration, then, to presume that his death might have elicited a collective sigh of relief across the USSR.

Adolf Hitler

How does a country allow itself to be ruled by a tyrant? Simply by allowing itself to be mesmerized by his oratorical skills and penchant for drama, conveniently ignoring the oddity of him raising furore over race and genealogy despite his own ambiguous ancestry.

Anti-Semitism in Europe dates back to early years of Christianity when the clergy actively propagated the idea of Jews being responsible for the crucifixion of Jesus. This was accompanied by the branding of Jews as being diabolic, causing long-standing strained relations between the two religious groups. When Jewish traders immigrated into north-western Europe—including France, England and Germany—around the time of the First Crusade, they were subjected to several indignities including accusations of poisoning wells and ritual murder. Attempts were also made to convert the Jewish infidels, resulting in riots and massacres. Further, the inimical attitude of the local Christian clergy, royalty and traders resulted in their ostracization from trade and most other professions, pushing them towards the unpopular occupations of renting, moneylending and tax collection.

Moneylending, in particular, created a trap for the Jewish immigrants, with Judaism prohibiting the charging of high interest (usury) on loans. However, there existed a grey area pertaining to loans taken in case of illness, litigation or other unforeseen personal expenses. So, while the already impoverished debtors found it difficult to repay these loans, the Jewish creditors, whose only source of income was the interest on the loan, had no choice but to employ all the tricks of the trade to extract payments. It wasn't surprising then that local debtors soon came to hate their immigrant creditors and indulged in their persecution, hoping to destroy potentially incriminating bonds or pledges. Although other communities such as the Cahorsins, Catalans and Lombards too lent money on interest in the region, the Jews were particularly hated owing to religious animosity and their separate social identity. By the sixteenth century though, Jews had gained a foothold in the business and by the nineteenth century, despite the Jewish moneylender having become a familiar stereotype, they had already started establishing themselves in several other professions.

The concept of Aryan supremacy and racial purity that found patronage within the elite circles of Western Europe took shape in the eighteenth century with the publication of French aristocrat Joseph Arthur de Gobineau's *An Essay on the Inequality of the Human Races*. The book, for the first time, discussed in detail the differences between white, black and yellow-skinned races and suggested that amongst the white-skinned ones, the Aryan race was the pinnacle of all human development. The idea was expanded upon by British-German philosopher Houston Stewart Chamberlain who, in *The Foundations of the Nineteenth Century,* expounded his *volkisch* anti-Semitic theories on the superiority of the Aryans. What's more, Gobineau's book—which went on to become popular amongst slave-owners in the United States who saw in it a justification for everything they did—also vehemently discouraged inter-breeding of races in order to maintain racial purity.

Around the same time, Heinrich Gotthard Freiherr von Treitschke, a noted German historian, extreme nationalist and member of the Reichstag, was amongst the first German elites to club the idea of racial purity and anti-Semitism. Speaking against the influx of Jewish immigrants from Russian Poland in the 1870s, he popularized the phrase '*Die Juden sind unser Unglück!*' ('The Jews are our misfortune!'), that went on to become the motto of *Der Stürmer*, the propaganda newspaper started by the Nazis in the 1920s. His inflammatory essays painted Jews as being 'of no further use to the world' even as he praised the Aryans for adapting to the 'idiosyncrasies of finance', thus obliterating the need for Jews. The term 'anti-Semite' itself was first coined by the German thinker Wilhem Marr in his 1879 text *The Way to Victory of Germanicism over Judaism*. Marr supposedly used 'antisemitismus', meaning hatred of the Jewish race, rather than 'Judenhass', meaning hatred of Jews, in order to make sure that the hatred he talked about applied to not only the everyday Jew but also also those who had stopped practising Judaism or had converted to Christianity.

In 1900, when Adolf Hitler was a school-going child in Linz, Austria, Jews comprised less than one per cent of the town's population and were either merchants, professionals or manufacturers. In 1903, the number of Jewish peers in his school, including future mathematician and philosopher Ludwig Wittgenstein, almost equalled that of Protestant Christians at 19, while Catholic students totalled over 300. Despite this, none of the Jews faced any apparent hostility. The Deutsche Volkspartei, or German People's Party, that governed Upper Austria at the time accepted Jews as members without much ado. Hitler's family doctor, Dr Eduard Bloch, was a Jew too, as were some of his favourite theatre actors.

Why is it then that when it comes to the words anti-Semitism, Aryan supremacy and racial purity, the world gives history a convenient slip and associates them with Hitler and Hitler alone?

Linz

Adolf Hitler was born in Braunau, a small town along the German-Austrian border, on 20 April 1889 to Alois Hitler—an illegitimate offspring of Maria Schichlgruber with no knowledge of who his father was—and his third wife Klara nee Polzl. Although he was the fourth child borne by Klara, 23 years her husband's junior, Adolf was the first to survive. Not surprisingly, he was the apple of his mother's eye. In 1895, Alois retired after 40 years of service as a customs official and moved to a remote hamlet in Upper Austria. In May that year, Adolf, then six years old, was admitted to the only school in town, essentially a single room in which students of all grades were packed for lessons.

The Hitler family moved again when Adolf was nine years old, this time to Leonding where they lived in a house next to a cemetery and where Adolf attended school rather reluctantly. He was, after all, more interested in play than studies. What did excite him though, as it did the entire German-Austrian population at the time, was the breaking out of the Boer War in South Africa with the natives' fight against British imperialism reminiscent of a David versus Goliath situation. Soon, children were playing war games that Adolf took a particular liking to. At home, he enjoyed pretending to shoot at rats, perhaps as an extension of games played at school or perhaps as a reaction to his drunk father's constant berating comments.

At the age of 11, Adolf was sent to high school in Linz, an hour's walk from his Leonding home. Here too, he found it difficult to adjust and failed to perform well in studies. The only subject that interested him was drawing. Not surprisingly, when Alois took him to visit the local customs office in the hope of getting his son to follow his footsteps, Adolf was immediately put off. He would rather pursue something more exciting like the arts than spend his life cooped in a room doing boring paperwork. Upset with his son's reaction, Alois started giving Adolf a thrashing every night on one pretext or the other. His mother compensated for the harshness by pampering him even more, admiring his watercolour paintings and secretly supporting his artistic ambitions.

It was around this time that the steady influx of seasonal workers from Czechoslovakia started to worry the locals. Newspapers fanned anxiety, highlighting issues such as natives losing jobs to cheap Slavic labour and attributing the increase in crime rate to the undercurrents of a language war between the Germans and Slavs. The volatile political milieu in Linz did not go unnoticed by school kids who learned to take sides and indulge in anti-Slavic activity. This was perhaps when, Adolf, for the first time, started taking interest in the idea of race and racial differences. At the age of 14, he is said to have pointed out the non-German-ness of a dark-eyed, dark-haired classmate.

School kids in Linz were also heavily influenced by the growing rift between loyalists of the Austrian imperial family and the pan-German nationalists who sought the annexation of Austria into the German Reich. With the idea of Germanic identity being instilled in their minds by teachers, Adolf and his peers soon found themselves demonstrating allegiance to the nationalist cause by collecting ribbons, pencils and pins in the 'Greater German' colours of red, black and gold, singing 'Deutschland uber Alles' instead of the Austrian imperial anthem and greeting each other with the orthodox German *heil* instead of the imperial salutation *hoch*.

Alois's death in 1903 gave Adolf a respite at home. However, with political demonstrations distracting him, he continued to perform poorly at school and was asked to leave the following year. A distraught Klara sent her son to another school in the industrial town of Steyr, but to no avail. Separated from his mother and forced to board with strangers, Adolf remained a troubled child, unable to focus on studies. When he failed in German, math and stenography that year, he grew exceedingly bitter and faked a lung ailment to return to his mother.

Back home, Klara's pampering ensconced her son in a sense of false security and so, despite rising inflation and his mother's failing health, Adolf did not bother to find work. Instead, he took leisurely walks during the day and spent evenings indulging in painting and reading. Around this time, he also started taking a keen interest in newspapers through which he was introduced to the idea of anti-Semitism.

The newspapers that Adolf devoured were mostly editions of those printed in Vienna, which, being a larger city trying to deal with urban problems, had already embraced anti-Semitism as a strategy to safeguard the interests of locals. While some papers urged readers not to buy from the vile and dangerous Jews so their economic growth could be stifled, forcing them to leave the region, others clubbed the Jew problem with that of the Hungarians and Slavs and sought to promote the pan-German agenda. In these papers, Jews were alternatingly called 'a disgusting lice infestation', 'an abomination to human race', and 'the lowliest of human races'.

The inflammatory slogans and articles simmered in Adolf's thoughts, but did not immediately find a patron in him. He was only 16 and enamoured as he was by the arts, theatre had a deeper impression on him than the papers. One opera, in particular, had a lasting impact on Adolf. It was Richard Wagner's impression of *Rienzi: The Last of the Tribunes*, based on the life of the eponymous fourteenth-century Roman tribune. When, in the performance, Rienzi called upon his people to choose him as the protector of their rights, the actors and the audience chorused 'Rienzi, Heil!' in unison. The resounding energy in the theatre was infectious and soon had Adolf dreaming of being looked upon by his people, someday, as Rienzi incarnate.

Vienna

In 1906, Klara, to encourage her son's artistic ambition, paid for a trip to Vienna so he could visit the imperial art gallery. That was how, Adolf, now 17, arrived in Vienna for the first time. While this was the city he would ultimately harbour bitter hatred for, his relationship with Vienna did not start that way. In fact, his three-day visit made him fall in love with the city that was a hotbed of art, culture and politics. And although the purpose of his visit was to take in the marvellous works of art at the museum, it was the splendid and varying styles of architecture of buildings such as the Hapsburg Parliament, Court Opera, Court Museum, University, Stock Exchange, Church, City Hall and the several elegant hotels and mansions, spread across the four-kilometre stretch of the Ring Boulevard, that won his heart. Much later, he would record in his seminal memoir *Mein Kampf* that the whole boulevard seemed to him 'an enchantment out of the 1001 Nights'.

Needless to say, the glitz and glamour of Vienna stayed with Adolf much after he returned home. In the fall of 1907, he was back in the city despite his mother's failing health, hoping to get enrolled at the Academy of Visual Arts. Once there, he rented a shabby 10'x10' box of a bedroom that smelled of kerosene and had a solitary window offering a glimpse of a sooty sky, in the house of a Czech lady. In September, he took and cleared the first stage of the entrance exam to the academy along with 112 other candidates. However, despite enrolling under the expensive tutelage of Rudolf Panholzer to prepare for the drawing exam that followed, he was unable to clear it.

Dejected, Adolf returned to Linz, only to be heartbroken once again when his mother died of breast cancer in December. As she lay on her deathbed, he sat beside her and sketched her so he could preserve the impression of the only person he had loved and who had loved him back unconditionally.

After Klara's death, Adolf and his sister Paula were left with a miniscule inheritance that they would be able to access when they each turned 24. Until then, there was only a meagre orphan's allowance to live on. Yet, Adolf refused jobs from sympathetic neighbours saying he was preparing to become 'a great artist'. As luck would have it, their landlady at Linz was connected to one of the big names in Vienna's stage-craft scene, Alfred Roller, and offered to write a recommendation. Adolf was filled with gratitude. Soon, he returned to Vienna, leaving Paula behind with his step-sister Angela Raubal. It wouldn't be until 1921 that the Hitler siblings would see each other again.

Back in Vienna—this time with his friend August Kubizek who had enrolled himself in a Viennese music conservatory and moved in with Adolf into his rented room—Adolf felt confident of living his dream. However, that was not to be. Several years later, as leader of the German Reich in 1934, Hitler would request Roller to stage an opera for him; but in early 1908 he could not summon the courage to walk up to the artist's office and show his work, fearing rejection. So he loitered on the streets of Vienna during the day and lectured Kubizek on a melange of topics throughout the night. He also spent a great amount of time redesigning, in his mind, several of the buildings in Linz, such as the museum, the Wildberg Castle, the municipal hall and the tower of Lichtenberg. He would then show his sketches to Kubizek for critique. When he heard about plans of building a new concert hall in his hometown, Adolf created an extensive proposal, complete with details of columns, balustrades, the ceiling and even the acoustic design, only to be furious when the planning committee shelved the project.

In September 1908, Adolf once again took the entrance test to the art academy. This time, he did not get past even the first round. Although the dean noticed in their meeting that he had a skill for architecture, with sketches of buildings proliferating his portfolio, he did not have a high-school diploma that was a pre-requisite to attending architectural school. He was thus left staring at a dead end to his career in art. Frustrated and ashamed, he moved out of the room he shared with Kubizek without informing his friend and, with his orphan's allowance dwindling, moved into a smaller room farther downtown with a loan from his aunt.

Vienna, in 1908–09, was a city with no regard for its poor. With there being no law to protect tenants from being evicted for no apparent reason, rich landlords residing in the luxury of their bucolic villas became enemies of their tenants in the city. Poor working-class families were increasingly rendered homeless, a situation exacerbated by the never-ending influx of immigrants. Soon, several illegal quarters cropped up with people—sick and healthy, alcoholics and hookers, children and the elderly—

cramming into small rooms each night for the price of a few kroners. In these dilapidated, vermin-infested buildings with unspeakable living conditions, people slept with strangers in the same room, sometimes on the same bed. Not surprisingly, these soon turned into hotbeds for diseases of all kinds. While the rich held benefit balls in their mansions to collect funds ostensibly to feed the poor, the latter remained embittered and humiliated.

In the summer of 1909, 20-year-old Adolf found himself staring at the possibility of ending up in just these kinds of quarters. Stubborn about not getting a job despite his desperate financial situation, he constantly shifted from one room to another until he finally found himself homeless. Having to live on the streets changed his perception of Vienna. From a city rich in culture, it became to him 'one of the most backward cities in Europe'. By the time winter set in that year, Adolf had transformed from a well-dressed, determined 16-year-old with a plan to a young man in shabby clothes who stood in the soup-line at charities, prompting him to later record his miserable circumstance in Vienna as 'one of the darkest sides' of his life.

Luckily for him though, the city had several homeless shelters and soup kitchens run either by cloisters attached to the Church or private charities established by Jewish philanthropists. Having been raised in an exceptionally clean household, he grudgingly chose shelters run by the latter whenever he got a chance. It was during his stay at one such shelter that Adolf befriended another homeless person, Reinhold Hanisch, at whose suggestion he decided to paint postcards for a living. With no money on him to buy paper and paint for his new vocation, he wrote to his aunt for help and used the 50 kroner she sent him to buy himself a coat from a pawnshop and some paint supplies. He then sat in cheap cafes and painted postcards that Hanisch helped sell to tourists looking for inexpensive souvenirs. Between them, they managed to make enough in a day to avoid hard labour and filthy shelters and, by early 1910, the duo was able to move into a men's hostel.

The men's hostel provided Adolf with a safe and clean atmosphere in which to paint. Soon, he was not only able to make a living by painting postcards but also progressed to becoming a painter of commissioned work, thanks to the enterprise of Hanisch who almost exclusively sought out Jewish dealers such as Morgenstern, Landsberger and Altenberg since they paid better than their Christian counterparts. However, when Hanisch prodded him to work harder and paint more in a day in order to increase their meagre profits, cracks started to appear in their friendship.

For Adolf, it was an everyday ritual to spend his mornings in the common reading room of the hostel, going through newspapers with a fine-tooth comb. He would then take an active part in political discussions with fellow hostellers, making passionate speeches about the political ideals of pan-German advocates Georg Schonerer and Karl Hermann Wolf. He would also voice his support for the policies of the German Reich, however violent or prejudiced they were. It was here, perhaps, that Adolf first recognized the power of his oratorical skills that wowed many a hosteller. This was also when he realized the importance of reading, for most of what he spoke with *élan* in his speeches were not his own ideas but those that he had read, memorized and internalized. So, while he spent his afternoons and evenings painting, he spent his nights studying. Sourcing books and political pamphlets from public libraries and cafes, he read vastly about architecture, philosophy, German history, politics, stage-craft and the operas of Wagner. Naturally, he was exposed to ample anti-

Semitic texts; but while he diligently studied them, he also read pro-Semitic literature under the influence of his Jewish friends Josef Neumann and Siegfried Loffner, who helped sell his paintings now that Hanisch had become a rival.

Adolf's mind, although curious, was academically untrained. Consequently, his own ideology was a patchwork of bits and pieces gleaned from various philosophical and political ideas. One of the thinkers who had a profound impact on him at the time was the pan-German advocate Guido von List who claimed in his writings that the Aryo-Germans were destined by God to rule the world while people of mixed lineage were meant to be the servants. According to him, the former, belonging to the Nordic regions near the North Pole, had been driven southwards owing to the calamitous ice age and while they brought culture to the entire world, intermixing with the southern races had diluted their ethnic purity. Guido von List argued for the regaining of the pure Aryan master race by de-mixing and segregation, blaming the Jews in particular for 'spoiling the Aryan race' by way of mixed marriages. He went on to encourage readers to 'get rid of the Jews' and predicted an Aryo-German war that would establish a new world order.

As a 21-year-old, Adolf read all of von List he could lay his hands on. At the same time, while he did not harbour any apparent misgivings towards the Jews as people, the question of Jews became to him inextricably intertwined with the question of race and German-ness. His confusion was evident in that although he was generous in his praise for Jews such as Jacques Offenbach and Rothschild, he perceived them as a different race that had a 'different smell'. Further, while he himself did not sympathize with the poor—developing a sort of abhorrence for them instead—he could not understand the morality of pity that prompted Jews to lead labour movements in various parts of Vienna. Unable to fathom why they would want to take up the thankless task of leading a broken, degenerate group of labourers, he grew suspicious of them, attributing their choice to a secret, perhaps selfish, motive, although he was not sure what it could be.

The three years that Adolf spent at the men's hostel saw him deepen his understanding of politics and hone his oratorical skills. Conspicuously missing from his life at this juncture though, was a deep, meaningful relationship of any sort. After leaving Kubizek without notice, he had not been able to form a bond with any of his new friends. As for his relationship with women, it was almost non-existent. His only childhood crush had been Stephanie, a senior student at the Linz school, to whom he never professed his love, fearing rejection. In Vienna, despite being surrounded by hookers—or perhaps because of it—Adolf went into self-imposed asceticism. While widespread syphilis induced in him not only the fear of infection but also the fear of being touched by women, the books he read emphasized the racial inferiority of hookers and the need for an austere relationship between man and woman rather than a carnal one. The only entertainment he allowed himself then was an occasional visit to the opera, where he watched performances from the standing section to save money.

Despite having settled into a comfortable routine at the hostel, Adolf could not shake off his growing hatred for Vienna. Keen to leave behind the moribund Austro-Hungarian Hapsburg Empire, he started making plans in the spring of 1912 to move to Munich in order to be part of the larger German Reich. However, with the Austrian parliament having recently revised its Compulsory Service Law to introduce strict punishments, including prison time, for young men who evaded getting drafted into military service, travelling was risky. So, assuming he would be free from the obligation to serve once he turned 24 in April 1913, Adolf decided to lay low and bide his time before crossing the border. In the meantime, he continued to paint, read and debate in the safe confines of the hostel. With the statute for gaining access to his paternal inheritance also drawing to an end in 1913, he came upon a small fortune of 820 kroner just in time to facilitate the realization of his Munich dream.

And so, on 24 May 1913, Adolf Hitler left Vienna the way he had arrived—as a neat, well-dressed young man with an inheritance and a dream.

Munich

In 1913, the Bavarian capital of Munich was struggling to live up to its reputation as a 'Kunststadt', or 'art city'. Considered second only to Paris until then for art education, hosting world-renowned artists and pioneering the creation of exhibition spaces for the marketing of art, the city was slowly losing ground to Berlin. However, art and architecture still flourished in the city, with works of Renaissance, Baroque and Neoclassicism dotting its urban fabric and defining its identity. It wasn't surprising then that Munich went on to carve a place for itself in the heart of the future Führer, who would note in *Mein Kampf*, '...almost from the very first moment of my sojourn there I came to love that city more than any other place known to me. A German city! I said to myself. How different to Vienna.'

When he arrived in Munich on 26 May 1913, Adolf had with him nothing but a few sets of clothes, painting supplies and a renewed dream of becoming an artist. With him was another young man from the men's hostel, Rudolf Hausler, in whom he had finally found a friend as close as Kubizek but who, unlike

Kubizek, was self-motivated and less tolerant of Adolf's angry outbursts and bossiness. Their bond was evident from the way they endearingly addressed each other as Adi and Rudi. The two friends rented a room, with Adolf registering himself as an artist and writer. Knowing well that his inheritance wouldn't last long, he fell back upon painting pictures of local attractions to make a living. For the next 15 months, the duo explored Munich together with Adolf, in particular, frequenting artists' cafes across the city in the hope of getting spotted and nurtured by an established artist. And just like Hanisch in Vienna, Hausler helped sell his work.

As in Vienna, Adolf also continued reading newspapers, keeping abreast with political developments. Having followed the two Balkan Wars closely since their breaking out in 1912, he intuited that there would soon be another war and secretly hoped that Germany would join it, giving him a chance to serve for his new country.

His wish came true in August 1914 with the breaking out of WWI. Then aged 25, Adolf Hitler joined the 1st Company of the 16th Bavarian Reserve Infantry Regiment with a sense of belonging and purpose. Despite being an unusual soldier with sloppy mannerisms, his eagerness for action saw him getting promoted to lance-corporal and assigned as a dispatch runner whose job was to take messages to and from the command staff and the fighting units three kilometres away at the battlefield. A dangerous job, given that the enemy targeted runners in order to disrupt communication between the command office and frontline, it wasn't unusual for more than one runner to be killed or wounded every day. However, Hitler did not mind the danger. Not only did he like the excitement of it all, he felt—for the first time—a part of a larger group fighting towards a common cause. Consequently, he neither complained about the bad food nor the horrible living conditions like his fellow soldiers, nor did he ask for leave. In December that year, he was awarded the Iron Cross, Second Class, for saving the life of a senior.

In the barracks, Hitler preferred discussing art and history rather than women. During lulls in the battlefield, he took out his watercolours to paint the landscapes of war. His only other distraction was a white terrier that had strayed across the no man's land. Naming it Fuchsl, he taught it tricks, and delighted in how it waited for him to return to the barracks every evening. All wasn't upbeat for Hitler though. While he was constantly ridiculed for remaining a lance corporal for four years, he was also made fun of because of his disinterest in women. Fellow soldiers alternatingly called him a 'monk' and berated him as a homosexual who displayed womanish characteristics. Hitler allegedly remained unaffected by it all and by the time the war drew to an end, he had earned himself another honour, the Iron Cross, First Class for his 'cold blooded courage and exemplary boldness', as described by Lieutenant Hugo Gutmann, the Jewish officer who had nominated him for the award.

In October 1918, Hitler was temporarily blinded by a British mustard gas attack, requiring him to get medical attention. It was while recuperating at the military hospital back in Bavaria that he heard about Germany's surrender to the Allied Forces, marking the end of the war. Germany was not only defeated but also declared a republic after the signing of the armistice, transferring power from the grand old Kaiser regime to political parties that had no experience in dealing with democracy. The news shattered Hitler. Such was his faith in his country and the powers that ruled it that the unexpected defeat plunged him into a whirlpool of anger and depression. Questioning the purpose of war and lamenting the vainness of all the lives lost, he sat crying on his bed for hours on end, refusing to talk to anyone.

Returning to Munich after the war ended, the question simmering in Hitler's mind was, 'Who was responsible for the debacle?' So important was this question to him that he spent much of his time dissecting the idea of why an individual might fight and die for one's state. According to him, the reason for such a choice would be the fulfilment of an ideal rather than for monetary gains. 'As long as the German people continued to believe that they were fighting for ideals they stood firm,' he would later elaborate in *Mein Kampf*. 'As soon as they were told that they were fighting only for their daily bread they began to give up the struggle.' Embittered by this realization, he—like many others who assessed the German surrender through the same lens—dubbed the politicians who signed the armistice on 11 November 1918 as the 'November Criminals'.

The post-war restructuring of Germany in 1919 saw a palpable undercurrent of suspicion about the Marxists, social democrats and Jews, particularly following their ratification of the Treaty of Versailles that came as a slap on the face of the German people. Germany was forced to accept sole responsibility for causing the war, had to pay huge reparations, and cede large portions of land to France and Poland. The treaty also sought to limit the German army to 100,000 men while forbidding it from possessing any military aircraft or submarines.

In the years to come, Hitler would use his oratorical skills to remind the Germans of this humiliation and garner support for his ideology. He would also subscribe to the popular but unfair exaggeration of the role of Jews in 'stabbing Germany in its back', despite it being acknowledged that over a 100,000 German and Austrian Jews had fought for their Fatherland in WWI. Now though, Hitler was glad to still be enlisted in the army at a time when Germany was witnessing a bloodbath as Marxists tried to wrest power in several pockets, including Munich. Before long, he was recruited as an undercover informant, responsible for the arrest and execution of fellow soldiers who supported Marxist uprisings. He was also sent to the University of Munich for a course in political indoctrination where he was trained to use his oratorical skills to stir up feelings of nationalism amongst fellow soldiers and warn them of the dangers posed by communists and Jews. Delivering these tirades to war-weary soldiers who were looking for someone to blame for their misfortunes, Hitler delighted in the fact that he could hold the attention of an audience full of strangers and sway them to his point of view.

With anything associated with the word 'workers' automatically becoming suspicious for having ties with communists, Hitler was also asked to spy on a small group that called itself the German Workers' Party (Deutsche Arbeiterpartei in German). In November 1919, he attended a meeting of the group at a Munich beer hall dressed in plain clothes and listened with rapt attention to the speeches made. Enraged by one of the speeches that encouraged the idea of Bavaria leaving the German Reich and joining Austria, he spoke out vehemently against the orator and voiced his opinions for a full 15 minutes. His small sermon-of-sorts impressed Anton Drexler, one of the founders of the party, who invited him to attend the next meeting. With Drexler sharing his nationalist, pro-military and fledgling anti-Semitic ideologies, it was not long before Hitler became a party member. What also lured him was the small, almost-disorganized nature of the party that would allow him, when the time came, to shape it in a way he felt appropriate. He was soon part of the seven-member executive committee—the first real job he had held in his 30 years.

During his stint as committee member, Hitler used his artistic talent to create posters and meeting invitations to lure more

Germans into the party. His first speech was so emotionally high strung that it captivated the audience at a crowded beer hall and resulted in donations of over 300 marks towards the party's cause. His ability to pull crowds soon catapulted him as the main speaker at all party meetings where he spoke passionately, and sometimes hysterically, about his favourite themes of nationalism, anti-communism, anti-Semitism and the misgivings of the Treaty of Versailles. Hitting two birds with one stone, he also frequently associated Marxism with Jews, instilling in his audience the fear of a Russia-like communist revolution by the German Jews.

Hitler's rising popularity at these meetings saw his importance within the party grow. Not surprisingly, he was entrusted with charting the party's 25-point agenda, including the intent to annex provinces with a substantial German-speaking population and bring them into the larger German Reich, to abrogate all provisions of the Treaty of Versailles and, most importantly, declare everyone 'not of German blood' as aliens. The charter spelt out in as many words that Jews could not be considered countrymen and would have to live in Germany as foreigners. Shrewdly, Hitler also included populist issues in the charter—such as improving agrarian economy, opportunities for higher education, increase of old age pensions and nationalization of trusts—that would appeal to the masses and bring in the votes whenever the party contested elections. Outlining these points at a meeting attended by over 2,000 people in February 1920, Hitler drummed up fervour in the gathered crowd to a point of frenzy to gain their seal of approval. The resounding success of the four hour long meeting set the tone for many more to follow.

As the party grew from a mere 25 members in 1919 to over 3,000, including several disillusioned soldiers, by the end of 1920, Hitler recognized the need for a symbol to identify the party with—a symbol as powerful as the hammer and sickle of the communists. He found the perfect one in the *hakenkreuz* (popularly, the swastika), which means 'hooked cross', a symbol whose potential had been explored by his idol von List. In his 1908 book, von List had described the hakenkreuz as signifying the tool for lighting a fire—a whisk and a cross—that the Aryans had developed for their worship of light. For Hitler, this association of the hakenkreuz with communities that had been founded by the Aryan culture was enough to develop a powerful narrative around it. Placing it inside a white circle on a red background, he not only made it instantly recognizable but also a worthy competitor to the communist flag. In *Mein Kampf*, he would ascribe to the hakenkreuz the 'mission to struggle for the victory of the Aryan man' and in 1933, Hitler's minister for propaganda, Joseph Goebbels, would issue a decree against the commercial use of the symbol saying, 'When Hitler is absent...his place is taken by the hakenkreuz, which, like the image of the Führer, becomes a switching station for personal and national identities.'

Soon after adopting this symbol, Hitler also brought about a change in the name of the party of which he had practically become the unopposed leader. By including the term National Socialist, in a clear display of his aversion for the idea of democracy, the party now came to be known as the National Socialist German Workers' Party (Nationalsozialistische Deutsche Arbeiterpartei). The acronym NSDAP was soon shortened further to the infamous word Nazi that, along with the hakenkreuz, would go on to become symbols of unimaginable terrors.

Hitler's rise in the party ranks did not go uncontested though. Despite him being the star speaker who was now addressing crowds of over 6,000, founders of the party were not happy with his overbearing nature. So an attempt was made in mid-1921 to create a new alliance, sans Hitler, that would restore equilibrium within the party. However, the executive committee was thrown off-kilter when an irate Hitler tendered his resignation, announcing that he would return into the party fold only if he were made chairman with sweeping dictatorial powers. With the certainty of the NSDAP crumbling without Hitler, the committee grudgingly accepted his condition. And so, in July 1921, Adolf Hitler was introduced to party members as the Führer of the Nazi Party.

The next 10 years saw Hitler try passionately to find a place for the NSDAP in the political fabric of the German Reich. In 1923, he attempted a military coup against the ruling Weimar Republic in what is known famously as the Beer Hall Putsch. Although the coup failed, Hitler's dramatic defence of himself in the trial that followed won him the approval of the judges who cut his sentence short to just nine months despite the gravity of allegations, and allowed him a rather spacious private prison cell at the Landsberg fortress where he could receive visitors and have his own private secretary.

It was during his imprisonment that Hitler dictated his thoughts to his secretary Rudolf Hess—thoughts that would later be put together in a book titled *Four and a Half Years of Struggle against Lies, Stupidity and Cowardice*. Thanks to his Nazi publisher, the title was shortened to *Mein Kampf* (*My Struggle*) before going to print in 1925. An autobiographical account that exaggerated events and memories from his life in line with its propagandist agenda and discussed his pet ideologies in detail, the book was slow on the uptake but steadily grew in popularity. By 1933, it had earned Hitler 1.2 million Reichmarks (nearly five million US dollars at that time) in royalty against the sale of a whopping 240,000 copies. By the end of WWII, nearly 10 million copies had been sold or distributed in Germany alone.

Once out of prison, Hitler decided to throw the party's hat in the ring to contest elections. Setting his sights on eventually ruling over the Reich, he also effected an overhaul in the party organization and fashioned it into a 'government in waiting' that could seamlessly slip into power when the opportunity arose. To this end, he created departments such as Agriculture, Economy, Interior, Justice, Race and Culture, Foreign Affairs and Propaganda within the party, divided Germany into 34 districts, each with a Nazi leader of its own, and advocated programmes such as Hitler Jugend for 15–18-year-olds and Deutsches Jungyolk for 10–14-year-olds to rally the youth behind him.

Realizing the importance of having not only an administrative order in place but also an instrument to enforce implementation, Hitler then reorganized the Nazi storm-troopers, or the SA as they were popularly known. The group that had been originally formed to control crowds at party meetings soon got outfitted with striking brown uniforms bearing the hakenkreuz armband to help etch the presence of the party in the minds of the public. From among the SA, Hitler also carved out a specialized unit to serve as his body guards. This black-uniformed unit, called the staff guard or SS, would soon gain notoriety for its activities, especially under the leadership of Heinrich Himmler, who expanded it from 300 members in 1929 to 35,000 in 1933. Recruiting only those who could demonstrate their racial purity and blind obedience towards Hitler, Himmler ensured that the SS was perceived as the ultimate defender of the Aryan race and Nazi ideology.

Despite his fervent preparations to take over the reins of the country, Hitler would not get an opportunity to do so until 1933. Thanks to the Dawes Plan, Germany was considerably relieved of its war reparations burden in 1926 and finances from the US started to pour in towards infrastructural projects. With the economy stabilizing and unemployment rates dropping, the mood in the country was upbeat for the first time since WWI. Consequently, the Germans felt satisfied with the rule of the Weimar Republic, leaving the Nazi Party twiddling its thumbs.

As he waited for the tides to turn, Hitler shifted base to the scenic village of Berchtesgaden in Bavaria, from where he kept fine tuning the workings of his party. Renting a small country house that would later be converted into a sprawling villa, he invited his long-forgotten half-sister Angela Raubal to come live with him and take care of house affairs. The arrival of Angela with her two daughters, Friedl and Geli, changed the atmosphere of the Hitler household. Twenty-year-old Geli, in particular, brought in a vivacious charm that immediately attracted her uncle and for the first time since leaving Linz, Hitler fell in love. He fawned over Geli, 19 years his junior, and she in turn, at least in the beginning, enjoyed the attention he showered on her. While he took her shopping, dining and to concerts, he also allowed her to accompany him to party meetings, with her presence relaxing and cheering him up, much to the amusement of his colleagues. Hitler was careful though, not to let this strange relationship deter him from his political goal. Between the time spent with Geli and his party responsibilities, he also found time to dictate the second part of *Mein Kampf* to Rudolf Hess and continued inspiring crowds in Munich and Berlin with his exhilarating speeches.

In late 1929, the collapse of the US Wall Street plunged the world into an economic depression. This was just the change in status quo Hitler had been waiting for. With rising poverty and unemployment as hundreds of businesses shut shop, Nazi propaganda was quick to point fingers at the democratic policies of the Weimar Republic for all of Germany's woes. Not only were thousands of meetings and parades organized to raise awareness of the government's shortcomings, millions of special edition Nazi newspapers and posters with anti-government messages were also circulated across the country. With his administrative system already in place, the propaganda worked like clockwork to ensure that the party's message reached every German in every small town. As for Hitler's own rhetoric, the audience for it only grew in numbers, so much so that they filled the entire indoor arena of the Berlin Sportpalast during a campaign rally.

The well-planned Nazi campaign worked. That the disillusioned public had lapped up its propaganda was evident when the NSDAP won 107 seats in the German Reichstag in the September 1930 elections, catapulting it from a party with the smallest representation of 12 members in 1928 to the second largest party. In a historic moment, the elected Nazi members marched into the Reichstag dressed in their brown uniforms and proclaimed 'Heil Hitler!' when each of their names was announced. Outside, the SA, dressed as civilians, celebrated the victory by smashing windows of shops and restaurants owned by Jews.

Hitler, who had moved back to Munich before the start of the campaign, with Geli in tow, was now at the centre of everyone's attention. Industrialists lined up to please him and the world that had until now viewed him with scepticism, stood up to take note of the sway he held on a mesmerized country. At home though, things were not as upbeat. In the last few years, his fondness for Geli had progressively grown into an obsession, so much so that he could not tolerate the young girl talking to or flirting with other men as would be the wont of anyone her age. His jealousy ensured that Geli was never alone. Be it in their lavish nine-room apartment or anywhere else she went, she was always accompanied by Nazi chaperons who reported every detail to their boss. A frustrated Geli threw tantrums and argued with her uncle but it only tightened Hitler's grip on her. Perhaps feeling trapped when he refused to let her return to Vienna to become a singer, Geli shot herself with Hitler's pistol in September 1931.

Geli's death had a devastating effect on Hitler. Although rumours about his possible hand in her murder were quickly dismissed and an inquest into her apparent suicide quelled, Hitler fell into a deep depression from which he would never fully recover. In what seemed to be a morbid reaction, he converted Geli's blood-stained room into a personal shrine that he would fill with flowers to commemorate her birth and death each year. While he had been toying with the idea of turning vegetarian for some time now, the incident made him swear off meat, confiding to a friend that eating meat now felt like chewing on a corpse.

Berlin

Hitler did not have time to grieve for Geli though, what with the volatile political scenario in Berlin begging for his attention. With the Social Democratic Party lacking a clear majority and the Communist Party of Germany refusing to help form a coalition government, the capital city was host to intense politicking. Sensing a chance for the NSDAP to gain from the chaos, the party's leader in the Reichstag, Hermann Göring, drew Hitler back into politics. Soon, a coalition had been formed with the German National People's Party and, in October 1931, Hitler flew to Berlin to meet the 84-year-old German president Paul von Hindenburg in the hope of gaining his trust before staking claim to the chancellorship of Germany as leader of the coalition.

Hindenburg, however, wasn't impressed with Hitler whom he considered a pseudo-nationalist trying to lead the country with the help of a rowdy and uncontrollable SA. With his mind made up even before the meeting, he remained indifferent to Hitler's overtures and remarked in private that Hitler was nothing but a Bohemian corporal, at best suited for the role of postmaster general. Feeling slighted by the president's refusal to acknowledge his bid for chancellorship, Hitler decided to challenge Hindenburg himself, announcing his candidacy for the 1932 presidential election. Despite Hitler's fiery campaign speeches and efforts to reach out to the masses, he lost the elections, held in April, to an ailing Hindenburg who chose to do nothing but rely on his reputation.

With the presidency returning to Hindenburg, Hitler tried to salvage his pride by bidding for chancellorship once again. Through a strategic alliance with a scheming army officer, General Kurt von Schleicher, he first got reigning chancellor Heinrich Brüning ousted. The duo then installed their puppet, Franz von Papen, as chancellor before the Reichstag was dissolved in preparation for re-elections. Presented with another chance to prove their majority, the Nazis campaigned hard and won 230 votes in the July election to become the single largest party in the Reichstag for the first time. Yet, with the NSDAP lacking a governing majority, the chancellorship was still out of Hitler's reach. Moreover, with Hindenburg more receptive to von Papen continuing as chancellor and the latter itching to be more than just a puppet, backdoor politics now took centre stage. Soon, Schleicher turned on his promise to support Hitler's bid for chancellorship and asked him to settle for the post of vice-chancellor instead. Adopting an 'all or nothing' stance, Hitler rejected the offer. Withdrawing support for von Papen in the Reichstag, he forced the country to go into yet another round of elections.

By the time elections to the Reichstag were held again in November 1932, the masses had grown weary of the process. In what was a frustrating outcome for the NSDAP, it once again fell short of a clear majority despite emerging as the largest party with 196 seats. Although Hitler's hopes were raised when von Papen tendered his resignation after failing to form a working coalition, Hindenburg soon shot them down. Still resistant to the idea of an anti-democracy Nazi goon at the helm of the country, the president, in a surprise move, appointed Schleicher as chancellor.

The loss of face a third time over was too much for Hitler to digest. What made it worse though was Schleicher's offer of vice-chancellorship to Gregor Strasser, a key founding member of the NSDAP, making good his attempt to break the party. With Strasser tempted by the offer, a war of words ensued between the once good friends and ended in him leaving the party, but not before accusing Hitler of being a congenital liar. Seeing the party he built unravel, Hitler slipped into depression and even as Germany celebrated Christmas that year, he contemplated suicide. It once again fell upon his trusted aides Göring and Hess to bring him back to his senses and to politics. It helped that most German industrialists and bankers were willing to throw their weight behind him in his quest to oust Schleicher.

And so, in January 1933, as Schleicher struggled to put together a workable coalition, a reinvigorated Hitler convinced von Papen to support his bid for chancellorship in exchange for positions of power for him and his ministers in the coalition government. Then, to ensure that the president did not deny him his rightful position this time, he buttressed his claim with rumours about Schleicher's plot to arrest Hindenburg and stage a military takeover of the country. His ploy worked. With a rattled Hindenburg finally giving in, Hitler was appointed chancellor of the German Nation on 30 January 1933, much to the jubilation of the Nazis who celebrated the victory with a torchlight procession through Berlin. Men, women and children thronged outside the chancellery along with the SA and SS for a view of their Führer, while across Germany people listened to the momentous broadcast on the radio. When Hitler finally made his appearance in the balcony above, the crowd burst into chants of 'Heil! Sieg Heil!' (Hail! Hail Victory!)

With Hitler's appointment as chancellor, the Nazis were finally in a position of power. However, conscious of their lack of majority in the Reichstag, he called for elections to be held immediately and plunged back into fervent campaigning with posters that read, 'You gave these parties 14 years to ruin Germany! Give Hitler four years to rebuild it!' As elections drew near, the Nazi's came upon an unexpected windfall when a Dutch communist arsonist set fire to the Reichstag building. Not only did the Prussian police that controlled Berlin under the commandership of Göring do nothing to stop the symbol of German democracy from burning to ashes, it also stirred up mass hysteria to turn the public against the communists.

Hitler himself allegedly relished the sight of the burning Reichstag, remarking that the incident marked 'the beginning of a great epoch in German history'. The next day, he coerced President Hindenburg into issuing the Emergency Decree for the Protection of the German People, giving the Nazis a legal basis to arrest and prosecute opponents by simply labelling them as traitors. The decree did away with basic personal freedoms of people, including the freedom of speech, right to property and right to a fair trial before imprisonment, paving the road to a future dictatorship. Soon, over 10,000 communist supporters found themselves behind bars. Many of those arrested were placed in the first concentration camp set up by the SS in Dachau, 12 miles north of Munich, just a few days before the country went to vote.

The March 1933 elections once again proved to be a damper with the NSDAP falling short of a clear majority despite shoring up 288 seats. A frustrated Hitler was left with no choice but to manipulate other political parties by coaxing, luring and, if required, imprisonment, so that when the Enabling Law, giving him the power to rule by decree rather than passing laws through the parliament, was brought to the floor of the Reichstag, it was passed with a whopping 444 votes. Significantly, the law—officially called the 'Law for Removing the Distress of the People and the Reich'—was the last law passed by the Reichstag before Germany fell into the lap of dictatorship.

Soon after assuming dictatorship, Hitler initiated Gleichschaltung, or the process of consolidating every aspect of Germany under Nazi control. Within a year, all other political parties ceased to exist, making Germany a single-party state. Next, employees of non-Aryan descent were removed from their roles as civil servants, teachers and professors, as were judges deemed unfavourable to the Nazis. The People's Court, constituted of pro-Nazi judges, was set up in 1934 to try cases of treason, diluting the powers of the Supreme Court. In schools, Racial Science was made a compulsory subject even as the number of sports hours were steadily increased from one to five a day in an attempt to de-intellectualize education and discourage future generations from asking questions. Teachers were required to not only become party members but also compulsorily attend indoctrination courses. With Joseph Goebbels being appointed 'Minister for Public Engagement and Propaganda', the Nazis soon had full control over Germany's cultural policy, including the national media, theatre, arts and cinema—whether literature, music or art, the only conditions for works to survive unscathed was for them to be 'good' and 'Aryan'. Predictably, books written by Jewish or communist writers were burned, goods sold by Jews were boycotted and enterprises run by them were forced to shut down.

Initially, Hitler's intent was only to force the Jews to leave Germany by making it unbearable for them to live there. Consequently, he introduced more than 400 laws and decrees targeting Jews over the next 12 years, robbing them of their rights one after another. With Germany being home to more Jews than any other country in Western Europe at the time, there was palpable anger and frustration within the community, not to mention fear and anxiety. Not surprisingly, some of the finest minds in the world, including writers, scientists and artists, left Germany. Notable among these were Sigmund Freud, Walter Gropius, Marlene Dietrich, Fritz Lang, Thomas Mann, Hannah Arendt and Albert Einstein. On the other hand, the NSDAP found patrons—if only initially—in eminent names like Martin Heidegger and Carl Jung who were swayed by the ideals of national socialism.

Even as the brain drain caused a flutter across Germany, Nazis appeased the public by replacing trade unions with a state-run private club of sorts called Kraft durch Freude, or Strength through Joy, that provided workers with vacations, ocean cruises, concert tickets and opportunities to go swimming and skiing. With Germans taking to criss-crossing the country for their trips, the automobile industry witnessed a boom as did the construction of state-controlled highways or the *autobahn*. Soon, the party set up the Reich Labour Service that used unemployed and unskilled workers to aid the building of the autobahn and other infrastructure projects. Hitler's Minister for Economics, Hjalmar Schacht, also introduced Germans to the concept of autarky or 'self-sufficiency' that would remove dependence on foreign investment, trade and imports and render the country less vulnerable to the fluctuations in world economy. While autarky dramatically reduced unemployment and improved the economy on paper, workers were in reality being paid much lesser than before the economic depression while being made to work far more hours a day to fulfil production targets.

With the common man kept busy in building Germany anew, Hitler turned his attention, in 1934, to the rising clout of the SA that had grown to over 3,000,000 members under Ernst Röhm. Feeling threatened by the rowdy organization that he had helped nurture; he established the Gestapo, or secret police, as a countermeasure. Soon, in an incident known as the Night of Long Knives, the Gestapo and SS rounded up all SA leaders and executed them without trial. Having been loyal to Hitler through the years, Röhm himself was given the choice of suicide or execution and, having chosen the latter, was shot dead by SS guards. A similar purge of political opponents resulted in the execution of Kurt von Schleicher amongst several others. Those who were spared were sent to Dachau to be treated like prisoners.

By mid-1934, Germany saw the setting up of three more concentration camps modelled on Dachau, housing over 200,000 political prisoners and Jews, headed by Theodor Eicke—the 'Inspector of Concentration Camps'. Responsible for designing the entire camp system down to the rooms occupied by prisoners, the uniform they wore, the food they ate and the work they did, Eicke was not only completely shorn of empathy towards his prisoners, he also trained junior officers to become like him—cold and inhuman. So, while prisoners entering the camps were stripped off their individual personalities and reduced to being just numbers, they were constantly referred to as 'filth' and 'pigs', especially if they were Jews, and made to work on 12-hour-long torturous shifts without breaks.

Amidst the upheaval of Germany under Hitler came the death of President Hindenburg in August 1934. With the last link to the erstwhile democracy having disappeared, Hitler lost no time in merging the posts of president and chancellor and appointed himself Führer of the German Reich. It was soon mandated that every German soldier would swear an oath of allegiance, not to the country but to the Führer and address Hitler as 'Mein Führer' instead of the earlier 'Herr Hitler'. In September, he addressed a crowd of one million Germans at the Nuremberg rally where he famously proclaimed, 'The German form of life is definitely determined for the next thousand years. The Age of Nerves of the nineteenth century has found its close with us. There will be no revolution in Germany for the next thousand years.'

The next five years saw an unchecked rise in Nazi power, which translated into a reign of terror for the German Jews. The Nuremberg Laws passed in 1935 officially stripped them of their citizenship and forbade marriage or sexual relations between them and the racially pure Germans. A supplemental decree went on to define 'full Jews' as those with at least three Jewish grandparents, effectively ensuring that Jews who had stopped practising their faith or converted to Christianity too could be persecuted at Nazi will. Complicated charts depicting Aryans in white, full Jews in black and 'half-breeds' or mixed-race Jews in grey were created to identify the 'degree of Jewishness' of a person. As part of a segregation drive, Jews were forbidden from attending public schools, visiting cinema halls and vacation resorts, and even living or walking in German sections of cities and towns. Then, even as they were forced to sell their businesses and properties, the Nazis destroyed synagogues and vandalized Jewish-owned stores and homes. Although Jews were the larger target of Nazi hatred, 'genetically inferior' Germans, such as blacks, gypsies and around 350,000 physically and mentally challenged citizens, were forced to undergo sterilization so they could not produce children, while homosexuals were promptly imprisoned.

Jews were also at the receiving end of Hitler's megalomaniacal mission to change the less-than-appealing urbanscape of Berlin that remained architecturally poor in his eyes compared to Munich and Vienna. To rebuild Berlin into Germania, a capital worthy of the Thousand Year Reich, homes of thousands of ordinary Germans were razed, forcing them to relocate to homes belonging to Jews. The Jews, in turn, were shifted to cramped ghettos and concentration camps.

Hitler's plans for Germania included a grand seven-kilometre-long avenue along the north-south axis with an array of business and civic buildings on either side that would culminate at the Great Arch, a WWI memorial of sorts, at one end, and the Grand Hall at the other. The latter, inspired by the Pantheon, was to be the largest covered space in the world with a dome 16 times higher than St. Peter's in Rome and designed to accommodate 180,000 people. The Nazi-style of architecture that emerged during this period was marked by simplicity, uniformity, monumentality, solidity and eternity, in keeping with the party's ideology. The building craze—sparked by the idea of Germania—also meant an escalation in demand for both material and labour. The Nazis had both at their disposal. Soon, concentration camps were built next to stone quarries and thousands of Jews, communists and other 'misfits', such as beggars, tramps, gypsies and homosexuals, were put to work at construction sites.

Even as plans were underway for a grand Germania that would dwarf capital cities across the world, Hitler started the process of rearmament in defiance of the Treaty of Versailles. A year earlier, France and the Bolshevik USSR had signed a treaty of mutual support that Hitler had deemed hostile to Germany. Now, in March 1936, he used it as a pretext to send troops to take back Rhineland, including the important cities of Bonn, Aachen, Cologne and Dusseldorf on the Franco-German border that had been demilitarized under the Locarno Agreement after WWI. The surprise move created a rift between the WWI allies, with Britain refusing to support a French armed conflict to push Germany back, partly deeming the Treaty of Versailles as having been unduly harsh on the latter and partly reluctant to start another war. When the League of Nations met that month to deliberate on the breach of the treaty, all nations, save for the USSR, opposed the imposition of economic sanctions on the Germans. Consequently, in what was a loss of face for France, Germany soon reoccupied Rhineland.

The success of the Rhineland operation gave Hitler the confidence to revisit one of his oldest beliefs that Germans deserved to have more land to live their lives on. And so, with annexation on his mind, he began to prepare Germany for war. Factories were set up to manufacture weapons, the German Air Force was established with a fleet of 8,000 planes and youth were recruited in large numbers to create a million strong army. The world, however, seemed to be in a forgiving mood. Just months after the remilitarization of Rhineland, it allowed Hitler to score another win on the global stage with 49 nations participating in the 1936 Berlin Olympics, up from the count of 37 nations that had participated in the 1932 Los Angeles games.

Despite Hitler having to compromise on his 'no-Jew-athlete' policy and tolerate the historic wins of black athletes that defied the ideal of Aryan supremacy, the games were conducted impeccably and received rave reviews across the world. What went unnoticed though was the suicide of Captain Wolfgang Fuerstner soon after the games concluded. Fuerstner had been the man in charge of designing and constructing the 130-acre

Olympic Village that was appreciated globally for its state-of-the-art housing and services. However, just days before the games commenced, he was demoted owing to his Jewish ancestry which meant that all the praise meant for him was lapped up by another non-Jewish officer. Frustrated, Fuerstner shot himself after attending a lavish banquet that would have honoured him rather than his colleague if only he hadn't been a Jew.

In 1937, buoyed by the world turning a blind eye to his expansionist ambitions, Hitler set sights on Austria, which had a large pro-Nazi German-speaking population that favoured merging with the Reich. With the Austrian government torn by internal fights between various factions and Chancellor Kurt von Schuschnigg suitably threatened by the Nazis, there was practically no opposition to the annexation plans. On 15 March 1938, Hitler's army marched into Vienna to a jubilant reception. Addressing the city from the balcony of the Hofberg Palace he proclaimed, 'This country is German and therefore in this hour I can report to the German people the greatest accomplishment of my life. As Führer and Reich Chancellor of the German nation I am announcing to history, my homeland's entrance into the German Reich.'

Hitler's next target was northern Czechoslovakia's Sudetenland, which too had a large German-speaking population. This time he pursued a diplomatic strategy, shrewdly inviting the British, Italian and French leaders to discuss Germany's rightful claim on the region. To his surprise, the talks culminated in the Munich Pact that allowed Germany to annex Sudetenland peacefully provided Hitler refrained from making further claims on the rest of Czechoslovakia. Remarkably, Czechoslovakia, the country to be annexed, had no representation in the meeting and no say in its outcome. When German troops marched into Sudetenland on 1 October 1938 and brought it under the banner of the German Reich, Hitler is said to have commented, 'I did not think it possible that Czechoslovakia would be virtually served up to me on a plate by her friends.' And, in what was an obvious expression of contempt for the Western Allies, he remarked, 'Our enemies are little worms. I saw them at Munich.'

Hitler's stupendous success with annexations earned him the 1938 'Time's Man of the Year' title in the US. However, unlike politicians who shied away from calling him out for his potentially disastrous expansionist ambitions and human rights violations, the iconic magazine offered an unflattering view of his policies. While the magazine cover depicted him playing the 'hymn of hate' in a desecrated cathedral even as victims dangled on a St. Catherine's wheel with the Nazi hierarchy looking on, the pages within delved critically into his politics of hatred and persecution of Jews. That, however, was all the world was willing to do. Consequently, despite the Munich Pact, Germany invaded the Czech provinces of Moravia and Bohemia within a year and although these weren't annexed into the German Reich, they were placed under Nazi rule as protectorates. The province of Slovakia soon declared itself an independent Catholic state with ties to Nazi Germany, while Hungary, taking advantage of the confusion, annexed southern Czechoslovakia. Thus, by the end of 1939, Czechoslovakia ceased to exist as a nation as the WWI Allies watched from a distance.

Heady with his success with Czechoslovakia, Hitler turned his attention to Poland. Having secured the diplomatic win of getting USSR's Joseph Stalin to sign a non-aggression pact with Germany in exchange for the latter getting a slice of East Poland, he sent troops marching into Poland on 1 September 1939. In what was conceived as a 'lightning strike' that would give

Britain no time to come to Poland's aid, Germany annexed the latter in just 18 days, stunning the world.

The conquest of Poland came with a problem for the Nazis though. The three-million-strong Jewish population occupying large parts of Polish cities meant that there would be less land for the Germans. To correct this perceived imbalance, Jews were soon gathered into hundreds of ghettos across Poland until the Nazis could find a way to deport them all to Madagascar. With overcrowding, lack of clean running water, absence of proper sewage systems and an extremely sparse supply of food and medicines, the ghettos became hotbeds for diseases and death. However, offering a higher possibility of living with one's family, they were much better than the concentration camps where tens of thousands perished in isolation.

Hitler's annexation of Poland sounded the bugle for WWII and soon, both France and Britain started to prepare for the inevitable conflict. Over the next six years the world would witness unprecedented carnage and destruction with close to 40 million people losing their lives and much of the cultural heritage of Europe, including Germany, being destroyed, thanks to the Führer's unquenchable ambition. In 1940 though, Germany's annexation of Denmark and Norway were quick and bloodless, with the former capitulating in just one day and the latter within two months. By early 1941, the Reich had been extended from France in the west to Ukraine in the east. Then, in the middle of that year, Hitler decided to disregard his pact with Stalin and attack the country whose Bolshevik ideology had long irked him. For Hitler, the trouncing of communists was as important as that of the Jews. However, Russia wasn't an easy enemy to conquer. With German troops having to fight Britain on the Western Front and Russia in the east, Hitler finally started to run out of luck.

Although the war started with big and quick wins for Germany, the country soon started to struggle for resources to sustain its growing population while also keeping the war going. With a shortage of both food and land for the Germans, it became all the more urgent to address the question of what was to be done with the large number of Jews in ghettos and concentration camps across Greater Germany. At the Wannsee Conference of 1942, attended by senior SS leaders, it was decided to arrive at a 'Final Solution' to the Jewish problem. This meant creating extermination camps with gas chambers to facilitate the mass murder of Jews, housing and providing for whom had become an unwanted burden.

In the horror that followed, documented as the Holocaust for the world to know, specialized killing centres were constructed in Poland's Auschwitz, Belzec, Chelmno, Majdanek, Sobibor, and Treblinka regions, featuring large gas chambers with adjacent crematories or burial pits for the disposal of corpses. Once these became operational, Jews were no longer sent to ghettos, they were directly transported by trains to their deaths. Between 1942 and 1944, 300,000 Jews were gassed to death at Belzec, 700,000 in Treblinka and over a million in Auschwitz. Not only did the death of these Jews relieve the human burden of the Reich, it also offered temporary financial gains for the SS. Upon arrival at the extermination camps, the Jews were required to deposit all their belongings, including foreign currency, gold, jewels, clothes and shoes, with the guards. These valuables were sent to the SS Headquarters of Economic Administration that in turn sent clothes and accessories to German families or soldiers at the front and funnelled the gold and currency into secret bank accounts.

While there was no doubt that Hitler was privy to the gruesome happenings at the death camps, he was careful not to leave a paper trail in the form of written orders or decrees to carry out the heinous crimes perpetrated against the Jews. At the same time, although the secrets of the death camps leaked out of Greater Germany and reached the Allies through eye-witnesses, escapees and informants as early as 1942, the rest of the world did nothing to stop the crimes for reasons as varied as disbelief, economic concerns, xenophobia, and anti-Semitism. With military and political leaders in the US and UK believing that diverting resources to rescue operations would jeopardize the war effort, appeals to bomb railway lines leading to the extermination camps were frequently rejected even as Germany's industrial infrastructure, some within as little as 50 miles of Auschwitz, were bombarded instead. What was also not justified was the reluctance of most countries to open their borders for the fleeing Jews. While several countries introduced restrictive immigration policies to avoid an influx of refugees, officials in US president Roosevelt's administration reduced the issuance of immigration visas to 10 per cent of the regular quota—and even obstructed approval at times—until it was too late in 1944.

In early 1943, Germany was trounced by the Russians in the Battle of Stalingrad after a bitter winter combat that saw over two million casualties on both sides. Forced to retreat from Russia, Hitler and his entourage tried to scramble together pieces of Europe and Africa to add to the Reich, albeit with little success. At the same time, Britain and the US upped their ante, carpet bombing Germany to destroy weapons factories regardless of civilian fatalities. The incessant bombings flattened major cities, including Berlin, Munich, Frankfurt, Cologne, Dresden and Nuremberg, wiping out entire civilian populations and their centuries old cultural heritage. In Hamburg, 40,000 people lost their lives in a single week. For German citizens, it was an unanticipated nightmare. Until now, they had silently witnessed what the horrors of ghettos, concentration camps and death camps did to their fellow Jews, believing in their Führer's vision for the Thousand Year Reich. Now, when a scorching death came knocking home, their faith in Hitler was shattered. Public morale across the country plummeted.

Hitler too was shaken by the turn the war had taken. Instead of touring the bomb-wracked cities, meeting with injured soldiers and providing moral support to his grieving citizens, he chose to isolate and surround himself with a few Nazi officers who would shield him from reality. Despite knowing that victory had slipped out of his grasp, he was keen on indefinitely sacrificing the lives of both civilians and soldiers to keep the war going.

In mid-1944, frustrated with the Führer's indifference to the ravages of war, a small Nazi faction attempted to assassinate him using a briefcase bomb. Unfortunately for them, luck intervened in favour of Hitler, perhaps for the last time. The bomb went off six feet away from him, with an oak conference table shielding him from the full force of the blast. While three of his staff died on the spot, he managed to get away with minor injuries. Paranoid after the incident, Hitler ordered another purge of the SA and SS ranks to ensure the elimination of all internal enemies, ordering officers found guilty of the bombing incident to be 'hung like cattle'. The Gestapo obliged and soon, in the execution room of the prison, eight meat hooks were fixed to the ceiling from which officers were hung with piano wire so they could die slow, painful deaths.

Hitler was not the same again after the attempt on his life. Although he did not sustain external injuries, his hearing and eyesight were adversely impacted. A persistent ringing in his right ear and an odd flicker in his right eye disrupted his balance, causing him to stagger as he walked and lean on walls or furniture to stay upright. Doctors overseeing his treatment put him on a regimen of pills and injections that triggered severe stomach cramps, necessitating further medication. These, combined with growing insomnia, left Hitler with a hazy memory and stunted his power to recall details. Not surprisingly, the man for whom control was an all-important asset was frustrated and became increasingly irritable.

Poor health, however, did not deter Hitler from dragging every last bit of his country to ruins. In the winter of 1944, he made a last-ditch effort to turn the tides in Germany's favour by ordering his men to invade US troops in what is famously known as the Battle of the Bulge. Adopting a novel war tactic, nearly 2,000 German commandos were trained to dress and talk like American soldiers so they could infiltrate the American camp, kill their dispatch runners and confuse troops with wrong instructions and directions. Although it began on a successful note, the operation crumbled within a week, putting the Americans back on top of the game. With British and American troops closing in on Berlin from the west and Russian troops from the east, the war was all but lost. Yet, Hitler refused to sign an armistice.

With Germany staring at certain defeat in March 1945, the Führer withdrew into an ideological cocoon, concluding that the turn of events proved that Germans as a race were neither strong nor ruthless enough to achieve victory. Issuing the Scorched Earth Decree that called for the destruction of all German infrastructure, be it industry, agriculture, mines, communications, railways, roads, bridges, ships, stores, food or shops, so that the victors would have absolutely nothing of value to claim, he asked his officers to spare no thought for the common citizen. Making it clear that he wanted the entire nation to perish for it had proved itself to be weaker than the nations of the East, his last ideological defence was, 'those who will remain after the battle are only the inferior ones, for the good ones would have all been killed.' Luckily for the common Germans, Hitler's officers did not carry out his final order in its entirety for they did not want their nation to commit suicide. The same could not be said about their leader though.

With the continuous Allied bombing of Berlin, Hitler abandoned the Reich Chancellery building in April 1945 and moved into the underground Führerbunker, 28 feet beneath the chancellery gardens. On 29 April, he heard about the fate of his Italian ally Benito Mussolini who had been executed the previous day and hung by his feet at a public square in Milan before being thrown into the gutter. Fearing a similar fate if taken prisoner, Hitler decided to take his own life. Early that day, he dictated his will and married his secretary and girlfriend, Eva Braun, in the map room of the bunker. The newlyweds proceeded to have a celebratory breakfast with two of Hitler's closest aides, Joseph Goebbels and Martin Bormann, even as Russian troops continued to close in. In preparation for his own final solution, he ordered the burning of all personal and political records and instructed his doctor to put down his dog Blondi, a gift from Bormann. After lunch on 30 April, Hitler gave Eva a cyanide capsule that she bit into and died instantly. He then shot himself in the right temple and fell onto the bunker floor, marking the end of the darkest period of German history.

Years before, during the peak of his reign, Hitler had mused about a time when he would retire with Eva and Blondi to a simple, anonymous life in the Danube hills once the great war had been won. He had also decided that when he died, he wanted his body brought to his favourite city, Munich, to be interred in a small, simple neoclassical mausoleum that he had already designed. 'No ornaments, no adornment, just a simple stone sarcophagus on the ground and the open sky above,' he had described to a friend. 'It will become a cult centre, a shrine as famous in the modern world as the mausoleum of Halicarnassus was in the ancient.' On 30 April 1945 though, Goebbels and Bormann carried his body, along with Eva's, to a small garden above the bunker, poured gallons of gasoline over it and lit it with a petrol-soaked rag. And as the two loyal officers watched the bodies burst into flames, they made their last Hitler salute.

Ayatollah Khomeini

Erstwhile Persia was both the birthplace and seat of Zoroastrianism, one of the world's oldest religions with an antiquity dating back to nearly 3,500 years. The monotheist religion, which venerates Ahura Mazda as the one and only God, is largely a peaceful one, engaging harmoniously with Jews, early Christians and Muslims and propagating the ideas of 'good words, good thoughts and good deeds'. It dominated the region from the second millennium BCE *to the sixth century* CE *during which Persia saw some of its golden years both culturally and politically. How then did the country become an Islamic Republic? How then did it fall into the trap of religious dictatorship despite its rich cultural and intellectual heritage? And how then did its fate, and that of its unsuspecting citizens, come to rest in the hands of fanatical clergymen?*

In the second millennium BCE, tribes from Central Asia migrated to what we now know as the Iranian Plateau. By 550 BCE, the Persian state had emerged as a distinct entity in the region and established itself as a force to contend with. With the accession of Cyrus the Great as emperor of the Achaemenid Empire, the Persians conquered much of erstwhile Mesopotamia, the region considered to be the 'cradle of civilization', what with it being the epicentre for the development of everything from pottery, agriculture and irrigation to writing, construction technology, beer brewing and code of laws. Then, under Xerxes I, the empire went on to become the largest of its times, spanning 5.5 million square kilometres from the Balkans in the West to the Indus Valley in the East. Persepolis, one of the four capital cities of the empire, was thought to be the richest in the world at the time.

It all came crashing down though, when Alexander the Great laid siege on Persepolis. From then on, Persia slipped in and out of the hands of several empires including the Hellenic, Seleucid, Parthian and Sassanian before getting finally conquered by Arab Muslims in the seventh century CE and getting absorbed into the Islamic Caliphate. Slowly but surely, Arabic influence swept across every aspect of life in the region, including the Persian language itself, which, by ninth century CE, was being written in Arabic script. Moreover, Zoroastrianism, the state religion of Persia since the times of Cyrus the Great, started to decline, giving way to Sunni Islam.

Then, in 1501 CE, Shah Ismail I of the Safavid dynasty conquered Persia. Descended from and belonging to a unique Sufi order called Safaviyyeh, he forcibly converted people of the region from Sunni to Shia Islam and established a version of Shi'ism known as 'Athnā ashariyyah' ('Twelver' in English) or 'Imamiyyah' as the state religion. Over the next several centuries this version of Shi'ism, which believes that the last of the 12 divinely ordained Shia imams, Imam Muhammad al-Mahdi (or the Hidden Imam), has been living in hiding since his birth in the ninth century CE and is expected to surface one day to liberate the world from all evil, gained more and more acceptance in Persia and almost completely replaced all other religions. In the Islamic world, the Sunnis constitute a majority, the Shias, a minority, and the Twelver Shias, an even smaller minority. Despite this marginal following, the religion managed to retain a stronghold on Persia through the centuries, establishing an inimical hegemony on every aspect of life that continues to exist even in current-day Iran.

Climbing up the Beanstalk of Modernization

The advent of the eighteenth century saw the establishment of connections between Persia and Europe that resulted in a curiosity amongst Europeans—traders and rulers alike. Soon, the Russian and British empires posed both political and ideological threats to Persia, influencing the intellectual elite of the country with their revolutionary ideas regarding organization, constitution and administration of the state and its economy. These intellectuals and activists found their detractors in a monarchy (which had changed twice since the fall of the Safavids) that was reluctant to change the status quo. Not surprisingly, the friction between the two groups resulted in several revolutions. The first, in 1906, heralded a parliamentary system based on the British constitutional model that separated the executive and monarchy during the rule of the Qajar dynasty. The second, a military coup by Reza Khan against the reigning Qajars, resulted in the establishment of the Pahlavi dynasty in 1925, headed by Reza, who adopted the name Reza Shah Pahlavi. No doubt influenced by the Europeans, Reza Shah nurtured ambitious plans for a modern Persia, including the development of industry, road and rail infrastructure, public education systems, healthcare and judiciary. He sent hundreds of Persians to study in Europe so they could return to join the government and help implement his vision over the next 16 years, transforming Persia into an industrialized country with an urban heart.

The Shah's biggest achievements were the construction of the Trans-Iranian Railway, the nationalization of communications and finances, and the emancipation of women through a decree to discard their veils. It was also during his reign that Persia formally changed its name to Iran in 1935, the Shah arguing that the name 'Persia' (originating from 'Parsa', the name of the group of people Cyrus the Great belonged to), represented only one of Iran's many ethnic groups. 'Iran', on the other hand, had been the name of the region long before the rise of the Achaemenid Empire, perhaps tracing its etymology to the word 'Aryan'.

Despite his progressive measures, the religious and intellectual elites in Iran were disenchanted with the Shah's dictatorial style—the state was vested with disproportionate power while the provision of basic civil rights to the common man left much to be desired. Furthermore, after the British-owned Anglo-Persian Oil Company failed to honour its 1933 agreement to provide better wages for labourers, build schools and hospitals, and establish a telephone system, the Shah sought to distance himself from the British and Russians, turning instead to the Germans, French and Italians for technical expertise in his developmental projects. The choice proved costly, for when WWII began in 1941, the Shah found himself on the wrong side. Although Iran had declared its neutrality, the continued presence of German and Italian technicians provoked Allied suspicion and hostility. The Shah's refusal to expel these technicians fearing the premature termination of his projects only deepened the mistrust of the Allies who soon invaded Iran, arrested the Shah and exiled him, first to Mauritius and then Johannesburg, where he died in 1944.

Fumbling through Democracy

Following Reza Shah's exile, the British and Russian authorities dismantled the political system established by him even as they allowed his son, Mohammad Reza Shah Pahlavi, to ascend the throne of Iran. The next four decades saw Iran grapple with the challenge of balancing democracy and monarchy. Although Mohammad Reza sought to continue the developmental agenda initiated by his father, he faced increasing interference from foreign powers. This included a 1949 attempt on his life attributed to the Russians and a 1953 coup against his nationalist prime minister, Dr Mohammad Mosaddeq, orchestrated by Britain and the US after Mosaddeq's bid to nationalize Iran's oil fields. Not surprisingly, the new Shah tried to revive and control the army, and expanded his constitutional powers, much to the chagrin of the liberalists.

In the 1960s, Mohammad Reza launched the 'White Revolution' that brought about land reforms, extended voting rights to women and aimed at eliminating illiteracy. While these changes irked the religious Shia leaders who perceived a threat to their traditional authority, the Shah's failure in complementing these sweeping socio-economic reforms with similar reforms in the political arena led to unfulfilled promises and a disillusionment amongst the masses—particularly the intellectuals and activists. Further, large-scale industrialization and urbanization led to majority of Iran's traditional and conservative rural masses getting uprooted and placed in modern cities they could not identify with. Oblivious to the plight of his people, Mohammad Reza continued with his reforms, passing a new law in 1962 to eliminate the traditional practice of swearing government officials into office on the Quran. Even as his actions flamed public ire, he signed an agreement with the US in 1964 to grant complete judicial immunity for all American military personnel in Iran, allegedly in exchange for a $200 million loan. The same year, he exiled the popular Shia scholar, Ayatollah Ruhollah Khomeini, for speaking up against his policies and instigating the masses to riot.

Then, in 1971, the Shah hosted an extravagant five-day gala at Persepolis, near the tomb of Cyrus the Great, to celebrate 2,500 years of Persian monarchy. Arrangements for the event included the setting up of a tent city made from 37 km of silk in a specially created oasis to house over 60 kings, queens and presidents from across the world. While Maxim, the best restaurant in the world at the time, was roped in to serve five-course banquets and the rarest of wines, thousands of soldiers were made to parade in ancient Persian costumes followed by a light and sound show at the foot of the Temple of Darius for the entertainment of the guests. The celebrations ended with the opening of the 45 m tall marble gateway that was named 'Shah's Memorial' in honour of the Shah himself.

While the decadent display for the world might have stroked Mohammad Reza's ego, it only aggravated the disillusionment amongst his people, especially the Shia leaders who perceived the event as being anti-Islamic. In 1975, he introduced reforms to the Family Protection Law—raising the marriageable age of women to 18 and men to 20, granting men and women equal rights to divorce, mandating that a man could marry not four times but only a second time, that too with the consent of his first wife, and setting up Family Courts. Although these were progressive measures that benefited Iranian women, they reduced the power and authority of the clergy considerably. Moreover, the conservatives were left fuming over what they felt was an affront to Islam.

Things only got worse when, in 1976, the Shah replaced the Islamic calendar (also known as the Solar Hijri) that began with the year of Prophet Muhammad's journey from Mecca to Medina, with an 'Imperial' one that started with the year of establishment of the Persian Empire. Further, his blatant disregard for the opinions of the people, and the censorship, surveillance and suppression of opponents with the help of SAVAK, Iran's security and intelligence organization, made it seem as though he were on a mission to commit political suicide. Iran's economic collapse in 1977 and the subsequent rise in unemployment and inflation did nothing to mollify the situation.

Slipping into Theocracy

With the Shah having managed to alienate not only the intellectuals and religious groups but also the leftists, nationalists and majority of the rural masses, the late 1970s saw a growing resentment towards the revived autocracy backed by the United States. Further, secular intellectuals who had been wary of the orthodox perspectives of the Shi'a ulama (religious scholars) until then, sat up to reconsider their stance. Aligning themselves with the ulama seemed an attractive option if it resulted in overthrowing the Shah. And so, in 1978, the country came together to bring about a revolution.

What started out as a protest by students in Qom, the seat of Iran's largest seminaries, against slanderous remarks made by a newspaper about the exiled Ruhollah Khomeini, snowballed into an anti-regime agitation joined by thousands of unemployed Iranian youth. The streets of Iranian towns and cities filled up with demonstrators carrying pictures of Khomeini, portrayed in his signature black robe with a white beard and piercing black eyes. The anger of the masses took Mohammed Reza, then fighting a debilitating cancer, by surprise. His government immediately imposed martial law and ordered the killing of protesters, setting into motion a vicious cycle of protesting, dying and mourning by demonstrators who returned to the streets to commemorate the seventh and the fortieth days of mourning for the 'martyrs' as per Shi'a tradition. By the end of the year, strikes by disenchanted staff at government offices and industrial units alike became a common sight in Tehran. Sensing trouble, the Shah abdicated in early 1979 and went into exile, leaving behind him a country that eagerly awaited the return of his nemesis—Ayatollah Khomeini.

Two weeks after the Shah's abdication, Khomeini, who had by now attained the status of a high-ranking spiritual leader or 'Grand Ayatollah', arrived in Tehran to a rousing welcome by a million-strong crowd. The populist revolution to obliterate the 2,500-year-old monarchy had been a success. However, that wasn't the end game the 77-year-old Shi'a scholar had envisaged. No doubt the revolution could not have been possible without the support of the seculars, leftists and nationalists, but they did not figure in his vision for the future of the country.

In the early 1970s, Khomeini had given a series of lectures in Najaf, Iraq—where he lived in exile—that were later compiled into a book titled *Hokumat-e Islami: Velayat-e Faqih* (*Islamic Government: Guardianship of the Jurist*). The book, which went on to become his most influential work, laid out his thoughts on the strict implementation of Sharia (laws of God) through an Islamic government that would be headed by a *faqih* (an expert in the knowledge of Islamic law and justice). Emphasizing that both monarchy and democracy were 'wrong' according to Islam, Khomeini argued that since no one knew Islam better than the clergy, it was only natural to allow them to rule as guardians of the state until the return of the Hidden Imam. He also propagated the idea that clerical rule was required not only to prevent corruption, injustice and oppression of the downtrodden but also to destroy anti-Islamic foreign influences. While Velayat-e faqih had existed in Shi'a Islam for centuries as a system of limited clerical guardianship to support those incapable of protecting their own interests, such as orphans and the destitute, Khomeini's interpretation recast the doctrine into a mould that encompassed the entire nation.

During his exile in Najaf, Khomeini had also made several speeches—some mollifying, some motivational and some fiery calls for action—whose cassette recordings found their way into Iran and were listened to with adoration and anticipation by frustrated Iranians. Although the allusion to Islamic law in these speeches should have raised eyebrows of secular intellectuals, they went almost unnoticed or were misinterpreted. For instance, in the same breath as he promised a return to the traditional Iranian identity—that the masses culturally lost between the East and West during the Shah's reign could connect to—he also talked about the divine ordinances of the Sharia and the need to use Islam as an organizing force to form the future government. Similarly, he mixed aspects of religion and governance to convince the people that just as following Islamic faith would lead to happiness and a philosophically perfect human, implementing the tenets of Islam at the national level would lead to a perfect society. His careful choice of words gave the masses a sense of pride in being Iranians and in being followers of Islam.

And so, when he returned to Tehran after 15 years in exile on 1 February 1979 and turned what had essentially been a secular revolution into an Islamic one, his appropriation of the symbolic leadership of the country by acknowledging the 'religious and legal right the people of Iran had bestowed upon us through their demonstrations' went uncontested. The ambiguity of his use of the word 'us' worked in his favour with the nationalists and intellectuals interpreting it as an allusion to the larger collective that had led the revolution and not just Khomeini and his disciples. Further, Khomeini veiled his distaste for democracy with statements that sounded pro-democratic such as in his avowal that 'in Muslim countries, Islamic law is of the people, so essentially Muslim countries are democracies.' His denunciation, 'I must tell you that Mohammad Reza Pahlavi, that evil traitor, has gone... We are saying this man, his government, his Majlis are all illegal... I shall appoint my own government. I shall slap this government in the mouth. I shall determine the government with the backing of this nation, because this nation accepts me,' was met with rousing cheer from the crowds of common men and intellectuals alike. And no one stepped forward to question his decree—when appointing Mehdi Bazargan as the interim prime minister of Iran—that since this was not an ordinary government but a government based on the Sharia, those opposing it were effectively opposing the Sharia of Islam, and any revolt against God's government was a revolt against God.

There was one group, however, that remained wary of Khomeini's doctrine of Islamic Governance. Paradoxically, it comprised Shi'a scholars from Qom who opposed the Islamization of Iran and rejected the idea of the clergy's involvement in matters of governance. Several of them even abstained from travelling to Tehran to acknowledge Khomeini's leadership.

In a scenario where spiritual leaders such as Ayatollah Shariyatmadari and Ayatollah Mahallati presented a moderate face that he feared would be better liked by nationalists, Khomeini realized the need for scholars to publicly endorse his religious authority if he were to implement his vision of Velayat-e faqih. And so, in his choice of Bazargan as Prime Minister, he shrewdly played down the 'Islamic' component of his rhetoric and presented Iran with an engineer and a nationalist who had led the Freedom Movement against the Shah's regime—a man with spotless democratic credentials who was acceptable to all, including the Americans.

Further, well aware that a US-backed military coup could destroy all that he had achieved, appeasing the Americans and placating the Shah's armed forces was a crucial next step. In this direction too, the choice of Bazargan worked its magic. Within a week, the SAVAK had declared its neutrality on the advice of the US and acquiesced to support the interim government. Little did the Americans, or indeed Bazargan and the larger Iranian population, know then that everything Khomeini said in those early days about a pro-people democratic government was a deception. And although a glimpse of what lay in store for Iran was apparent in the months that followed, the excitement of overthrowing the Shah seemed to have inhibited the reasoning power of the entire country.

No sooner had Bazargan's government been sworn in, than Khomeini put into action his plans to turn Iran into an Islamic state. Within three days his disciples, comprising several radical clerics, formed a separate political entity—the Islamic Republic Party (IRP)—whose motto was 'one community, one religion, one order, one leader'. The leader, of course, was the Imam—the title by which Khomeini was fondly addressed. With the goal of recruiting as many members for the future government as possible, the IRP distributed propaganda leaflets across government offices, universities, army establishments, industries and revolutionary groups, and allegedly gained as many as two million members in its first 100 days. While Khomeini was clear that he did not want clerics to hold government posts, he went on to sanction their appointment as heads of parallel committees to the judiciary, police and army to oversee every conceivable public activity including the offering of Friday prayers.

Then, even as the IRP Komiteh (committee) expanded influence across the country under the guidance of its Imam, steps were taken towards the Islamization of the army. Under the leadership of Ali Khamenei and Hassan Rouhani, both of whom would go on to occupy the top posts of 'Supreme Leader' and 'President' of Iran, respectively, after the demise of Khomeini, 'religious' army officers, irrespective of their rank, were promoted to senior commanders while every last nationalist associated with the Shah's army, including janitors, were removed from their posts. In mid-February, many of the Shah's military commanders who had trusted Khomeini's assurances of clemency were arrested and executed after summary trials, much to the horror of the world that saw the naked and bloody pictures of some of Iran's top officers in their newspapers over the next several days.

In March 1979, Khomeini ordered the replacement of Iran's existing judiciary with Islamic Revolutionary Courts headed by clerics as judges. Soon, alcohol was prohibited, with those caught producing or drinking alcohol getting lashed in public. Broadcasting and listening to music other than Komiteh-approved revolutionary songs was also banned and veiling was made mandatory for women. The last order created a flutter in the womenfolk who had been active participants in the revolutionary struggle. When, during a speech in Paris in the early days of the revolution, Khomeini hinted at the role of women in the Iranian society being defined within the Islamic framework, nobody had thought it prudent to ask for clarification. Now smacked on the cheek by the veiling order, women took to the streets in thousands on 8 March, celebrated globally as International Women's Day, to protest the regressive rule. Even religious scholars such as Ayatollah Taleqani, who wielded as much power and had as many followers as Khomeini, questioned the need for veiling.

Taken by surprise, Khomeini backtracked, but only regarding the veiling law and only for the moment. In the coming days, he would force the interim government to rescind the Shah's progressive reforms to the Family Protection Law, bringing back the marriageable age of girls to nine years, taking away child custody from women, and allowing men to take four wives and stop their wives from working or going out into the streets, and also divorce at will.

Even as the Komiteh started interfering in the workings of the interim government, appointing radical clerics to important posts and imprisoning and executing dissident clerics who refused to accept the new order, Iran prepared for what would be a fate-changing referendum for its people. On 30 March, the Iranians were to vote for whether or not Iran should be an 'Islamic Republic'. Khomeini's disciples spread themselves across the country to convince every individual to vote with a 'Yes'.

Despite being given a whiff of the future through the blatant interference of the Imam's Islamic radicals in the workings of the interim government, publicly known executions carried out by them and their imposition of arbitrary bans, 98.2 per cent of Iran's population, including ethnic minorities, women and secular intellectuals, chose to walk into that future. On 1 April 1979, a jubilant Khomeini announced, 'I am declaring today the day of the Islamic Republic of Iran, and I would also like to declare that such a referendum is unprecedented in history—to establish a Government of righteousness and to overthrow and bury the monarchy in the rubbish pile of history.' He then went on to proclaim 1 April as the 'first day of the Government of God'.

Anointing the Supreme Leader

The referendum's outcome marked the first step towards the complete Islamization of Iran and the subsequent takeover of the nation by radical clerics. The next step was to draft an Islamic Constitution and once again put it to a public referendum. Even as Khomeini negotiated with Bazargan's government, and the clerics and nationalists drew up a Constitution acceptable to all, his followers worked on the sidelines to silence dissident voices. Between April and December 1979, the Komiteh suppressed several spurts of rebellion—some nationalist, some Marxist-Islamist—that rose against the clerical takeover of the government.

Careful not to step on sensitive toes before the approval of the new Constitution, Khomeini had initially forfeited the mention of Velayat-e faqih in the draft Constitution. However, the assassination of his disciple Ayatollah Morteza Motahari by rebel Marxist-Islamists made him change his stance. Realizing that the unfortunate event was a result of a weak interim government and his own tolerance, he voiced his discontent with the nationalists and started campaigning towards the institutionalization of the Velayat-e faqih in the Constitution. In July that year, another of his disciples, Ayatollah Montazeri, called for the new president to be either a faqih himself or to be appointed by one. Soon, Islamic radicals were asking Khomeini to step in as their political leader and the IRP projected itself as Khomeini's party in the run up to the Constituent Assembly elections to be held in August.

Despite vehement protests by Shariatmadari and accusations of rampant election rigging, the IRP secured 55 of the 73 seats in the Constituent Assembly, 65 per cent of which were held by clerics. With the sweeping majority paving the way for the incorporation of Velayat-e faqih into the Constitution, Khomeini issued a congratulatory message to the Majlis-e Khobregān, or Assembly of Experts in charge of writing the Constitution, emphasizing the need for every law they created to be 100 per cent Islamic. He then coordinated to constitute a 12-member Guardian Council, including six grand ayatollahs, to ensure that every law passed by the Majlis was in line with the Sharia.

Even as the Majlis debated and formulated new laws for what was soon to be a brand new 'Islamic State', Iran witnessed increasing incidents of rebellion by the anti-clerical and anti-American Marxist-Islamist groups. The Imam's ambivalent stand on the country's relationship with the US and his propitiations to President Carter, such as 'You will see we are not in any particular animosity with the Americans,' in particular, were used to drum up anti-Khomeini sentiments amongst labour unions, university students and factory workers. Their rhetoric found favour with left-leaning masses who were still livid with—and suspicious of—the US for supporting the Shah's eccentricities. Then, in late-October 1979, the ailing Shah was allowed to enter the US for treatment. The seemingly innocent event sent both the leftists and radical Islamists scrambling to prove that each was more anti-American than the other. Even as they competed to denounce their common enemy, Khomeini seized the moment and, labelling President Carter's government as a 'Great Satan' and an 'Enemy of Islam', urged his followers to demonstrate against the Americans. However, even he hadn't anticipated the events that unfolded next.

On 4 November nearly 300 armed students—who called themselves 'Muslim Student Followers of the Imam's Line'—stormed into the US embassy in Tehran, took its staff of 63 American men and women hostage and demanded the extradition of the Shah so he could be tried and executed in Iran. Although Khomeini was as surprised as the rest of the world, he realized that the incident had stolen the thunder from the leftists—nothing could have showcased anti-Americanism better than this. So, after waiting for a few days to gauge President Carter's response, which, incidentally, was rather tame, he stepped up and declared his support to the hostage-takers with his now famous line—'America can't do a damn thing'.

With the leftists also supporting the taking of hostages, the 'Iranian hostage crisis' as it came to be known, continued till early 1981. For Khomeini, though, the benefits were immediate. His support for the action of his student followers and the accompanying anti-American rhetoric managed to divert the attention of the masses from the controversial Islamic Constitution getting framed by the Majlis. And so, when the Constitution was put to a referendum on 2 and 3 December 1979, it was approved by an astounding 99.5 per cent votes. The country had agreed to the idea of having a faqih as its *rahbar* or supreme leader, and who better to occupy that post than Ayatollah Ruhollah Khomeini himself.

Descending into an Ideological Abyss

When Iran approved a Constitution that had Velayat-e faqih governing each and every aspect of its citizens' lives, it also knowingly or unknowingly chose clerical sovereignty over popular sovereignty. This meant that the authority to govern the Iranians now rested in the hands of the faqih or jurists who purportedly understood God's laws. Moreover, not only did Khomeini now get to don the roles of the supreme jurist and supreme commander-in-chief, he also had the sole authority to appoint or remove from office the president, members of the Guardian Council, heads of the armed forces, and heads of all government branches. And under Article 107, Khomeini could hold his office for life.

Born on 27 May 1900, in the town of Khumayn, 180 miles south of Tehran, Khomeini belonged to a family with a long tradition of religious scholarship. His ancestors, descendants of the seventh Imam of the Ahl al-Bayt, had migrated from Lucknow, India, to Khumayn towards the end of the eighteenth century. Not surprisingly, he spent his entire life as a writer, teacher and religious scholar who engaged deeply with the interpretation of Islamic laws based on the Quran. However, while his expertise and single-minded pursuit of what he thought was the ideal political and social order that helped him rally support for the Islamic Revolution, it also created in him a tunnel vision that now, in his eightieth year, left him ill-prepared to rule a country. This wasn't a reality he would acknowledge though. With his eyes on the target that was Velayat-e faqih, he went about implementing his vision without a thought about what its fallout might be.

Among the first steps taken by Supreme Leader Khomeini was to call for an *inqilab-i-farhangi* or a 'cultural revolution' to redefine the educational system. Declaring that Iran was afraid not of economic sanctions but of Western universities that were diverting the country's youth away from their culture and religion, he ordered the purging of all non-Islamic influences from schools and colleges, replacing them with systems compatible with his idea of revolutionary Islam. However, while university students had played an important role in the Iranian revolution, many of them harboured ideological differences with Khomeini and were more sympathetic to Marxist ideals. In fact, several universities had become political hotbeds since the success of the revolution, with students focusing more on ideological debates than education. Consequently, there was considerable resistance to Khomeini's radical move, prompting him to call for the closure of all universities in the spring of 1980. Soon campuses across the country saw violent clashes between left-wing students and followers of the Imam, leaving hundreds of students injured and a few dozen dead. Finally, in June, universities were forced to shut down indefinitely to allow the 'Committee for Islamization of Universities' to complete its task of revamping textbooks and courses to conform to the ideals of Islam.

When schools and colleges reopened after three years in 1983, the first perceptible change was that of gender segregation, with female children as young as six years having to veil themselves and female faculty having been relieved of their posts and responsibilities in all except 'only women' colleges. Erasing the progressive strides made by Iranian women in the past, school textbooks depicted women wearing veils and performing stereotypical roles of managing homes and children while men were depicted as the key providers of families. In universities, both professors and students were screened before getting accepted, their admission being confirmed only if they were practising Muslims with a declared loyalty to the Velayat-e faqih. Although female students were allowed to pursue higher education, they could choose from only a few curated subjects and were allowed scholarships to study abroad only if they were married and had their husbands accompanying them. Non-Muslim students were worse off, being allowed to study nothing but accounting and foreign languages. Further, while new courses such as Islamic sociology and Islamic psychology were introduced in colleges, music was removed as a subject in line with the Supreme Leader's assertion that it was 'no different from opium, stupefying listeners and making their brain inactive and frivolous'.

Similarly, while Khomeini asserted in his speeches that Qom was the centre from where science had been exported to the rest of the world, his disciples promoted universities as places to create pure people with pure Islamic values rather than professionals. These sweeping changes in the education system left several students, professors and scientists frustrated and soon resulted in a massive brain drain from Iran, with many of them fleeing across the borders on foot fearing the Komiteh.

The next area that Khomeini focused on for Islamic reform was the judiciary. Observing that cases that took only a few days for a Sharia judge to decide were prolonged to over several years under the Westernized judicial system, he shut down the Ministry of Justice and brought in mullahs to serve as judges, jury and prosecutors. Further, banning the system of appeals, he declared that all judgements passed by mullahs would be final with punishments being meted out swiftly as per the Sharia. This meant that anyone found to be on the wrong side of the Sharia—be it for consuming alcohol, listening to non-Islamic music, cheating customers, committing adultery, women wearing lipstick and so on—would be flogged in public, the number of floggings commensurate with the gravity of the crime. Those found to have committed more serious crimes, such as homosexuals, prostitutes and married individuals committing adultery, were sentenced to death without the possibility of an appeal.

Political opponents of the Khomeini regime, including leftists, nationalists and intellectuals, bore the brunt of his ire during 1980–82, with an estimated 4,500 people being executed and nearly 30,000 imprisoned. Amongst the latter was his arch-rival Ayatollah Shariatmadari, whose boycotting of the December referendum had incited most Azerbaijanis, Kurds and Baluchis that made up nearly half of Iran's population to do the same, resulting in a barely 75 per cent voter turnout. Presented with a chance for revenge, Khomeini accused him of spying for the US during the hostage crisis and placed him under house arrest, defrocking him and denying medical care for his cancer. Such was his animosity towards Shariatmadari that Khomeini also denied him a formal funeral when he died in 1986.

Even as Khomeini set about reforming the Iranian society, the country was grappling with deep economic sanctions imposed by the US following the taking of hostages at its embassy. However, neither the supreme leader nor any of his followers knew how to handle the oil-dependent economy they had inherited from the Shah. All they knew was the need to undo everything the Shah had done. And so, Iran cut its daily oil production by half and stopped work at most infrastructure projects started by the Shah, rendering millions of workers unemployed. At factories, most of the management staff were declared unworthy of their posts by the Islamic committees and subsequently arrested or fired, costing the country a large pool of technical experts.

At the same time, inspired by non-capitalist developmental models, all large-scale industries, foreign trade, power generation, large-scale irrigation, communication and transport networks, banking and insurance were nationalized under Article 44. While this in itself would not necessarily have impeded economic growth, the problems were exacerbated owing to the near absence of experienced economists and bureaucrats, thanks to extensive purging. Moreover, with properties of top industrialist families having been confiscated for alleged unjust accumulation of wealth through bribery and exploitation, almost 80 per cent of the Iranian economy now rested with an inexperienced, oversized and incompetent bureaucracy that based economic decisions on naïve ideologies. For instance, the decision to cut down on oil production was based on the petroleum minister's assertion that 'Iran did not need nor want to be an industrial power at any cost.'

While the implementation of the Velayat-e faqih dragged down the country into a social, political and economic abyss, the most devastating of Khomeini's decisions was perhaps the one to allow the Iran-Iraq War of 1980 to continue for eight long years. The war had no doubt been started by Iraq's Saddam Hussein, who had seen an opportunity to annex parts of Iran during the fluid period after the revolution. However, it was Khomeini's stubbornness to not sign a ceasefire that sustained it.

Despite historical border disputes between the two countries, Saddam had supported Khomeini in Najaf for several years during pre-revolution Iran, hoping to overthrow the Shah whose close ties with the US was seen as a problem. In 1978 though, Saddam signed a mutual agreement with the Shah, forcing Khomeini to flee to France just months before the revolution. Further, although nearly 50 per cent of Iraqis were Shi'a, Saddam, himself a Sunni, was wary of the Iranian supreme leader's intent to dislodge him by inspiring an Islamic revival in Iraq along with other Muslim nations such as Lebanon, Afghanistan, Pakistan and Bahrain. Not surprisingly, Khomeini regarded Saddam an obstacle to his global Islamic Revolution and saw in the Iran-Iraq War, an opportunity to replace him with a friendly ally. Consequently, when Iraq sensed the futility of the war in mid-1982 and repeatedly sought a peace agreement, even voluntarily withdrawing forces from all captured Iranian territory, Khomeini refused to blink.

Drumming up Islamist fervour in his speeches with exhortations such as 'you are fighting to protect Islam and he (Saddam Hussein) is fighting to destroy Islam,' and 'this is not war, but a divine cause,' Khomeini urged Iranians to raise a 20 million strong army to defend the Islamic Republic. Soon, the Iranian youth, some as young as 12 years of age, were being brainwashed to lay down their lives for the country, either as soldiers or members of suicide squads, with assurances of attaining a place in *jannat* (paradise). Those who did not report for recruitment were threatened with imprisonment and execution. On the other hand, the overzealous but poor and illiterate followers of the Imam interpreted his speech as a call to increase the country's population, which, coupled with heavy child subsidies announced by state programmes, drove the fertility rate of Iran to an all-time high of 6.5 children per woman in 1983.

By the time the war ended, with Khomeini reluctantly agreeing to a ceasefire in 1988, the booming number of children had become a burden rather than an asset for Iran, forcing the coming governments to rethink the state's family planning policies. More disturbing than that, however, was the 'martyrdom' of close to three lakh Iranians in a war that achieved nothing for the country except social and economic doom. While the war had sapped the collective energies of the nation, what with nearly seven lakh injured soldiers and civilians, the destruction of over 150 towns and obliteration of 1,800 villages along the Iraqi border, it also depleted Iran's coffers by over $700 billion. Blame for the disaster could be squarely placed on the shoulders of Khomeini, for according to Article 110 of the Constitution he helped draft, the responsibility for declaring of both war and peace rested solely with the supreme leader.

Stuck in a Revolutionary Time Warp

Despite the socio-economic crisis the country had been plunged into in just a decade after the revolution, despite nearly 4.2 million Iranians fleeing the country during the same period and despite the debacle that the Iran-Iraq War was, Khomeini managed to retain the veneration of his fanatic followers who claimed to have seen his face on the moon and were ready to die to preserve his rule. So, when the man—who popularized the word *fatwa* by issuing it liberally during his reign—passed away a year later at the age of 89, millions of mourning Iranians poured out into the streets to catch a glimpse of his casket in what was perhaps one of the largest funeral processions in history. Not surprisingly, the gold-domed tomb that was constructed for him at Tehran's Zahra cemetery soon became a shrine for his followers. For the rest of the world though, it was, and perhaps still is, as difficult to comprehend the extreme love and respect Khomeini had managed to garner from his people as it was to dissect the dichotomy of him being both deeply spiritual and aggressively political.

Now, with him gone, the question that faced Iran was who would fill their beloved Imam's shoes. It is perhaps this moment of reckoning that reveals Khomeini's biggest error—having dragged his country into theocracy, he had not bothered envisioning a future beyond him. It seemed as though he had visualized the titular role for himself when writing the *Velayat-e Faqih*, with him being the only person in Iran who could fulfil the precise qualifications of the Supreme Leader. Being one of the six grand ayatollahs, he had been an authority on religious matters and was regarded by other scholars as a *marja-e taqlid* or spiritual source worth emulating, being the torch-bearer of the revolution, he had been a leader whom people respected and obeyed, and being an expert on the Sharia, he knew how to interpret it to suit every scenario.

The only person who came close to being all that he was, was Ayatollah Montazeri, Khomeini's lifelong supporter and designated successor. At the time of Khomeini's passing, Montazeri was a grand ayatollah himself and was perhaps the only person other than Khomeini to have an implicit faith in the concept of Velayat-e faqih. However, he had changed from being a fiery proponent of the concept to one who questioned Khomeini's interpretation of it through the years, even criticizing the latter's orders to execute thousands of leftists and Kurds towards the end of the Iran-Iraq War in the name of Islam. Perhaps confident of having been Khomeini's favourite disciple, he hadn't expected to have angered his mentor to the extent that Khomeini would dismiss him as his successor just eight weeks before his death. He was also left stunned when Khomeini ordered the withdrawal of the title of grand ayatollah from Montazeri along with the removal of his portraits from government offices and mosques, and the stoppage of any and all of his scholarly publications.

With the only eligible contender for the top post being sent back to languish in Qom, Iran faced a dilemma. And so, knowing that the Constitution in its current form would pose a hurdle in ordaining Khomeini's successor, the Guardian Council compelled him, during the last days of his life, to make key constitutional amendments. These amendments would go on to not only dilute the concept of Velayat-e faqih but also bestow greater authority in the presidency, ushering in corruption that had been evaded thus far. It wasn't surprising then that the 50-year-old Sayyid Ali Khamenei, who was neither an ayatollah nor a marja-e taqlid, neither an expert in interpreting the Sharia nor a well-respected leader of the masses, was chosen to be the new supreme leader, ignoring at least two other grand ayatollahs.

Of course, Khamenei, along with Ali Akbar Hashemi Rafsanjani, had been a staunch follower of Khomeini during and after the revolution and had been tasked by his mentor to hold important positions, including that of the defence minister for a brief period in 1980, the supervisor of the Revolutionary Guards at the start of the Iran-Iraq War and, as a testament to his oratorical skills, the influential post of the Friday Prayer leader in Tehran. After the 1981 assassination of President Mohammad-Ali Rajai, he also served as president of Iran until Khomeini's demise. However, he was only a *hojjat al-Islam* or middle ranking cleric and to allow him to occupy the top post, it was necessary to elevate him to ayatollah. This blatant political move was met with resistance from several senior clerics, with Montazeri bemoaning the trivialization of the clergy and questioning the legitimacy of Khamenei's ascension as the Velayat-e faqih. In response, Rafsanjani, the sitting speaker of the Majlis and a close aide of Khamenei, sent state-sponsored goons to attack Montazeri's house and placed him under house arrest.

Aware that it wasn't enough to silence just the clerics, Rafsanjani mobilized radio and television broadcasts to popularize Khamenei and get the masses accustomed to looking upon him as a venerable grand ayatollah. The need to use state propaganda to hoist the new supreme leader, something that was never employed during Khomeini's reign, was perhaps another sign that Khomeini had failed to look beyond his own tenure, that he had failed both himself and the Iranians who had put their implicit faith in his idea of a revolutionary Islam.

Despite the devious appointment of Khamenei as supreme leader, Khamenei was not Khomeini for the masses—not in 1989, not now. In the 36 years since he occupied the top post, Khamenei has been just a shade of his predecessor—neither has he been able to replicate the fanatical veneration and popularity that Khomeini enjoyed, nor has he steered Iran in a direction that could be said to portray his interpretation of the Velayat-e faqih, except perhaps promoting Iran's nuclear programme that he feels is key to keeping the 'Satanic' US at bay. His sole agenda through the terms of six presidents including Hashemi Rafsanjani, Mohammad Khatami, Mahmoud Ahmadinejad, Hassan Rouhani, Ebrahim Raeesi and the recently elected Masoud Pezeshkian has been to maintain the revolutionary status quo, constantly reminding the masses of the virtues of being an Islamic state, favouring conservatives over reformists and keeping the anti-American rhetoric alive.

And so, current-day Iran seems to be stuck in a time warp, struggling to break free from the outcome of a 46-year-old revolution. Women still have to veil themselves, girls are still married away upon attaining puberty, voluntary sterilization and free distribution of contraceptives are still prohibited, religious and ethnic minorities are still oppressed, freedoms of assembly and expression continue to be curbed, journalists, activists and lawyers continue to be imprisoned, homosexual activities, consumption of alcohol and adultery continue to attract severe punishments, death penalties continue to be doled out, with over 970 offenders being executed in 2024, and the economy is still floundering under heavy US sanctions. Amidst it all, the march towards substantial socio-economic reforms seems to be excruciatingly slow, with the shackles of Khomeini's Velayat-e faqih refusing to yield.

In his historic speech after the 1979 revolution Khomeini had proclaimed, 'Great people of Iran! The history of Iran, even world history, has never witnessed a movement like yours; it has never experienced a universal uprising like yours.' It is for the best, perhaps, that such an uprising was never experienced elsewhere.

Francois Duvalier

Haiti occupies one-third of Hispaniola, the second largest island of the Greater Antilles chain in the Caribbean Sea, the other two-thirds being the territory of the Dominican Republic. Despite the shared piece of land, the two neighbours could not have been more different. Haiti, a French colony until 1804, has a black population of 95 per cent, largely descended from the hundreds of thousands of African slaves brought in by the French colonizers. On the other hand, the Dominican Republic, an erstwhile Spanish colony, has a mixed-race (mulatto) population of European ancestry. While the economy of Haiti is in shambles, with the country being the poorest in Latin America and amongst the poorest in the world, that of the Dominican Republic has grown robust through the years and is nearly seven times larger than Haiti's. More importantly, although both countries endured the rule of despots, even the nature of their dictatorships

couldn't have been more different. While the Dominican Republic's Rafael Trujillo was a violent and brutal army man who tried to modernize the country, Haitians, in 1957, found themselves being ruled by a doctor and self-proclaimed Voudou priest who claimed to be one with the Ioa, or God himself.

The recorded history of Haiti is neither too old nor too complex, mostly because of the dearth of information regarding Caribbean natives before the arrival of Christopher Columbus in 1492. In December of that year, after a historic landing in current-day Bahamas—assuming it to be India—Columbus set out to explore nearby islands and upon arriving on the shores of Hispaniola, established the first European settlement of La Navidad in current-day Haiti. Soon, the native Amer-Indian tribes of what he called the 'Pearl of the Caribbean', were mercilessly tortured and decimated. By the early-sixteenth century when gold mines in the region had been scraped clean, the colonizers abandoned the island, save for areas around Santo Domingo in the east.

During the next century, what started as the occupation of the north-western coasts by French pirates metamorphosed into the thriving French colony of Saint-Domingue, thanks to the cultivation of sugar. However, with cultivation requiring labour that was scarce in a region wiped of its natives, the French uprooted hundreds of thousands of Africans belonging to the Iho, Yoruba and Ashanti tribes from coastal West Africa and brought them to work as slaves on the plantations. In no time, Saint-Domingue became the crown jewel of the French Empire and the most lucrative colony in the world, notwithstanding the cruelty and harsh conditions of bondage meted out on the slaves.

The slave revolt of 1791 set the ball rolling for the independence and unification of the island under the Republic of Haiti in 1804, making it only the second oldest independent nation in the Americas after the US. With the slaves having won a surprise victory over their oppressors, Haiti also became the first country to permanently ban slavery. However, independence came at a great cost to the island nation. In return for diplomatic recognition as an independent entity, France, in 1825, demanded a payment of 150 million francs against property and slaves lost during the revolution. It took Haiti 122 years to pay off the amount with interest, severely crippling the nation's development. Further, the incompatibility of the two sets of native populations—the white elites of European descent and the black Haitians of African descent—resulted in a protracted civil war and the eventual separation and founding of the Dominican Republic in 1844.

After the split, Haiti's geographical area reduced to a mere one-third of the entire Hispaniola. However, it remained a politically volatile region until the end of the century, with the country witnessing the rule of no less than 18 presidents between then and 1907, each leaving the country worse off than what was inherited and almost always getting assassinated by his successor. To complicate Haiti's governance further, a highly rigid class structure evolved through the years that saw the blacks dominating the army and the mulattos owning land, controlling the economy and running the country. It was sometime during this calamitous period that Florestal Duvalier, a tailor and son of a Haitian peasant, moved to the capital city of Port-au-Prince with his wife Marie-Louise Etienne and son Duval Duvalier to test his fortune.

Nationalism

By 1907, when the Americans took financial control of the neighbouring Dominican Republic, Duval Duvalier had established himself as a primary school teacher in Port-au-Prince and had taken a nubile bakery worker, Ulyssia Abraham, for his wife. On 14 April that year, a son, Francois Duvalier, was born to them. Soon after the birth though, 17-year-old Ulyssia became mentally ill. Consequently, it was Francois's aunt (some say grandmother), Madame Florestal, who took care of him during his early years.

Although the Duvalier family was poor, belonging to the Haitian lower-middle class, Duval himself was seen as a minor intellectual, wearing the additional hats of journalist and magistrate. During the first six years of Francois's life, even as Haiti saw the comings and brutal goings of five different presidents, Duval railed against the self-centred political elite and promoted ideas of nationalism in his articles. And despite earning a pittance, he ensured that his son was admitted to the Lycee Petion, a school of excellent repute in Port-au-Prince.

By the time Francois turned eight in 1915, two more Haitian presidents had been killed. However, the last assassination, or rather lynching by an irate public, of President Vilbrun Guillaume Sam, changed the course of Haiti's history. Irked with Germany's growing influence in what had until then been a French and US bastion, President Woodrow Wilson had already been contemplating invading Haiti under the Monroe Doctrine. The killing of Guillaume Sam provided a timely and more acceptable justification for reasserting American influence in the region. Consequently, thousands of US Marines landed in Haiti within hours of the incident and took charge of the country without opposition. The Haitian-American treaty that followed, virtually bullied Haiti into giving the US full control over its security and economic concerns for a decade. Within no time, over 2,000 US Marines were stationed across the country, all of Haiti's public institutions, including the banks and treasury, were taken over by the US, press censorship was introduced and martial law imposed on an unwitting population.

Although the marines, in-charge of most administrative operations, detested the Haitian mulattos for trying to pretend to be *blanc* (white), they detested the free blacks even more. Consequently, mulattos were given preference over blacks for employment in almost every department, kicking off racism in a manner the country had never seen before. Soon the Haitian blacks were being called niggers, coons and monkeys. The marines would send home letters and media reports filled with racist slurs and jokes demeaning the natives, and their white wives did not bother hiding their squeamishness when meeting or talking to local men and women. To add to the indignation of the natives, the US installed a mulatto as Haiti's puppet president.

In 1918, a new Haitian Constitution, allegedly personally drafted by future US president Theodore Roosevelt, imposed compulsory corvée labour, a sort of serfdom, on the natives. Clearly, the idea of a country owned and run by freed black slaves did not appeal to the new occupiers as it challenged the world order, especially at a time when slavery, in all its inhumane manifestations, was booming in the US. To its own economic advantage, the US also changed Haitian laws to allow foreigners to own land in the country, setting off a race by American business owners to set up factories on cheap peasant land for producing goods for consumption in the US mainland. Finally, the American regime cracked its whip on the country's centuries-old Voudou religion.

Of African origin, Voudou was not merely a religion but a way of life in Haiti. Based on certain codes of ethics, it had its own systems of traditional medicine, education and morality-based justice that were orally transmitted down generations through songs and folklore. However, for the marines and their families stationed in the country, the everyday loud drumming and conch shell sounds that accompanied the perceived barbaric rituals of the black natives were not only annoying but also intimidating. Consequently, even as they sent back home stories with eye-grabbing titles such as 'Cannibal Cousins' and 'Voodoo Fire in Haiti' that stereotyped the religion, *houngan*s and *mambo*s (Voudou priests and priestesses) were arrested in Haiti, their sacred ritual objects destroyed, and the practice of voudou itself driven underground.

It was in the midst of these oppressive circumstances that Francois grew up, acutely aware of the persecution and humiliation of the black people, their religion and their way of life. Around the age of 12, Francois made up his mind to pursue a career in medicine, allegedly inspired by the scene of a Haitian mother treating her child's tropical bacterial infection. After finishing secondary school in 1922, he joined the University of Haiti's School of Medicine in Port-au-Prince as one puppet president was replaced by another at the helm of the country.

Having taken a fascination to politics, Francois worked only hard enough to pass his exams at medical school. Often participating in student protests and trying to mould himself into an intellectual, he wrote articles under the pseudonym Abderrahman for *Action Nationale*, an anti-American-occupation, nationalist newspaper. Further, while the university opened up avenues for Francois to discover the ideology of negritude that encouraged blacks to reclaim their cultural identity by shunning colonialism, he also came across Haitian poets and writers such as Jacques Roumain who, in the late 1920s, were questioning their own national identities under American occupation. Soon he joined an intellectual group influenced by Jean Price-Mars, a black doctor who had studied in France and returned to Haiti to advocate the African roots of Haitian culture.

In 1929, 22-year-old Francois's slant towards ideas of

nationalism and ethnology brought him in contact with lawyer and journalist Lorimer Denis, and Louis Diaquoi, the editor of the nationalist journal *Le Petit Impartial.* Together, the three of them formed a group called the 'Trois D' ('Three Ds' denoting the common starting letter of their second names) that expressed their overlapping ideas through articles in both the *Le Petit Impartial* and *Action Nationale.* In 1932, after the premature death of Diaquoi, Francois and Lorimer continued the tradition under the name 'Griots', the African word for tribal storytellers and sorcerers.

With Jean Price-Mars as their idol, the Griots wrote articles that promoted *noirisme* and pan-Africanism, criticizing the mulatto elite for embracing the French language, Christianity and other European cultural practices instead of the Haitian peasant culture that placed value on the native Creole language and Voudou. The duo also discussed the need for the black middle class to join hands with peasants to overthrow the selfish mulatto from positions of power.

In the meantime, the Americans, under President Herbert Hoover, were already preparing to withdraw from Haiti after overstaying their welcome, thanks to the public furore generated by the bombing of the town of Cayes and subsequent killing of several Haitians in December 1929. Irked by the unapologetic stance of the US Marines, who went on to decorate the commander in charge of the operation, members of the Haitian National Assembly voted in a nationalist, Stenio Vincent, in the 1930 elections, instead of the pro-American candidate. The next four years saw the US securing its financial assets in Haiti and training Haitians to handle the administrative intricacies of their country in preparation for a complete withdrawal.

Indigenism

The departure of the US from Haiti coincided with Francois's graduation from medical school in 1934. As the masses erupted with cheer and celebration when the last of the US Marine vessels left Haitian shores in August that year, Doctor Duvalier prepared to intern at the Hospice Saint François-de-Sales. Although his poor eyesight prevented him from becoming an army medical doctor, he went on to gain experience working at several other hospitals, subsequently taking up the job of a government medical consultant at a retirement home south of Port-au-Prince. It was here that Duvalier met Simone Ovide, an abandoned mulatto child who had grown up in an orphanage and become a nurse's aide. Although Duvalier hadn't been charitable towards mulattos in his writings, he fell for her good looks, shy demeanour and rational outlook, and started to court her.

Although his job at the retirement home barely allowed him to make ends meet, it gave Duvalier a peek into the workings of government organizations and left him with ample time to continue his journalistic activities. In 1938, even as the dust was settling down on the 1937 massacre of Haitian migrants in neighbouring Dominican Republic by its dictator Trujillo, Duvalier and Lorimer started the *noiriste* quarterly *Les Griots*. The publication, whose contributors included well-known Haitian writers and poets of the time, focused its energies on indigenism, a doctrine that narrowed the concept of negritude to address the specific identity of the Haitian people.

A year later, 32-year-old Duvalier married Simone Ovide in a small church ceremony. With her, he would later sire four children: Marie-Denise, Nicole, Simone and Jean-Claude. In 1940, though, the socio-political landscape of Haiti was witness to turmoil when, under the patronage of the newly elected mulatto president Elie Lescot, the Catholic Church began an 'anti-superstition' campaign that targeted and persecuted Voudou practitioners. Soon, in a deja-vu of sorts, houngans and mambos were being imprisoned, their ritual drums and objects vandalized, and Catholic ministers were delivering inflammatory speeches that equated Voudou to Satanism. Churches across the country also forced their congregations to renounce Voudou ceremonies that had been an inseparable part of their lives. In response to this act of religious cleansing, a group of Haitian intellectuals, including Jaques Roumain and Jean Price-Mars, set up the Bureau d'Ethnologie in 1941 to research, popularize and preserve Haitian heritage, especially the Voudou religion. Duvalier too became an active member of the Bureau through which he delved into Haitian religious life in the provinces.

In 1943, despite his disdain for the US, Duvalier enrolled as an interpreter and assistant to the lead doctor in the American Sanitary Mission, a US-Haiti joint effort to eradicate tropical diseases such as yaws, malaria and typhus. The mission, which required travelling extensively across the countryside, allowed him to acquaint himself with the Haitian hinterland and gain the trust and goodwill of poor rural peasants who lovingly bestowed upon him the moniker 'Papa Doc'. Additionally, the mission allowed Duvalier to conduct his ethnological research on the sidelines and establish lasting friendships with regional houngans and mambos. His embracing the Voudou culture also reinforced the trust of the Haitian peasantry in him and would later become crucial to his electoral victory. The immediate consequence of his studies though, was the publishing of *The Gradual Evolution of Voodoo* in 1944, where, apart from tracing the history of the religion, he tried to establish a cosmic, philosophical, spiritual and scientific basis that would make Voudou relevant to current times.

In appreciation for his efforts towards the American

Sanitary Mission, Duvalier earned an opportunity to join the post-graduate medical programme at the University of Michigan in the US in 1944. The subject of his choice, public health, proved to be an astute one, for upon his return to Haiti in 1946, he was invited by the newly elected black president, and his former teacher, Dumarsais Estimé, to serve as the director general of the National Public Health Service. The same year, Duvalier joined the Mouvement Ouvrier Paysan (Worker-Peasant Movement or MOP)—a labour party started by Daniel Fignole, a young populist Haitian leader—as its general secretary. Although the association between the two was short-lived owing to their contradicting stances on Estime's policies, the MOP gave Francois a taste of party politics and brought him closer to the president and his offices. Consequently, when he left MOP in 1948, he was immediately offered the position of 'Secretary of Labour' in the Estime government. A year later, Duvalier became cabinet minister in charge of public health and labour, a position that allowed him access to important political and military figures.

With his interest in noirist ethnology still alive, Duvalier co-authored the book *Le Problème des classes à travers l'histoire d'Haïti* (*The Problem of Classes Throughout Haiti's History*) with Lorimer Denis in 1948. Drawing upon their favourite themes of negritude and indigenism, the book discussed Haitian history through the lens of colour and class, distorting facts to present their thesis that skin colour, as manifested in the conflict between the blacks and mulattos, was the main historical problem plaguing Haitian society, a problem that could be resolved only via a reverse racism of sorts. Extolling the black masses as the true repositories of the 'national soul', the duo argued that it was their art, songs, dances and folklore that constituted the spirituality of the nation. The book concluded with the radical thought that it was time for the blacks to take back the political power that had historically been concentrated in mulatto hands. This thought would later translate into Duvalierism, a word much dissected to understand the unique political ideology of Duvalier.

Even as Duvalier and Lorimer were immersed in their theories, the political landscape of Haiti was getting volatile by the day. In 1950, Estime was overthrown by a military coup led by Gen. Paul Magloire, who went on to declare himself the new president. With several members of the toppled government leaving the country or going into exile, Duvalier too stepped into the shadows, temporarily going back to work with the American Sanitary Mission. However, he was now surer than ever of his political calling and worked on the side lines to chart his route to becoming Estime's heir. The coup also made Duvalier aware of the power of the military, which he decided he would rein in and use to his advantage when he became president.

The flamboyant Magloire had a four year dream run in office with US support, with Haiti witnessing unprecedented infrastructure development and a surge in tourism owing to an influx of American tourists and visits by stellar names such as Truman Capote, Irving Berlin and Graham Greene. In late 1954 though, the unforeseen destruction wrought by Hurricane Hazel and the subsequent mismanagement and theft of relief funds by government officials tarnished his image and marked the beginning of the end of his rule. At this juncture, Duvalier's outspoken opposition provoked a frustrated Magloire to deploy the military against him, forcing him into hiding.

The two years Duvalier lived in hiding changed him as a person. Aware of the brutal ends met by majority of Haiti's past leaders, the constant fear of being caught by the military turned him into a paranoid wreck who suspected everyone around him. Not only did he start carrying firearms on his person, he constantly changed addresses, moving from one place to another allegedly disguised as a woman, and often swapped dinner plates with companions, fearing getting poisoned. Despite his paranoia, Duvalier remained politically active during the time, befriending low-ranking black military officers and gathering foot soldiers from the black middle class to form underground revolutionary groups against Magloire. He also re-established connections with Clement Barbot, a schoolteacher turned dispatcher from his days with the American Sanitary Mission, whom he tasked with scouring Port-au-Prince's poor black community to create a gang of loyalists who would not shy away from violent acts against his rivals if and when required.

In 1955, Magloire banned the Marxist Popular Socialist Party and the MOP, shut down the Haiti Democratique and closed schools across Haiti fearing their role in subversion. The subsequent rioting and striking by students and revolutionary groups through 1956 saw its culmination in a series of bombings in November that were attributed to Duvalier supporters. Within a month, Magloire was forced to step down from his post and, abandoned by the army, he fled to New York, leaving behind a vacant presidential seat. Duvalier immediately seized the opportunity and threw his hat into the presidential elections, positioning himself as the legitimate heir of the much loved Estime.

When elections were finally held in September 1957, Duvalier astutely played the pro-black card in his campaigns while going soft on his anti-mulatto stance and made populist promises of democratic pluralism, improved living conditions, better agricultural infrastructure, and a free press to the Haitian middle class. Moreover, having learned early-on that he would need to keep the military on his side if he were to ascend to power, Duvalier strung along the black military leaders in their assumption that he would be their puppet at the helm.

Consequently, in what was alleged by his mulatto opponent Louis Dejoie as a rigged election, Duvalier emerged winner by more than four lakh votes. On 22 September, the short, soft-spoken, bespectacled doctor who had a fancy for black suits, Homburgs and top hats was formally sworn in as the thirty-fourth president of Haiti.

Macoutism

In his first speech after becoming President, Duvalier declared that his 'Government of Unity' would reconcile the nation with itself. What transpired in the first few months of his reign was quite the contrary. Astounding Haitians, and indeed the rest of the world, with his overnight transformation from a soft-spoken doctor into a callous ruler, Duvalier let loose Barbot's gang of *cagoulards* or hooded thugs to vandalize shops and businesses owned by Dejoie supporters barely a month into the new regime. Then, to consolidate his position, Papa Doc, as he had now started calling himself, shut down pro-Dejoie newspapers and radio stations, and arrested their editors on charges of sedition. They were soon being sent to Fort Dimanche in the outskirts of Port-au-Prince, along with over a 100 opposition figures, to be interrogated, imprisoned, tortured and executed. Not surprisingly, many of his political rivals, including Dejoie, fled the country.

Duvalier's next target was the fledgling trade union movement in Haiti that had taken root during his tenure as minister of labour in the Estime government. Despite having promised in his election campaigns to extend the rights of the unions, he had progressively grown wary of them, finding in them a probable opposition that would woo away his support base of the working black middle class. Consequently, executing a u-turn on his promises, he not only cancelled May Day celebrations that year but also arrested union leaders and issued warnings against attempts to revive the movement. He then went on to fill every government and bureaucratic post with Duvalierists, his loyal supporters from the medical fraternity, the Voudou leadership and the publishing community from his *Les Griots* days. At the same time, all potential points of political subversion, including school teachers, professors, students, journalists and critics within his own party were placed under surveillance.

With the fear of a military coup feeding his paranoia, Duvalier trained his eyes next on the Haitian army. Soon, most senior officers were transferred out of the capital to remote postings and the very military leaders who had propped him up to the presidency were relieved of their duties. Over subsequent years, the army would shrink to barely 5,000 men, commanded by officers who swore loyalty to the president. Despite these precautions, three exiled army men attempted a coup in mid-1958 with the support of American mercenaries. Although the plot was uncovered and all men involved were killed, the episode only heightened Duvalier's paranoia. He soon fortified the Presidential Palace with a 600-man-strong Presidential Guard trained by US Marines and ordered the transfer of all military arsenal and ammunition from the army barracks to the palace, allowing him full control over their use. Finally, he sanctioned the creation of a parallel civilian militia, the Tonton Macoutes, under Barbot's leadership that not only kept the by now toothless army in check but also roamed the streets armed with machine guns and machetes to intimidate the masses.

In Haitian Creole, *tonton* stands for 'uncle' and *macoute* stands for 'gunnysack'. The two words come together to form the ominous moniker for an evil Voudou spirit, the *tonton macoute*, who snares unruly children in a gunny sack and carries them away to be had for breakfast. Under Duvalier, just as the masses learnt quickly to fear the once benign Papa Doc, they also learned to live in the terror of these new uncles on the block who sported blue denim shirts and straw hats and were never seen without dark glasses covering their eyes and a machete in their hands. Hailing from varied social and economic backgrounds, they only needed to be black and loyal to Duvalier to a fault to qualify for the enviable job of roaming freely in jeeps to scour for possible rebels and transgressors, kidnapping and torturing Duvalier's political opponents, extorting money from businessmen and intimidating the common man enough to keep him from causing trouble.

While goons and henchmen have been part of politics since antiquity, Duvalier's tontons were different in that they embodied institutionalized, state-sponsored terror, resulting in a gangster government of sorts. Not surprisingly, they inspired the coining of the term, *macoutism*, which came to represent the ideology of committing violent acts in fanatical loyalty to a leader. In the words of a tonton chief, a good macoute was one who was prepared to kill his children (for Duvalier) and expected his children to kill their parents for him as well. And so, while the tyranny of the tontons ensured that no one dared question Duvalier's policies, they were in turn rewarded with guns and the opportunity to loot their victims, grab their lands, houses and vehicles, and rape their women. Moreover, although they had initially been organized to counter the army, with their operations concentrated in and around the capital, the tontons soon became a ubiquitous presence across the Haitian countryside, their terror penetrating the lives of students, professors, church clergy, peasants, bureaucrats in foreign embassies, businessmen, traders and the working class alike. And while their operations were covert at first, they became more public and brazen by the day, with victims with their throats slit left tied to chairs or hanging in busy marketplaces for all to see and dread.

With the Tonton Macoute also being a secret police of sorts, the system bred feelings of mistrust and caution amongst the masses who had no way of knowing if their own close family members, friends or colleagues were tontons, eavesdropping on their conversations and watching their every move. The only way to survive the regime was to either become a tonton oneself or to please a tonton enough to be protected by him, even if it meant betraying someone else. And so, just a few years into his rule, Duvalier had ensured that the entire country was looking over its shoulder, experiencing paranoia the way he did.

President-for-Life

In 1959, Duvalier suffered a near-fatal heart attack. The US, which had by now cozied up to him despite his cavalier rule thanks to his anti-communist leanings, flew in a team of cardiologists from Guantanamo Bay, Cuba, for his treatment. As he recuperated in the hospital for the next four months, Barbot, who was by now the obvious second in command, took charge of a country that had plunged back into rioting and anti-Duvalier guerrilla attacks. Although his deft moves and an alliance with the US Marines prevented a political catastrophe for Duvalier, the latter doubted Barbot's intentions and threw him into prison as soon as he got back on his feet. Addressing a large gathering of Haitians soon after, he sounded an ominous warning to 'never forget that I am the supreme authority of the State. Henceforth, I, I alone, am your only master.'

Barbot's place was taken by Luckner Cambronne, who soon went on to become the most feared face in Haiti with his unique brand of cruelty. Not only did he oversee the routine kidnappings and killings made at the behest of Duvalier, he also unapologetically embezzled public funds to finance his own businesses. One of these businesses involved providing human cadavers and blood to universities and hospitals in the US. To maintain a constant supply of what he called 'raw material', Cambronne allegedly picked innocent and unsuspecting civilians to be murdered and shipped to his clientele, earning him the sobriquet 'Vampire of the Caribbean'. Although well aware of his actions, Duvalier turned a blind eye to them in exchange for complete loyalty.

By the end of 1960, all of Duvalier's opposition was either in prison, exiled or dead; trade unions had become extinct, the Haitian army had been rendered toothless and the tontons were everywhere, ensuring his regime was safe from internal and external threats. However, if the time seemed ripe for him to implement his election promises and take Haiti to great heights, he was not keen on it. With most intellectuals and professionals having already fled Haiti and his cabinet populated by inexperienced men, Duvalier lacked both the skill and will to draft viable developmental policies. Rather than striving to put together a team of experts, he chose to abandon productive government activity altogether and instead devised alternative strategies that would ensure that Haiti was never left wanting for funds.

Identifying America's Achilles heel during the Cold War, Duvalier blackmailed the former occupiers into doling out more and more dollars in exchange for Haiti's remaining anti-communist, even forcing the US into financing an airport in Port-au-Prince. At a time when Cuba had turned to communism under Fidel Castro, whom Duvalier regularly courted if only to irk the US, keeping the dreaded C word from spreading across the Caribbean and Latin America was top priority for US president John Kennedy. And so, he sanctioned a $15 million aid to Haiti under the 'Alliance for Progress' economic aid programme in 1961. However, the aid money vanished into thin air even before the country could get a whiff of it, with

Duvalier's mandate that a sizable chunk of the budget for every project be allocated to paying government salaries.

An example of this glaring incongruity was the allocation of $110,000—out of the $112,000 outlay for tackling the serious problem of soil erosion—towards payment of salaries, ensuring that Duvalier and his ministers always had their pockets full. Not surprisingly, soil erosion, coupled with other natural disasters, resulted in a 13 per cent slump in agricultural production, steering the country towards year upon year of acute food shortages. In a similar vein, almost all infrastructural projects across Haiti either remained only on paper or came to an abrupt halt like the tarmac roads in portions of Port-au-Prince beyond the Presidential Palace.

Duvalier's other economic policies involved extortion of money from domestic and foreign businessmen alike to finance Duvalierville, a utopian housing project that never got built, siphoning millions of dollars of tax money to fund and maintain the Presidential Guards and tontons and ordering government employees to go out and 'have fun' in the evenings to maintain Haiti's international image as a coveted tourist destination with a thriving night life. Even as he levied heavy taxes on essential food items such as rice, sugar and edible oils, government employees were compelled to park part of their salaries in government bonds and lottery tickets.

With no industrial or agricultural policy in place, Haiti was the only country to record negative growth in the 1960s when the economy was booming in the rest of the world. An all-time low GDP, per-capita income of less than $70 and a skyrocketing cost of living meant that there were no takers for goods and services in the Haitian market. Yet, to keep up appearances, businesses were forbidden from filing for bankruptcy and hotels prohibited from closing down. In the countryside, the impoverished blacks, who had pinned their hopes of emancipation on a president who championed black nationalism, languished in silence, while peasants helplessly watched both the government and tontons usurp their land holdings. With no alternative, most displaced peasants migrated to Port-au-Prince to seek jobs for meagre incomes, causing the uninhabitable and disease-ridden slums in the capital to burst at their seams.

Unperturbed by it all, Duvalier focused his energies on changing the Constitution to do away with the inconvenience of elections. In 1961, he circumvented the problem of the Constitution forbidding a president to succeed himself by issuing ballots carrying the words 'Doctor Francois Duvalier, President' on top without specifying whether or not he was contesting. When the votes were counted, the confused masses were told that they had elected him for a second term of six years because his name figured in the roughly one million ballots that were cast. In a speech, Duvalier humbly acknowledged the people's will saying, 'As a revolutionary, I have no right to disregard the will of the people.'

If the world media thought this to be an outrage, Duvalier outdid himself in 1964 when he declared himself 'President-for-Life' after a sham referendum in which 99.9 per cent of Haiti apparently voted in his favour. The changes to the Constitution also legitimized the sole control of the president on virtually any institution in Haiti, be it the executive, legislative, judiciary, army or police. And so, on 22 July that year, Duvalier graciously accepted his new title of President-for-Life along with a slew of others such as 'Apostle of National Unity', 'Incorruptible Leader of the Great Majority of the Haitian People', 'Renovator of the Republic', 'Worthy Heir to the Founders of Haiti' and 'Spiritual Father of the Nation'.

Voudouism

Even as he dragged down the country's economy, Duvalier did not lose contact with his original vote base, the black middle class, from which hailed all the local leaders of the Tonton Macoutes and several of Haiti's influential houngans and mambos. The latter had progressively become an important part of the president's life, what with the forever-paranoid Duvalier turning to Voudou for spiritual strength. Consequently, not only did he have a houngan serving in his cabinet, Voudou ceremonies became frequent occurrences in the basement of the Presidential Palace. In fact, his interest in ethnology and Voudou were the only aspects of his life before becoming president that had successfully transitioned to the life after.

Although himself a Roman Catholic, as was every other Haitian citizen, Duvalier had always resented the foreigner-dominated and racist Church that dragged its feet in appointing black clergy and consistently supported mulatto candidates, including Dejoie, during elections. While the Catholic newspaper *La Phalange* was openly anti-Duvalier, he was also wary of the Church's role in setting up schools and colleges with mulatto dominated student and teacher populations that often rose up to strike against the government. Moreover, the bishops and priests persistently disparaged Voudou during masses, proclaiming it to have Satanic associations and scaring congregants into abandoning its practice even as they persecuted those who did not toe their line.

These acts of bullying by the Church did not sit well with Duvalier, who considered Voudou an important expression of Haiti's African heritage. Consequently, the clergy faced a reverse persecution of sorts after he became president. Not only were several of them arrested, tortured or deported, Duvalier also expelled Archbishop François Poirier on charges of aiding communist students' agitations, inviting the ire of the Pope himself. Not surprisingly, he was soon excommunicated. The Pope's response did not trouble him though. With the Church being the single richest private entity in Haiti, he was well aware that it made for a lucrative target of extortions and lootings by the tontons. Moreover, even as he ignored Vatican's order and continued attending mass, albeit flanked by rifle-toting bodyguards, he worked out a strategy to woo the Haitians through Voudou.

Soon, Duvalier consciously cultivated the mystical behaviours of houngans such as hyper-slow physical movements, staring gaze and whispered speech and eventually elevated himself to the position of a houngan. In Voudou, the Gede spirit Baron Samedi, considered the Ioa or spirit of the dead, is depicted wearing a top hat, black tail coat and dark glasses with cotton plugs in the nostrils, resembling a corpse dressed for burial in Haitian style. Perhaps to intimidate the largely illiterate peasantry and his adversaries alike, Duvalier fashioned his own appearance to mimic Baron Samedi, often appearing in public dressed as the demi-god and spreading rumours that he had spirits living with him in the palace to make sure no human could overthrow him. Addressing the masses in one such appearance, he declared in an inimitable Baron Samedi nasal twang that his enemies would not be able to 'get' him because he was 'already an immaterial being'.

His innumerable spiritual ramblings were also broadcast on radio to build around him an unparalleled cult of personality that equated him not only to the Ioa but also to Jesus Christ. Much to the chagrin of the Church, a propaganda poster showed Jesus standing with his right arm on Duvalier's seated figure with the caption, 'I have chosen him.' In a bizarre act that brought together his obsession with Voudou and nationalism, he slept on the tomb of Jean-Jacques Dessalines, the hero of Haitian independence, to commune with his ghost, and proclaimed himself to be the physical embodiment of the island nation. As his paranoia grew, he also allegedly ordered the beheading of several rivals, with their heads being brought to the palace so he could 'chat' with their spirits and gather information about any future rebellion they might have had planned against him.

Although Duvalier's cult of personality seemed alternately exotic and comical to the world media, it had its intended effect on the Haitian masses who believed it to be dangerous to even think bad thoughts about their mystical president, leave alone act on them. In 1963, it turned out that the danger loomed over dogs as well. That year, following the failed kidnapping attempt of Duvalier's children Jean Claude and Simone, he ordered a man hunt to find the culprit—a vengeful Clement Barbot who had recently been released from prison. When, after weeks of pursuit he had still not been captured, rumours started to float that Barbot had the occult power to transform into a black dog and escape at will. Although Barbot was eventually found and executed, Duvalier ordered the killing of every black dog in Haiti.

Duvalier also believed in his share of superstitions. For instance, the number 22 was so important to him that he ensured that every key event in his life took place on that date. Consequently, he won the elections on 22 September, was appointed president on 22 October and was installed as President-for-Life on 22 June. In 1962, after an attempted insurgence by rebel army men that the tontons successfully quashed, leaving behind several tortured and dead officers, Duvalier announced the celebration of the Month of Gratitude from 22 April to 22 May where officials were to praise him in public rallies, either in their own words or in pre-written speeches handed to them. The following year, Duvalier claimed credit, in private, for the assassination of his friend-turned-foe

John F. Kennedy on 22 November and sent an envoy to gather a vial of air, a pinch of earth and frayed flowers from the late US president's grave for Voudou rituals.

Towards a Numbing Tranquillity (or Defeatism)

The years between 1964 and 1968 saw several attempts to overthrow Duvalier's regime, each of them failing and ending badly for the rebels involved. The attempt to kidnap his children in 1963 had already amped up his paranoia, resulting in the indiscriminate massacre of entire families of innocent military officers for their suspected involvement before Barbot had come forward to claim responsibility for the act. In a chilling display of both the cold-bloodedness and arbitrariness of killings sanctioned by Duvalier, an elderly lawyer named Benoît Armand was murdered merely because he shared his first name with Francois Benoît, an army chief under suspicion.

In 1964, months before Duvalier installed himself as President-for-Life, 13 exiled mulatto guerrillas sailed in from the Dominican Republic to launch an attack on government forces at Cap Dame Marie. The skirmish that followed lasted 83 days, ending with the Haitian army overpowering the inexperienced rebels who called themselves 'Jeune Haiti'. While eleven of them were killed immediately, Duvalier ordered the public execution of two of the rebels at a cemetery in Port-au-Prince as a warning to his detractors. Not only was a national holiday declared on the day of the execution to ensure maximum attendance to witness the gruesome event, it was also televised and broadcast across the country. Not satisfied with the killing of the rebels, Duvalier also slaughtered their families and distant relatives before unleashing the terror of the tontons on the city of Jeremie, which had a largely mulatto population. Soon, hundreds of innocent mulatto families, including children and the aged, were wiped out. In a public display of Duvalier's macabre side, the body of one of the rebels was left to rot under a sign outside the Port-au-Prince airport that read 'Welcome to Haiti'.

In 1966, Duvalier signed a contract to send 20,000 Haitians every year to harvest sugarcane in the Dominican Republic through which he not only earned a commission of $10 per worker, but also pocketed $49 from every worker's salary. The contract did not surprise anyone in Haiti for by now, Haitians had gotten used to graft, corruption and government inaction. They had also resigned themselves to a numbing, zombie-like existence under Duvalier. Yet, turning a blind eye to the gross violation of human rights, President Lyndon Johnson resumed US aid to Haiti the same year, and the Pope retracted his excommunication of Duvalier. In what was seen as a resounding victory for the Haitian president, the Vatican also acceded to the installation of the country's first black archbishop, something Duvalier would later gloat about in his book *Memoirs of a Third World Leader.*

In 1967, Haitians were made to celebrate the completion of 10 years of Duvalier's regime that coincided with his sixtieth birthday. The nation-wide festivities included scores of beauty queens being flown in from Miami, US, glorious tributes being lavished on the president by intellectuals, businessmen, politicians and army men alike, stamps and coins commemorating the event being released, and a carnival parade being arranged in his honour. During the parade though, bombs went off within the palace grounds, killing four and injuring several revellers. An irate Duvalier ordered an immediate purge of the Presidential Guards, personally supervising the execution of 19 officers who had once been close to him and his family.

Towards the end of 1968, when myriad small political parties in Haiti came together to form a communist opposition to Duvalier's oppressive regime, every last member of the new party was hunted down and executed. The wiping out of the Haitian Communist Party before it could take root earned Duvalier vital brownie points with the US administration, normalizing the blow-hot blow-cold relationship between the two countries. Before long, he was shaking hands and posing for photographs with visiting New York governor Nelson Rockefeller. In the meanwhile, Clinton Knox, the new US ambassador, was conferred with the unofficial title of Honorary Tonton Macoute for recommending increased financial aid to Haiti. With a thawing in the US-Haiti relationship, tourism started to flourish again, as did the reestablishment of American businesses in the country. The next year, a final clumsy attempt was made to dislodge Duvalier when Haitian exiles used a WWII bomber to drop bombs on the Presidential Palace. However, with the bombs missing their target, the fate of the rebels was sealed when Duvalier sent 200 troops to 'mop them up'.

Following the incident, Haiti fell into the humdrum of life under Duvalier who, secure in the knowledge that his rule was no longer under threat, decided to loosen his grip on the masses. Consequently, the rigorous 'stop and search' of cars passing through Port-au-Prince was relaxed, fewer tontons were visible in and around the city, and wealthy mulattos who had fled the country in the preceding years were wooed back with statements such as 'Haitian soil belongs to every Haitian.' However, if these were perceived as signs of change, nothing could have been farther from the truth. Every Haitian knew that it would only take the raising of an eyebrow to any of Duvalier's orders to find themselves in Fort Dimanche.

In 1970, Duvalier suffered a second heart attack after which his health started to deteriorate rapidly. Keen on keeping the presidency within the family, he started preparing the country to embrace its future leader, his son Jean Claude Duvalier.

However, despite the senior Duvalier hinting at passing the baton of power to the youth and promising the masses a 'young leader' in several of his speeches, no one in Haiti expected the 19-year-old Jean Claude to succeed his father. Not only did he clearly lack experience in running a country, the Haitian Constitution was unambiguous in its mandate that the president would have to be at least 40 years of age. What the masses did not anticipate, rather surprisingly, was the ailing Duvalier's response to what was by now a mere technicality. And so, Haitians were called for a referendum on 22 February 1971 and asked 'Citizen Dr. François Duvalier has chosen Citizen Jean-Claude Duvalier to succeed him to the Presidency for Life of the Republic. Does this choice answer your aspirations and your desires? Do you ratify it?'

When the votes were put to count, it seemed that the whole of Haiti was keen to see junior Duvalier as their next president, with not a single 'no' vote having been cast. In keeping with their wishes, Duvalier had the Constitution changed to lower the minimum age requirement for the presidency from 40 to 18 and to empower himself to designate his successor.

Duvalierism

Francois Duvalier died on 21 April 1971 of complications arising from his heart condition and diabetes. Just as he would have liked it, the announcement was made to the world on 22 April, with 22 soldiers of the Presidential Guards and 22 tontons guarding his body as mourners streamed in to pay their respects. The same day, Jean Claude Duvalier, aptly nicknamed 'Baby Doc', took over the reins of the country. With the older Duvalier already having struck a deal with the US and Dominican Republic to ensure a smooth transition of his regime, US warships and Dominican troops stood guard at the borders to prevent exiles from returning to Haiti to launch fresh rebellions. What followed was another 15 years of Duvalier rule with what Jean Claude claimed was the 'same inexhaustible energy and intransigence' he had observed and learned from his father.

There were, of course, two aspects to the senior Duvalier's rule. The first, the executions and massacres of at least 30,000 Haitians, was a result of his extreme paranoia of being dislodged from presidency and being assassinated like most of his predecessors. However, the doing away with of perceived rivals soon gave way to arbitrary killings of innocent citizens and it was this arbitrariness that helped the Duvalierist machine sustain a foreboding climate of fear and suspicion across Haiti. The second aspect was Duvalier's extreme nonchalance to the desolation surrounding him. Not only was he not worried about poverty and peasant rights, he also did not care for infrastructural development or—for that matter—development of any sort. So, while Duvalier revelled at having consolidated black middle class dominance across all spheres in Haiti, instilling a sense of black pride in them, virtually nothing in the country functioned. Roads, factories, ports, businesses and even electric supply lay in utter disrepair.

This was perhaps because Duvalierism, derived from the ethnological treatises written by Duvalier and Lorimer in the 1940s, was an incomplete ideology. While it successfully appealed to the emotions of the blacks, it didn't address questions of economy. Not surprisingly, Haiti was reduced to begging and blackmail to sustain itself, with a communism-wary US playing along rather enthusiastically.

Yet, despite Duvalier's regime fated to be remembered for the thousands of lives lost to executions and the stereotyping and comodification of its Voudou affiliations by the world media, the once-gentle doctor managed to achieve what no other leader in the Western Hemisphere could. Not only did he have the Americans pandering to him, he got the Vatican to bend to his wishes and held fort for 14 years at the helm of a country that had seen presidents change sooner than one could say Haiti. And, in the words of a Haitian worker, by putting Duvalierism into action, Duvalier taught an entire country to sustain without money, eat without food and live without life.

Kim Il-sung

What do you do when the leaders of your country are near-divine, can walk on water, be in two places at the same time, turn invisible and travel great distances in a single night, turn pine cones into bullets and grains of sand into rice, and change the weather of an allegedly sacred mountain simply by visiting it? You build monuments to commemorate them, get married in front of their statues, renumber the years of human history to start from their birth year and become an ideological slave who allows a single leader to rule over you, unchallenged, for a whopping 46 years.

The centuries-old kingdom of Korea under the rule of the Choson dynasty was historically the coveted bone that both Japan and China vied for. While the kingdom became a tributary state of China under the Qing dynasty in the mid-1800s, the crushing defeat of the latter at the hands of the British and

French forces in the two Opium Wars exposed its outdated military and bureaucratic systems, giving Imperial Japan a chance to snatch Korea from under the nose of the Chinese. The consequence was the First Sino-Japanese War (1894–95) that resulted in a decisive victory for the Japanese Empire. With China relinquishing all influence over Korea, the now-defunct kingdom became a protectorate of Japan before being completely annexed in 1910.

The Japanese takeover came with a plethora of changes and restrictions for native Koreans. First up was the conscription of several thousand Koreans as forced labour in Japanese factories, mines, and military bases while Korean women were forced into prostitution to serve Japanese soldiers and officers as 'comfort women' or bluntly, sex slaves in military brothels. Next came a deluge of Japanese families who settled on Korean land, displacing the locals. When millions of trees across Korea were felled to supply wood for large-scale projects in Japan they were replaced with non-native species, allegedly to make the new settlers feel at home, in turn transforming the once-familiar landscape into an unrecognizable one for the Koreans. While Korean peasants were forced to continue tilling their lands, land ownership was transferred to the Japanese, kicking off a phase of indentured labour. To add to the farmers' woes, they could hardly get a taste of the crops they nurtured and harvested, for most of these were sent to Japan to combat food shortages.

While pledging loyalty to the Meiji emperor was an expected demand, the Japanese went further and imposed a complete ban on speaking Korean in schools, universities and public places. Teaching history from non-approved texts became a crime and thousands of documents related to Korean history were burned down, obliterating the country's antiquity. Within months of annexing Korea, the Japanese also looted the country's priceless artefacts, razed a big chunk of the

Gyeongbokgung, the historical royal palace built by the Choson rulers, and forced locals to worship Japanese gods and spirits in Shinto shrines. Then, as a final blow to the morale of the Koreans, they were forced to abandon their family names and take up Japanese surnames.

It was in the middle of these sweeping changes in Korea that Kim Il-sung was born in 1912.

Early Years

In 1912, Kim Hyung-jik was a teacher at a Western missionary school in the modern-day province of Mangyung-dae near Pyongyang. On 15 April that year, his wife Kang Ban-suk gave birth to a son whom they named Kim Sung-ju. Soon after, perhaps foreseeing a grim future under Japanese rule, the family fled to the Chinese province of Manchuria. Here, the relatively peaceful atmosphere gave little Sung-ju a chance to grow up shielded from Japanese terrors. However, his father's involvement in anti-Japanese revolutionary activities ensured that ideals of nationalism constantly hung around him. So, when Hyung-jik died in 1926, Sung-ju joined the Whasung Military Academy hoping to follow in his father's footsteps. Upon completing eighth grade though, Sung-ju was disillusioned with the orthodox ideologies propagated at the academy. A gradual surge in juvenile ideals of vengeance within made him drop out to join various anti-Japan groups before becoming an active member of a communist youth organization. In the 1920s, despite waves of Marxist ideology washing through parts of China, the country was still under an imperial rule that viewed communists with suspicion. Consequently, Sung-ju's activities with the communist organization landed him in prison when he was still a teenager. After his release, he changed his name to Il-sung, meaning 'the sun', and joined several anti-Japanese guerrilla resistance movements. In one such movement in 1937, now known as the Battle of Pochonbo, a small troop executed a daring raid on a Japanese outpost in Korean territory, with the guerrillas burning down a post office, police station and fire station before retreating into Manchuria. Although not much is known about the raid, including whether or not any casualties were inflicted on the Japanese side, it went on to become the first of many incidents that Il-sung would distort to his advantage. Years later, he would claim in his biography to have led the raid that, according to him, heralded the dawn of Korean liberation, contradicting popular belief that it was perhaps another guerrilla fighter of the same name who had been the leader.

Whether or not it was indeed Kim Il-sung who commandeered the raid of 1937, the incident is said to have made the Japanese army sit up and take note of him. His name was soon on several 'most wanted' lists, and a special unit was purportedly assembled with the sole purpose of killing him. Around the same time, he was also noticed by the Soviet Red Army for his abilities as an organizer. Consequently, when Koreans in Manchuria had to flee to the Soviet Union in 1940 at the height of the Second Sino-Japanese War (1937–45), Il-sung found himself being picked out to be trained as a Soviet Special Ops agent. With WWII looming, he was also made captain of a battalion comprising Korean and Chinese exiles in the 88th Special Independent Brigade near Khabarovsk.

Nothing much is known about Il-sung's life as an exile in Khabarovsk except that it was here that he married fellow Korean comrade Kim Jong-suk and, in 1942, sired a son, Kim Jong-il. It was also at Khabarovsk that he received formal political training under the Soviets before joining the local communist party.

Although the 88th Special Independent Brigade was

almost never called upon to contribute to the Soviet army's manoeuvres during WWII, Il-sung made sure to keep himself in the good books of the Red Army. His strategy paid off, for when Soviet troops trounced Japan at the end of the War in 1945, he was made puppet chairman of the Korean Communist Party and put in charge of forming a provisional government in Soviet-occupied northern Korea.

Dreaming of a Unified Korea

After Japan's surrender in WWII, the Soviet army occupied the area north of the 38th parallel on the Korean Peninsula while US forces occupied the southern region. With ideological differences between the two occupying powers, Korea was effectively split into half with the Soviet North turning into a communist regime and the American South adopting a democratic system of government. Kim Il-sung had no choice but to accept this division. Although he deeply yearned to reunify the Koreas, his priority now, as the first premier of the Democratic People's Republic of Korea, was to bring back a semblance of order to the country. So, with economic help from the Soviets, he started rebuilding North Korea, introducing sweeping reforms to improve the standards of living.

A key initiative was to redistribute land that had now been vacated by the fleeing Japanese. In a bid to ensure self-sufficiency amongst his people, Il-sung divided the over 2.6 million acres of land in North Korea among nearly 700,000 families such that every family had its own five acre parcel of land to sustain itself. The move immediately made Il-sung popular with the masses. To bolster this small victory, he took a leaf out of his idol Stalin's book and legally granted equality to women and started training an army to protect the country. In 1949, after being elected chairman of the Korean Workers' Party (KWP),

Il-sung initiated more reforms to strengthen the industrial and agricultural sectors along with health and education.

However, while the layman in North Korea rejoiced a newfound freedom after years of subjugation under the Japanese, Kim Il-sung had moved on from being a passionate nationalist to a person consumed with the idea of unifying the two Koreas at any cost. By mid-1949, he had already travelled to Russia several times, hoping to gain Stalin's blessing and support for his unification agenda. Stalin, however, didn't immediately see merit in Il-sung's grand plans, especially given the inadequate experience of the Korean People's Army (KPA) that could easily be quashed by US forces assisting the South. He preferred to wait and watch rather than initiate a conflict.

The refusal stung Il-sung. He returned home with an iron-will to reinforce his army and transform it into a formidable force. A year later, when he approached Stalin once again, his idol approved the invasion. On 25 June 1950, the KPA, with assistance from the Soviets, crossed the 38th parallel and marched into South Korea. By August, the well-equipped and disciplined army had swept across most of the South, inflicting several thousands of casualties amongst South Korea's ill-prepared armed forces and civilians. With only a small south-eastern province near Pusan remaining to be conquered, victory seemed near, as did Il-sung's dream of a unified Korea.

However, tides changed in September that year when the UN-backed US army, determined to thwart the spread of communist forces, launched a surprise counter-offensive at Inchon on the west coast. With their supply lines choked, the KPA was forced to retreat across the 38th parallel and watch helplessly as the US army crossed the border and ran over the country all the way up to the Yalu River at the Korea-China border. Sensing defeat in the tug of war being played across the 38th parallel, Il-sung reached out to the Chinese for assistance.

General Mao Tse-tung, the Chinese premier, had been keeping an eye on the events unfolding in Korea and had himself been alarmed at the rapid advances made by the US troops. Fearing an American invasion on Chinese territory he immediately sent tens of thousands of soldiers to help Il-sung push the US troops back to the South. Thus, the Korean War, bolstered by Mao's newfound interest in helping unify the Koreas after tasting initial success, continued for two more years with fierce fighting and several thousands of casualties. However, with neither party making substantial inroads into enemy territory, the conflict finally ended in a stalemate in 1953 with the signing of an armistice on 27 July. This agreement established a status quo at the 38th parallel, with the North ceding an extra 1,500 square miles of land to the South and both parties agreeing to a two mile wide demilitarized zone between the countries.

For Kim Il-sung, the outcome of the war that he had staked his dreams and reputation on was far from agreeable. Although he grudgingly accepted the armistice on the advice of the Soviets and Chinese, he would remain staunchly against the division of his country until his death, making several covert attempts to destabilize the South Korean government and assassinate its rulers. He would also act on his 1946 decree titled 'On Transporting Intellectuals from South Korea' to bring back thousands of North Koreans who had fled to the South during the years leading up to the war. His tool to achieve this end was an elaborate kidnapping system through which almost 84,000 South Koreans were abducted and brought to the North during and immediately after the war. State-sponsored kidnappings would go on to become an important bequest in the politics of the Kim dynasty.

Consolidating Power

In the immediate aftermath of the Korean War, Il-sung turned his focus back to his portion of the pie. With North Korea being a one-party state, the KWP that had started taking shape in 1949 was the only group that existed in the country's political fabric. However, as is wont with most single parties, several factions existed under the larger KWP umbrella—factions with similar ideologies but different approaches to the implementation of political agendas. Key amongst these were four groups including the guerrilla faction led by Kim Il-sung, the Soviet Korean faction led by Ho Ka-I, the Chinese Yanan faction led by Mu Chong, and the Workers' Party of South Korea faction led by Pak Hon-yong. After the Korean War debacle, Kim Il-sung sensed an undercurrent of disillusionment and rage both within the KWP and amongst the people of North Korea. His astute sense of politics warned him of a possible rebellion to counter which, he once again drew inspiration from Stalin and systematically converted what was a decidedly humiliating defeat into a means that would ensure his iron-grip over the country.

It started with Il-sung vindicating himself by shifting blame to other officials within the KWP. Insinuating that they had covertly collaborated with South Korea and the US during the war, he got them either exiled or executed. For instance, Pak Hon-yong and his counterpart Yi Sung-yop were charged with spying for the US and planning a coup against Kim Il-sung and were subsequently sentenced to death. The remaining members of their faction were sent to *kwan li-so*, or forced labour camps, created purportedly for the 're-education' of political opponents. In 1951, Ho Ka-I was removed from office citing the delayed repair of a water reservoir under his watch and was subsequently found dead with a hunting rifle by his side. Although officially ruled a suicide, dissident voices alleged Il-sung's role in orchestrating the death.

Irked by Il-sung's blatant lies and misuse of power, Nikita Krushchev, who had become premier of the Soviet Union following Stalin's death, summoned the former to Moscow for six weeks in the summer of 1956, allegedly for a dressing-down. During his absence, the Soviet and Chinese factions of the KWP plotted to confront and overthrow Il-sung at the next party meeting. However, getting wind of their plans through his network of spies, Il-sung effortlessly crushed his opponents upon his return in what is popularly known as the August Incident. Dismissing anyone and everyone in the KWP who seemed to sympathize with the Soviets or Chinese, he purged nearly 2,500 of his rivals between 1953 and 1960, leaving more than a quarter of the seats in North Korea's Supreme People's Assembly vacant.

In 1966, tired of Il-sung's extreme actions, the guerrilla faction led by him broke into two. The new Gapsan faction, which sought to turn the focus on implementing economic reforms in the country, proposed replacing Il-sung with Pak Kum-chol. Il-sung lost no time in cracking his whip on the new faction. In a series of speeches at party meetings, he accused Kum-chol and his cronies of poisoning the party's core ideology and removed them from positions of power. Although many members of the Gapsan faction had fought beside Il-sung during their days as guerrilla fighters in Manchuria and had remained loyal to him until now, he unflinchingly had them either executed or sent to labour camps.

With the elimination of the Gapsan faction, Kim Il-sung was finally able to establish a totalitarian rule within the KWP. Having accomplished what he claimed was an important task of purging the country of evil and incompetent officials, Il-sung altered the Constitution and, in 1972, declared himself the president and absolute ruler of North Korea.

Cult of Personality (or True Lies)

Tell a lie a million times and the lie becomes the truth. Even as he purged his rivals, Il-sung undertook another mission that was key to salvaging his pride following the Korean War. It involved creating a cult of personality around himself—again, much like Stalin. To this end, he organized an elaborate apparatus for propaganda that involved badgering the public with speeches that glorified him, plastering the entire nation with posters that elevated him to the status of a legendary hero and publishing several books, including his own hagiography, which twisted and invented facts to bolster his larger-than-life image. The engine that would orchestrate the production and indoctrination of this elaborate web of lies was the North Korean Federation of Literature and Art that employed hundreds of writers and artists to create the required fabricated content.

Amongst this content was the revival of an ancient Korean myth about Tan'gun, the semi-divine 'First King of Korea', dating back to 2333 BCE. With artists and writers commissioned to establish a connection between him and Il-sung, legends and intricately detailed paintings were created to include the role of a white war horse, similar to the one Tan'gun rode, into Il-sung's biography. For instance, while an elaborate fresco portrayed Il-sung holding his toddler and galloping across the mountains on a white horse adorned with golden accessories, another depicted a young Kim Jong-il perched atop a majestic white horse in the mountains with his proud parents and guerrilla warriors looking on. Such was the importance given to the horse by Il-sung's propaganda machine that it went on to become a permanent feature of the propagandas of Kim Jong-il and his son Kim Jong-un. After Jong-il's death in 2011, a giant bronze statue of him and his father astride galloping horses was erected in Pyongyang.

With artists instructed to portray Il-sung as a gentle, nurturing, father-like figure, the country was also flooded with posters of him embracing children, sharing words of wisdom and compassion with factory workers and farmers, and inspiring soldiers with gentle assurance. Even as orphans of the Korean War were indoctrinated to look upon him as their father, posters depicting his supposed affection for these children were created for circulation, and stories and poems based on his childhood were inserted into school textbooks. Within no time, Il-sung was being addressed as 'Father of the People'.

Satisfied with this soft, compassionate image that brought him closer to the masses, Il-sung set out to change the narrative of the Korean War to ensure that even as the tortures suffered during it remained fresh in public memory, the humiliating outcome was obliterated. So, while posters depicting the brutality of the US attack were pasted across the country, speeches blaring through loudspeakers and radios glorified Il-sung's tremendous leadership that had brought the US to its knees, forcing it to surrender and beg for a ceasefire. People were forced to keep their radios (that ran only one channel) on 24x7 to ensure the speeches were being heard by all. Finally, declaring 27 July as Fatherland Liberation Day, an event celebrated with much pomp to this day, Il-sung painted himself as the 'saviour of the nation' and liberator of the country.

Once he had convinced the citizens of his invaluable contribution in North Korea's astounding victory in the Korean War, Il-sung got down to changing history itself. Although neither the anti-Japanese guerrilla unit nor the Soviet 88th Special Independent Brigade that he had been part of in his youth had made as much as a dent in the Japanese regime during the early 1940s, Il-sung's speeches exaggerated and glorified his own valiant military achievements while underplaying the role of the Soviets and Chinese. In his biography, he wrote about single-handedly saving the Korean people from Japanese oppression by launching the daring 1937 raid and later delivering a historic speech 'Let Us Fight on Staunchly for the Liberation of the Motherland' to a cheering crowd.

In an attempt to impress upon the people that valour and heroism ran in his family, he went further back into history to concoct a story of how his great-grandfather, Kim Eung-u, led an attack on the US merchant ship *General Sherman* that had sailed into Pyongyang in 1866 to force the conservative and isolationist natives to establish trade relations. The skirmish that, according to him, marked the country's first great victory over Western powers was, in fact, fought and won by unknown locals. Il-sung also devoted a large portion of his eight-volume, 2,000-page biography to discussing his father, about whom little was otherwise known. Through several chapters, he waxed eloquent about Kim Hyung-jik's ideal of *ji-won* and his contribution to the Korean struggle against Japanese occupation.

Having rewritten his family history, Il-sung went on to unabashedly rewrite his own childhood to portray himself as an obedient child who resonated with ideas of righteousness and nationalism from a very young age. Recalling his father's arrest in 1917, Il-sung talked about how he took a vow at the tender age of five to defeat imperialist forces even as he played in his mother's arms. In his biography, he wrote:

> One day, Mother took me to a playground located at Mangyong Peak and got on a swing holding me on her lap. She told me: 'Sung Ju, your dad is not coming back, even after the ice in Taedong River over there is all melted and gone. Your dad fought for Korea and he has committed no crime. You will have to grow up fast and get even with your dad's enemies. You must become a hero and recover our lost nationhood.' I swore to her that I would follow her wish.

Il-sung also portrayed himself as a juvenile hero when he wrote about winning a wrestling match against a Japanese kid much bigger than him, smuggling bullets and gun powder in his school bag for his father's revolutionary group and lining roads with spikes to puncture the bicycles of Japanese policemen. When he was 12, his father allegedly sent him back to Korea to continue studies and 'observe Korea suffering under the yoke of foreign domination'. The young Il-sung purportedly travelled a distance of 1000 ri (roughly 250 km), walking all alone through uninhabited mountainous lands infested with wild beasts.

Discussing his teenage years, he also wrote about how he stole *The Communist Manifesto* into his class at the Whasung Military Academy that was decidedly anti-communist, how he influenced students to embrace the anti-Japanese revolutionary movement and how, as a 14-year-old, he asked pointed questions such as 'What kind of society should Korea be after independence?' during class debates. He further recollected, with modesty, how members of the New Age Children's League, a communist organization for teenagers founded by him, nicknamed him 'Han Byol', meaning 'One Star', despite his protests and wrote a song 'Star of Korea' in his honour.

A similar story is repeated when discussing his days as a guerrilla fighter. Contrary to information that he had himself changed his name from Sung-ju to Il-sung, his biography highlights the role of his comrades in conferring the title on him in 1931, looking up to him as their leader and expressing their innermost feelings by singing songs about him. To portray Il-sung as a loving husband, a section of the biography also focused on his wife Kim Jong-suk, with him fondly recollecting how 'love blossomed' between them 'on the hard rocks of Mt. Paektu'.

While it might not be impossible for many of the events

described in the biography to have actually taken place, the obvious and purposeful exaggerations, omissions and additions revealed a mind with great imagination and an intense yearning to be liked, and perhaps, even worshipped by the people of North Korea. With no known witnesses to either corroborate or deny most events, it wasn't difficult for Il-sung to get away with telling these half-truths. At the same time, witnesses to a select few incidents, such as the 1937 raid, preferred to remain silent either out of blind devotion to their 'Great Leader' or the fear of incurring his wrath.

To complement the paintings and books, Il-sung's propaganda also included several monuments built and dedicated to himself. By 1960 there were an estimated 10,000 statues, portraits or murals of Il-sung in Pyongyang alone. In 1972, a 66-foot-tall bronze statue of the Great Leader was inaugurated in the capital to mark his sixtieth birthday and it was made mandatory for tourists visiting Pyongyang to lay fresh flowers at the foot of the statue. By 1992, over 30,000 monuments, referred to as 'places of worship', had been built in his honour. Further, while school students were taught to owe their food, clothes and other comforts to the 'grace of the Chairman', the masses were instructed to place his portrait in their homes.

Rebuilding and Isolating

The Korean War had vastly depleted the country's economic resources. While carpet bombing by the Americans had flattened several towns, including Pyongyang, which needed to be rebuilt, industry and agriculture needed to be revived from the brink. Fortunately, Il-sung's relations with the Soviets and Chinese were still intact despite the unimpressive outcome of the war. To ensure a constant flow of funding from them, he strategically remained impartial in the issues of contention between the two communist powers for the first 10 years, focusing instead on developing heavy industry and modernizing the country.

In 1956, Il-sung initiated the Ch'ŏllima movement (named after a mythical flying horse) to rapidly achieve self-sufficiency in food, housing and clothing through nationalization of agriculture and industry. Even as a 'drink no soup' campaign was started to deter workers from wasting time by using restrooms too often, Il-sung undertook a nationwide tour to exhort the masses to produce more and over-fulfil his visionary five-year-plan ahead of schedule. In return, he promised them the title of 'Ch'ŏllima Rider' along with symbolic gifts, such as Ch'ŏllima embossed notebooks and flags. The workers apparently did not mind the non-monetary bargain, for amongst the early successes of the movement was the supposed doubling of production at a steel factory in Kangsong from 60,000 tons to 120,000 tons in just one year. By the end of the 1961, Il-sung's charisma ensured that North Korea's state-run economy was entirely self-sufficient with registered annual industrial growth of over 36 per cent during the preceding five years.

The success of the five-year-plan gave Il-sung the pluck to re-evaluate North Korea's relationship with its communist allies. Already wary of them after the attempted 1956 coup, he was not keen on remaining their puppet particularly now, in 1963, what with Krushchev adopting a staunch anti-Stalinist stance and the Chinese giving him a cold shoulder. However, severance of ties with his biggest allies meant that he could no longer depend upon them for economic and military support. To compensate for the loss, Il-sung launched a new work-day model that required people to work, study and rest for eight hours every day. He also inducted more women into the labour force.

These steps, however, could not help replicate the economic

surge of the late 1950s. Not only had the Ch'ŏllima movement led to a lopsided development where industries benefited at the cost of education and healthcare, it also resulted in worker exhaustion and deterioration in production quality. With the movement unable to sustain, North Korea's GDP soon started to plummet. Yet military expenditure soared from a mere 2.6 per cent of the national budget in 1960 to over 30 per cent in 1971 to ensure that the defence mechanism of the now completely-isolated country did not slack.

Although Il-sung resumed ties with the Soviet Union in 1965 following the deposing of Krushchev, he realized the need to develop new allies in order to improve the economy. Consequently, he started to befriend other dictators across the world, including Libya's Colonel Muammar Gaddafi, East Germany's Erich Honecker and Romania's Nicolae Ceausescu. North Korea was soon filling its coffers by supplying arms to Libya, Syria and Iran. The absence of Soviet and Chinese influence also allowed Il-sung to shift away from the predominantly Marxist-Leninist ideology of the communists towards the ideology of *juche* that had been simmering in his mind for a while.

Juche

Juche, which translates roughly as 'self-reliance', was at first a concept introduced by Kim Il-sung to encourage military independence, economic self-sufficiency and ideological autonomy for North Korea. While he had lived his life believing in his father's ideology of 'ji-won', justifying all his actions as the outcome of 'righteous aspiration' towards his country and people, his growing disenchantment with communism propelled him to look for an alternative ideology that could sustain itself for posterity. That was when he came across juche, an abstract concept that draws inspiration from sources as varied as Korean nationalism, Japanese imperialism, Marxism and Confucianism. At its core, the ideology stipulated that people of a country were the masters and motive forces of both revolution and construction.

In 1967, following the elimination of the Gapsan faction, Il-sung delivered a speech entitled 'Let Us Defend the Revolutionary Spirit of Independence, Self-Reliance, and Self-Defence More Thoroughly in All Fields of State Activities' to the Supreme People's Assembly. The speech, while outlining the governing principles for the establishment of a monolithic ideological system, was also an introduction to juche.

Il-sung went on to explain to the masses that establishing juche meant 'rejecting dependence on others, using one's own brains, believing in one's own strength, displaying the revolutionary spirit of self-reliance, and thus solving one's own problems for oneself on one's own responsibility under all circumstances.'

Although juche seemed simple enough to understand at first, Il-sung's interpretation of the word was so fluid and ambiguous that no one in North Korea, or indeed elsewhere in the world, was able to comprehend what exactly it meant. For instance, he used juche to convince North Koreans that isolation had helped preserve their racial purity even as the rest of the world was nothing but mongrels.

He also twisted a Confucian idea of how a right mindset would help humans transform the world to explain why, according to juche, the North Koreans owed deep respect to their president. Finally, he argued the case of his being the only qualified person to lead the country by citing juche, which mandated that a *suryong* or leader could only be someone who possessed a genuinely correct conscience. This ambiguity in the meaning of juche also allowed Il-sung, and later his son and grandson, to change government policies to suit their whims. If the Kim family required something to be done, juche was cited to justify the requirement.

With no news leaving or entering the country unchecked and a propaganda machine that constantly glorified Il-sung's intellect, the people of North Korea believed every word of their Great Leader. Not surprisingly, juche rapidly rose from being just another ideology to the only ideology, and indeed, the only religion the North Koreans were allowed to follow. Soon, thousands of Buddhist temples and churches were destroyed and practitioners of Buddhism and Christianity were arrested in large numbers. While Il-sung famously remarked that it was he who had influenced Christian ideology and not the other way round, propaganda started including stories about how he was as loving as Christ, as benevolent as the Buddha, as virtuous as Confucius and as just as Mohammed.

With the enormous amount of propaganda associating Il-sung to juche, the two soon became inseparable—there was no juche without Il-sung, there was no Il-sung without juche. This special association no doubt demanded a monument in its honour. So, in 1982, the Juche Tower was built to mark the seventieth birthday of the Great Leader. Standing 170 metres tall on the banks of the Taedong River, the tower was designed to comprise 25,550 granite blocks, each signifying one day in the glorious life of Il-sung thus far. Further, when the years of human history were renumbered to start with the birth year of North Korea's Great Leader, the years were referred to as juche. So, 1982 was in effect Juche 70 while 2026 would be Juche 114. As a final hat tip to the ideology, the North Korean state media, to this day, refers to the tomb of Kim Il-sung and Kim Jong-il as the 'sacred temple of juche'.

Songbun

Even as Kim Il-sung went about propagating his new ideology and isolating North Korea, he slowly grew more and more paranoid about retaining absolute power. Although his cult of personality was being played up at every opportunity, there were rebels who still questioned his policies. In order to weed them out and ensure complete control over every aspect of Korean life, Il-sung introduced an elaborate, intrusive and diabolical system known as *songbun* in the mid-1960s.

Songbun, which means 'ingredient' or 'material' in Korean, borrowed heavily from race-based or caste-based segregation systems, dividing North Koreans in two ways. The first, based on their origins, was dictated by the socio-economic background of one's family and ancestors. The second, based on an individual's socio-political behaviour, trustworthiness and loyalty to the Kim family and the country, decided whether one was 'core', 'wavering' or 'hostile'.

The 'core' group comprised relatives and close friends of the Kim family who demonstrated extreme loyalty to Il-sung and the state, and were in return ensured a great lifestyle with high-ranking government and army jobs, the right to live in Pyongyang, and receive good education and healthcare. The 'wavering' group was made up of those whose loyalty was deemed suspect but who had the potential to serve the regime well through constant demonstration of loyalty. While placed under strict state vigil, they were allowed the privilege of living in smaller towns around Pyongyang. Although they would have no opportunity to climb up the songbun ladder, getting caught doing anything deemed wrong would immediately demote them and their entire family to the lowest songbun .

The latter, classified as the 'hostile' group, comprised everyone the state distrusted and deemed anti-party, including relatives of those who willingly shifted to South Korea after the war and North Korean prisoners of war who had been repatriated from the South. Considered enemies of the regime, they were deported to the most remote parts of the country, denied basic education and healthcare, and made to engage in the most menial and labour-intensive jobs. While it was unthinkable for someone from the 'core' group to marry a person of a lower songbun, the heredity-based system ensured that descendants of those from the 'hostile' group would forever remain part of the lowest songbun. When the system was first introduced, Il-sung, in a public speech, identified 25 per cent of North Korean population as falling under the core group, 55 per cent under the wavering group and 20 per cent under the hostile group.

Passing the Baton

The period between 1970 and 1990 saw North Korea struggling, sandwiched as it was between the lofty ideals of juche and the regressive songbun system. To add to its woes, the two seven-year plans introduced during the time failed to achieve their intended goals. Il-sung's isolationist policy, coupled with heavy military expenditure and a steady increase in population, led to a massive economic slowdown, a severe shortage in food and daily commodities, and an overall decline in standard of living. The battered morale of his people did not, however, seem to impact Il-sung, who persisted with efforts to annex South Korea, even sanctioning attempts to assassinate the South Korean president.

Further, having seen how atomic bombs had brought the Japanese empire to its knees in WWII, Il-sung was keen on developing North Korea as a nuclear super-power. Concealing his ambitions under the shroud of developing nuclear capabilities for peaceful purposes, he successfully sought Soviet help to set up a nuclear research centre. The strategic induction of North Korea into the International Atomic Energy Agency (IAEA) in 1974 allowed him to station a nuclear scientist at the organization's Geneva office to covertly siphon information and learn how to design a nuclear reactor. Not surprisingly, North Korea was producing weapons-grade plutonium and developing and testing its own nuclear weapons by the 1980s, much to the chagrin of the US and its allies.

Even as he steered the country towards his skewed vision of an ideal state, Il-sung also started to prepare for the eventuality of his death. Having seen the chaos unleashed on Soviet politics with Krushchev systematically undoing the legacy of his predecessor Stalin, Il-sung wanted to ensure that the country he had liberated and nurtured remained in his family, almost like an heirloom. Consequently, in the 1980 meeting of the KWP, he appointed his son Kim Jong-il to three powerful party posts and made him the heir apparent.

Despite being the eldest of six children, Kim Jong-il, did not start off as his father's first choice. However, he worked his way into his Il-sung's heart with a strategy and shrewdness that befitted him as his father's son. As a teenager, Jong-il was already accompanying his father on propaganda tours, watching with awe as he worked his charm on a gullible population. After graduating from college in the early 1960s, he joined the central committee of the KWP where his role was to ensure that members toed the party line and stuck to the ideologies laid down by his father. He also joined his father's propaganda team as director of the Motion Picture and Arts Division. Movies and operas produced under his guidance, which focused largely on glorifying Il-sung's role in the liberation of Korea from the Japanese, left the elder Kim impressed and made him take note of his first-born like never before.

To further cement his loyalty, Jong-il announced in a speech in 1973 that the national ideology of North Korea would henceforth be referred to as 'Kimilsungism'. During the course of the year, he ordered the construction of several monuments in honour of the Great Leader while also undertaking the task of exposing dissidents in the party and military ranks. Sure enough, his efforts paid off. At a party meeting in 1974, members of the KWP are said to have been asked to swear loyalty to Jong-il in case anything grave happened to Il-sung. Soon, the first large photos of Jong-il, alone and with his father, started showing up in the state's propaganda and a cult of personality started developing around the younger Kim too.

Jong-il did not rest on his laurels though. For the next decade and a half, he worked in the shadows of his father, creating a foothold for himself. Amongst his early interventions were the institution of policies that forced bureaucrats to work amongst subordinates for a month every year in order to bring them closer to the masses. He also oversaw the launch of the Three-Revolution Team Movement where teams of young, city-bred Koreans were sent to factories and villages to train workers for increased production and introduce new technologies. As with his father's approach, those who took part in the movement were awarded the Three-Revolution Red Flag and the Three-Revolution Honour Badge rather than monetary incentives. Although the campaign had negligible impact on overall production, with workers not taking kindly to the idea of untrained urban youth teaching them to work better, no one dared to oppose it.

While Jong-il wasn't as imposing as his father in stature, he was just as shrewd. Digging into his father's box of political tricks, he commanded a series of infamous kidnappings between 1977 and 1983 to flaunt his power. The abduction of numerous unsuspecting regular folk, mostly single men or young couples from countries as varied as Japan, South Korea, France, Romania, Thailand and Malaysia was ostensibly to fill in the posts of language teachers or translators. However, the undeclared reason for the kidnappings, as decoded much later by some victims, was to produce a generation of mixed-race children who looked nothing like North Koreans and could easily be recruited to spy on the Japanese, Americans and South Koreans. While the theory could be more than just conjecture, given the eccentricities of Il-sung and Jong-il, not all kidnappings had spying as the ultimate goal.

Although his father had been impressed with the propaganda films he produced, Jong-il himself was frustrated with the lack of talent and technological finesse in the North Korean film industry, a fact that was rubbed in every time he watched one of the 15,000 European, American and South Korean productions he had had smuggled in. Consequently, he ordered the kidnapping of Choi, a famous South Korean actress and her director husband, Shin, in 1978, to boost the industry and improve the quality of propaganda films. The husband-wife duo went on to create several popular movies in North Korea, casting, amusingly enough, abductees of European or American lineage as Western villains, before managing to escape to the US in 1986.

By the mid-1980s, Kim Il-sung, then in his seventies, started to show signs of slowing down, giving Jong-il the opportunity to take greater responsibility in the administration. With him having been anointed heir and appointed to senior posts in the Politburo, Military Commission and Secretariat, it was now also time to play up his personality to appeal to the people of North Korea. Although this propaganda was rather similar to that of his father's, it seemed as though Jong-il was keen to be seen as being just a notch better. So, details of his birth were fudged to show that he was born, not in Khabarovsk but a secret military camp on the sacred Mount Paektu, with a miraculous double rainbow appearing in the sky at the time of his birth. Stories were created and circulated about how, as an eight-year-old during the Korean War, he not only swore to liberate Pusan from the Americans but also impressed his father with war strategies. By the age of 10, he was apparently rebuking people old enough to be his uncles and teaching them the ideals of patriotism and socialism. The public of North Korea lapped up these stories just as they had done with Il-sung's and started to look upon the heir apparent with awe and respect. Soon, willingly or by design, Jong-il was conferred with the moniker of 'Dear Leader' and books, paintings and monuments in his honour started to flood the country. While a flower was named 'Kimjongilias' after him, he was catapulted to near-divinity by the disclosure that he never had to urinate or defecate owing to his astounding body configuration.

Even as Jong-il's persona was being pumped up, North Korea, in 1990, was stumbling under the weight of his father's isolationist policies. With Il-sung having virtually retired from active politics, it fell upon Jong-il to help the country navigate through the tough times. The dissolution of the Soviet Union in 1991 served as the last blow, ending whatsoever little aid the country had been receiving. Soon, while imports in the energy sector plummeted by 75 per cent, impacting industrial production, a standstill in agricultural imports dealt the agricultural sector a mammoth blow with farmers grappling with inoperable irrigation systems and non-availability of fertilizers and pesticides. As the economy went into a downward spiral, Kim Il-sung passed away in 1994, leaving the country in deep despair.

Strategically, Jong-il did not immediately ascend the presidential throne. Instead, he dissolved the office of president in deference to his father and waited in mourning for three years before declaring himself general secretary of the KWP and chairman of the National Defence Commission, posts that now defined the highest office of the 'Supreme Leader'. During these three years, North Korea was hit by record-breaking floods in 1995 and 1996 followed by drought in 1997, crippling the country's food production. With the party strictly adhering to the tenets of juche, importing grains or other food products was not an option. Consequently, what ensued was a famine that—exacerbated by the disproportionate distribution of the meagre harvests based on the songbun system—resulted in the loss of hundreds of thousands of North Korean lives.

Worried that the public would rise in rebellion, Jong-il immediately instituted *songun*, a 'Military First' policy that put the army at the top of the pyramid for disbursal of national resources. Thus pacified, the military remained in his control and gave him the muscle to defend himself from domestic and foreign threats. Jong-il then effected tweaks to the country's economic policy, popularly characterized as a 'flirtation with capitalism'. These—coupled with Chinese support, however meagre it was—ensured that the North Korean economy did not completely collapse, allowing Jong-il to divert his attention back to the country's nuclear ambitions.

In 1994, the US had helped set up two power-generating nuclear reactors in North Korea in exchange for the country abandoning its nuclear weapons programme. By 2000 though, Jong-il was issuing directives to covertly use the reactors to enrich uranium for the production of nuclear weapons. By 2003, North Korea had in its possession at least two nuclear bombs and, despite increasing pressure from the rest of the world, successfully conducted underground nuclear tests in 2006 and 2009.

Gen-Next

In 2008, Jong-il's health started to deteriorate, warranting the ordaining of an heir to his post. While he himself had had enough time to find a foothold in politics before assuming leadership of the country, the same wasn't true for any of his three sons from three wives who were likely to succeed him. Having lived most of their lives outside North Korea, speculation was abound as to their capability to lead the country. Jong-il put these to rest in 2009 by naming Kim Jong-un as heir, simultaneously promoting him to four-star general and bequeathing him with an important position on the Central Military Commission.

While the announcement of the 25-year-old, pudgy basketball fan being chosen to take on the reins of the Kim dynasty came as a surprise to the rest of the world, Jong-il, it seemed, had worked out the necessary propaganda material well in advance. And so, North Koreans were soon hearing about the momentous appearance of a bright star on Mount Paektu the day their 'Leader Comrade' was born, his stupendous ability to fire a gun by the age of three and drive a truck at 80 miles an hour by the time he was eight. And so, Jong-un, who was educated in Switzerland, with his aunt and uncle posing as his parents to ensure anonymity, and grew up in the lap of luxury, living in palatial homes, feasting on eclectic cuisines and travelling to exotic destinations, was soon given the moniker of 'Great Successor'.

Kim Jong-il died of heart attack in December 2011. Even as an entire nation marched to Pyongyang, grieving and mourning the loss of their Dear Leader, political analysts and media worldwide were already writing obituaries to the Kim dynasty. Kim Jong-un, however, went on to prove them all wrong. As though referring to an unwritten book on how to rule a nation by crippling it, he implemented all the tricks of the trade discovered by his grandfather and perfected by his father. Soon, North Korea was back to being the same isolationist, regressive and repressive state the world had always known.

Today, into the fourteenth year of Jong-un's rule, over 100,000 people are believed to be held in political labour camps and, in keeping with the songbun system, have their human rights violated every day of their lives. Building and testing of nuclear weapons, ballistic missiles, and chemical and biological weapons are more prevalent than ever, as are covert political kidnappings and murders. While propaganda stories such as 'Blessings in Disguise', 'Sky, Land, Sea', 'Gratitude', 'Teacher', 'Blooming Dreams', 'Red Persimmon', and 'A Promise of Fire' introduce to the masses the same wonderful qualities of their leader as were present in his grandfather, children in preschools across the country now have to spend more time learning about their leaders under the recently introduced 'Greatness Curriculum'.

Eternal President

A nationalist, a quasi-communist, a totalitarian, a benevolent and multi-talented leader, the world's last Stalinist dictator and the bellwether of the world's only dynastic dictatorship, Kim Il-sung ruled North Korea for 46 years until he breathed his last in 1994. Such was the cult of personality designed around him that the nation sank in grief at the news. As a mark of love and respect, his body was embalmed and put on public display in a glass coffin at the Kumsusan Palace of the Sun in Pyongyang. While it had been mandatory to address him with the most exalted titles such as 'Great Chairman', 'Father Chairman' and 'Heavenly One' when alive, he was now conferred the title 'Eternal President' of North Korea whose spirit, it is believed, continues to guide and steer the country towards greatness. To this day, 15 April, the day of his birth, is celebrated with pomp as the 'Day of the Sun', his photograph is often displayed alongside the North Korean flag and 'The Song of Marshal Kim Il-sung' is played before the national anthem during official events.

The stronghold of the Kim dynasty over North Korea is not only an unheard-of misnomer in the history of communism but also a lesson in public relations and propaganda. It goes to the credit of Kim Il-sung for single-mindedly pursuing a nationalist agenda, navigating the murky waters of international politics and yet, managing to embed his persona and ideology deep into the conscience of an entire nation. The enduring success of the dynasty is also testimony to the power of ambiguity and a comprehensive snub to the US and its allies who could not bring down what they concurred was a regressive state despite their superior economic and military power. A key reason for this is Il-sung's visionary decision to develop North Korea as a nuclear power—a power that allows it to engage in coercive diplomacy with the rest of the world. A bonus, of course, is the opportunity to propagandize the infallibility of the Kims, showing the people of North Korea how uniquely they are placed to defend the country with a nuclear button on their desk.

Nicolae Ceausescu

The Carpathian Mountains have been generous to Romania in their endowment of wildlife, flora, acres after acres of virgin forests and myriad geographical features, all packed into a tiny footprint of 235,000 square kilometres. The mountains purportedly derive their name from the Dacian tribe of Carpes that settled in the region during seventh–fourth century BCE. *It only seems right then, that Nicolae Ceausescu, who ruled Romania for 24 years and declared, in his propaganda, to be a direct descendent of the valorous Dacians, should claim for himself the title, 'Genius of the Carpathians'.*

The geography of Romania, comprising the four sub-provinces of Transylvania, Dobruja, Wallachia and Moldavia, is as rich as it can get. Apart from the aforementioned mountains flanked by the fertile Transylvanian and Moldavian plateaus, there are the Wallachian plains with their loess deposits and rich black soil making them ideal for agriculture. Then, there are the seven important rivers that criss-cross the country before emptying themselves in the Black Sea that kisses her south-eastern shores, and the Danube delta. Home to sturgeons, herrings and hundreds of species of rare birds—with ties to prehistoric times—it is a World Heritage Site today. However, it is perhaps geography that ensured invasion after invasion of the region by armies from near and far, with the Carpathian Mountains—snaking through the centre of the country—not doing much to protect Romania's land borders and the Black Sea inviting invaders along with traders. And so, the region has seen through its history, the comings and goings of the Greeks, Romans, Visigoths, Huns, Germanic Gepidae, Bulgarians, Hungarians, Ottoman Turks and the Russians.

The reason Romania held her own despite these attacks was her non-defensive stance against invaders. For instance, her recognition of the suzerainty of the Ottoman sultans ensured that Romania was not annexed and incorporated into the Ottoman Empire, allowing her to not only avoid an influx of Muslim settlers into her territory but also preserve her political institutions and social structure. However, WWI changed things for Romania. Although she managed to double her physical territory as a fallout of multiple land reconfigurations during and after the War, her cooperation with the Allied powers resulted in a gradual but tenuous transition from monarchy to democracy.

After a brief dalliance with democracy though, the common Romanian grew sceptical about its merits owing to a sudden collapse of agricultural prices and an unmitigated increase in unemployment during the Great Depression. Consequently,

Romania soon returned to monarchy with the ascension of Carol the Second to the throne. While the new king disliked democracy, he loathed communism. So, the Communist Party, formed in 1918 in the aftermath of the Russian Revolution, was outlawed in 1924. Then, vexed with the constant bickering between political parties, King Carol dissolved them all in 1938 and declared a royal dictatorship. However, WWII took him by surprise the very next year. With the German conquest of France in 1940, Romania lost its key Allied support and was soon torn into bits. While the Soviet Union claimed the provinces of Bessarabia and northern Bukovina, Bulgaria took southern Dobruja and Hungary annexed northern Transylvania.

The ensuing political chaos resulted in the abdication of King Carol, leaving the reins of Romania in the hands of General Ion Antonescu, the country's first military dictator. The iron-fisted reign of Antonescu did not last long though. Within three years, his dictatorship was overthrown by King Carol's son, Michael, and the country once again found itself in the midst of a power struggle between the democratic and communist parties. In the elections held in 1946, the Communist Party crept into power, marking the point from where Romania slowly but surely slipped into political ignominy. During the next 20 years, her communist leaders laid the foundation for a totalitarian regime that would be helmed by the 'Conductor', Nicolae Ceausescu.

The Shoemaker's Apprentice

Nicolae Ceausescu was born in early 1918 to a poor peasant couple, Andruta Ceausescu and his wife Alexandrina, in the hamlet of Scornicești in southern Romania. While being one of the nine children in a family struggling to make ends meet was bad enough, Nicolae's stutter, which remained with him until the end, and an abusive, alcoholic father ensured a turbulent early life. Although he attended the village school, and purportedly contributed to the family's income through tailoring, Nicolae was a frustrated boy by the time he turned 11. Consequently, he ran away from home to stay with his sister, Niculina Rusescu, in Bucharest.

In 1932, Romania was in the throes of the Great Depression. The government, under the orders of the king, imposed austerity measures including slashing of salaries of clerks and blue-collar workers by 25 per cent and cancelling rent allowances. It declared that workers would be paid only if they produced proof of taxes paid for the previous years, causing immediate dissent amongst railway workers. To champion their cause, the then-outlawed Communist Party oversaw the formation of a committee headed by Comrade Gheorghe Dej. It was in this milieu that Nicolae turned a teenager and started his apprenticeship with Alexandru Săndulescu, a shoemaker and an active member of the underground Communist Party. Săndulescu took young Nicolae under his wing, using him to secretly circulate anti-fascist pamphlets across Bucharest even as he tutored him on the tenets of communism. On one such errand, Nicolae was allegedly caught carrying a briefcase full of party flyers and thrown into a prison filled with communists. Before the end of the year, he had become a member of the Union of Communist Youth.

Barely 15, Nicolae got increasingly involved in communist activities in 1933 when the railway workers' strike was at its peak. In the next couple of years, he was arrested multiple times for charges ranging from street-fighting during protests to collecting signatures on protest petitions. By the time he turned 18, he had been branded 'a dangerous communist agitator' and 'a distributor of communist propaganda material'. In a trial following an arrest in 1936, he was convicted and sent to the Doftana prison to serve a two-and-a-half-year sentence.

During the inter-war period, Doftana was typically used to house political prisoners in near inhuman conditions. Its infamous H-cells, reserved for rebels, were dark and dungeon-like with no furniture and a single metal can that served as a toilet. Here, prisoners were forced to remain naked or barefooted on stone floors that were regularly soaked in cold water even during winters. In the 1930s, most of its prisoners were communists who were treated with particular malevolence in order to get them to relinquish their ideology. Not only were they repeatedly beaten with batons, they were forced to sustain on nothing but a daily bowl of soup and some polenta. Despite the harsh treatment that led to the death of many a prisoner, Doftana became a hotbed for communist intellectuals, with senior leaders imparting Marxist and Leninist teachings to younger members and holding covert discourses on political economics and philosophies. It was here that an impressionable Nicolae honed his own ideology and, despite the physical abuse and maltreatment, returned to civil life with a renewed fervour to promote communism. Later, during his dictatorial regime, Doftana would be turned into a museum and political pilgrimage for youth aspiring to join the Communist Party.

Once out of prison in 1939, Nicolae's continued contributing to the party's activities and was consequently in and out of prisons across the country. In 1940, the Ion Antonescu regime that actively supported Germany's fascist ideology in WWII sent him to the Targu Jiu internment camp on charges of 'conspiracy against social order'. Here, he found himself sharing a cell with Gheorghe Dej himself. During the next four years, as incarceration shielded him from the destruction wrought by the war, Nicolae won Dej over with his commitment to the communist ideology and went on to become his protégé.

In 1944, King Michael ousted Antonescu, restored

democracy and pulled Romania out of WWII. It was a step taken too late though. The Yalta Conference between the Allied forces in early 1945 bequeathed Soviet Russia with influence on and subsequently the occupation of almost 90 per cent of Romania, resulting in a sweep of communism across the country. However, with the reins of the country still in the hands of a monarch who supported democracy and a people that did not cosy up to an anti-fascist agenda, the Romanian Communist Party (RCP) faced an uphill task before elections. Now out of prison with his mentor, Nicolae was less than pleased with the situation. Not only was he concerned about how weak the party was, he was also frustrated with the step-daughterly treatment meted out to it by the Soviet leaders. Consequently, he advocated softening the party stance towards the bourgeois even as it waited for the right time for revolution.

Dej seemed to have agreed with him for, in the elections that followed, the RCP collaborated with King Michael to form the 'National Unity' government. Then, finding an opportune moment, he colluded with Prime Minister Petru Groza and forced the monarch to abdicate in December 1947, allegedly at gun point. Within days, monarchy was abolished from Romania and the country was declared a 'People's Republic'. Over the next few years, Dej ensured the mass purging of all political opponents, including 280,000 members of the democratic National Peasants Party, and went on to become not only the general secretary of the newly formed Romanian Worker's Party (RWP) but also the premier of Romania.

The Protégé

With the ascent of Dej to the acme of Romania's political landscape, it was but natural for his protégé to reap benefits. In the new scheme of things, Nicolae Ceausescu was appointed first as the minister of agriculture and then as deputy minister of armed forces. When the party promoted him to 'Secretary to the Central Committee in charge of Party Organization', he fell upon the rare power to whet all applications to various sub-committees. In a milieu where people vied with one another for privileges big and small, Ceausescu ensured that every appointee felt indebted to him for the opportunity.

Further, his training at the Frunze Military Academy in Moscow before his arrest in 1940 gave him a unique advantage of a familiarity with the Soviet way of thinking. It also helped that he knew a smattering of Russian. Consequently, Ceausescu was inducted into the Central Committee of the RWP at the insistence of Dej and given the responsibility of handling foreign policy issues. Amongst the early work under his purview were the strengthening of ties between Bucharest and Moscow and mediation efforts between the Soviet and China. In 1955, at the age of 35, Ceausescu became a full-time member of the Politburo and was made member of the Secretariat soon after.

In the decade that followed, Ceausescu learned from the deft political manoeuvres of his mentor and steadily rose to occupy the second-highest post in the political hierarchy. When Nikita Khrushchev replaced Stalin at the helm of Russia, Dej seized the opportunity to move Romania out of the Soviet shadow. Formulating a semi-autonomous economic and foreign policy, he initiated the establishment of heavy industry and reached out to leaders in Britain, France, West Germany and the US for trade agreements. He also pursued diplomatic tactics to ensure the withdrawal of the Soviet Red Army from Romanian territory and the removal of Russian as a mandatory language in schools.

In 1964, Dej issued the 'Declaration of Independence', asserting Romania's right to non-interference in internal affairs, a foreign policy based on national sovereignty and peaceful coexistence, which made him hugely popular both at home and abroad. So much so that both the Romanian masses and international media largely ignored the warning signs of an impending authoritarian regime, as Gheorghe-Dej persisted with repressive Stalinist measures—enforcing collectivization of rural land, establishing the Securitate (a Soviet-style secret police), building an extensive network of prisons and labour camps, and ruthlessly purging his rivals.

Such was his popularity that when Dej succumbed to cancer a year later, delegations from 33 countries, including a special envoy from General Charles de Gaulle of France, attended his funeral. For Ceausescu, his successor, this meant a ready audience to appreciate his interpretation of a communist regime.

The Prodigal

With Dej not having formally nominated Ceausescu as successor and with senior leaders vying for power, infighting ensued within the party soon after the former's death. Ceausescu, however, had already won over several comrades who were looking to distance themselves from Moscow, positioning himself as a 'home communist' who had chosen to stay back and fight during the reign of Antonescu while other communist leaders had fled to Russia. Moreover, he had the crucial support of three of Dej's key cohorts—Emil Bodnăraş, Chivu Stoica and Ion Gheorghe Maurer. Bodnăraş, in particular, had been an important figure who, as minister of defence in Dej's administration, had sent Ceausescu to Russia several times to gain training at Soviet military schools. Now, with the leader gone, his loyalists threw their weight behind Ceausescu to ensure his election as general secretary of the RWP. Thus, just three days after his mentor's death, Ceausescu ascended to the highest post in the country's hierarchy on 22 March 1965. At 5'2" with an awkwardly small build and a prominent stutter, nothing about the 47-year-old Ceausescu hinted at the future he was envisaging for Romania.

From his very first day at the helm, Ceausescu was clear that he did not want the spectre of his mentor looming over him, impeding his agenda to carve a political identity of his own. Hoping to start with a clean slate, he reinstated the older name of the party—Romanian Communist Party—marking a clear departure from Dej's ideology, and established a Marxist-Leninist single-party communism in Romania. During the next three years, he steered the country towards being a socialist state, changing its identity from Romanian People's Republic to Socialist Republic of Romania. While he manipulated the internal workings of the RCP to ensure undisputed power for himself, he also initiated several changes on the pretext of reforming the party's governing bodies. A crucial decision was to increase the number of party members, even accepting those who had been excluded from membership during Dej's regime, to ensure that numbers favoured him when it mattered. Within a year of his inauguration, party veterans—with the exception of Maurer, Bodnăraş and Stoica—were sidelined and loyalists were installed in positions of power, be it within the party or in the state bureaucracy, military and financial institutions.

In December 1967, Ceausescu was elected president of the State Council of the Socialist Republic of Romania by the Grand National Assembly. Not one to forget his supporters, his first act after assuming presidency was to appoint Bodnăraş as vice president and ensure that Maurer retained the post of prime minister. Stoica was given a position in the Secretariat and was later appointed chairman of the Central Auditing Commission.

In 1968, having created a strong power base for himself, Ceausescu openly denounced Dej for deviating from party ideals and abusing power during his regime. With Dej gone though, it fell upon his minister of interior and Ceausescu's rival, Alexandru Draghici, to face the accusations. Although he was subsequently dismissed from the party and put under internal surveillance, Draghici wasn't purged the way Dej's rivals had been. Instead, in keeping with Ceausescu's ideal of being regarded as a reformer and champion of the common man, he was sent to head a state-run factory in the suburban town of Buftea from where he retired in 1972 with a hefty pension. Similarly, Gheorghe Apostol, who had been Dej's deputy prime minister, was advised to switch to a diplomatic career that saw him becoming the Romania's ambassador to Argentina, Uruguay and Brazil, keeping him happy but out of Romania's internal politics. The next few years saw a cautious de-Stalinization in Romania's domestic affairs, much to the respite of the common man. Ceausescu not only welcomed back to Romania the purge victims of Dej's regime, he also granted new freedoms to writers, artists and intellectuals and encouraged younger people, especially academicians and technicians, to join the party's various bodies.

After being elected chairman of the Defence Council and being anointed 'Supreme Commander of the Armed Forces' in 1969, Ceausescu went on to implement economic reforms that promised to allow greater freedom to private enterprise, decentralize economic control, increase efficiency and boost incentives. Consequently, Romania went on to enjoy some of her most economically prosperous years in the early 1970s.

The Social Engineer

The Romania that Ceausescu inherited in 1965 was a country at the brink of starvation thanks to Dej's policies. A quick and long-lasting solution to the problem at hand had to be arrived at and Ceausescu's solution was simple—grow the population to reverse the situation. Deriving from the economic tenets of Stalinism, his logic was that a younger and larger Romanian workforce would dramatically increase production. Consequently, in 1966, a year after coming into power, Ceausescu instituted the infamous Decree 770, a law that advocated punishments for citizens opting for small families. With the objective of rapidly increasing Romania's population from 25 million to 30 million, he famously proclaimed that the foetus was the property of the entire society and anyone avoiding having children was a cog in the wheel of the laws of national continuity. He then instituted new rules, including a fine of up to 30 per cent of wages on childless couples over the age of 25 and a ban on sterilization procedures on women under the age of 45 who did not have at least five children.

Soon, in what would become one of the most notorious state-sponsored attempts at social engineering, women in Romania were prohibited from using contraception or opting for abortion. They were subjected to mandatory monthly check-ups by state-appointed gynaecologists who came to be known as the 'menstrual police', and had their pregnancies supervised to completion. Infringing on basic personal freedoms, the sexual lives of women who failed to conceive were investigated, while those who miscarried were suspected of having an abortion. The impact of the law was felt almost immediately across Romania. In the very first year, birth rate in the country jumped by 13 per cent and almost doubled by 1977. Yet, when condoms and birth control pills started to become available in Romania in 1980, they were banned, making their smuggling a lucrative business in the country.

While women from affluent families could afford these pills and even hope for authorities to turn a blind eye to the illegal interruption of their pregnancies, the situation of poorer women was most preposterous—they were forced to bear five children when they had no resources to raise even one. With no safety net to fall back upon, they either resorted to surreptitious and risky backyard abortions or abandoned the children altogether. Not surprisingly, the Human Rights Watch reported a 600 per cent increase in abortion-related deaths as well as an unprecedented rise in the number of orphans in Romania in the years following the decree.

With more and more children being abandoned, the focus of orphanages in Romania changed from providing care for children who had lost their parents to housing children whose families could not afford to nurture them. Far from being perturbed, the state assumed the role of a foster parent of sorts and encouraged couples to send their children to the orphanages, with government propaganda promising to take care of them and prepare them for adult life. The Ceausescu government also devised a controversial three-step structure where children were placed in a particular institution until they turned three, transferred to another one until they reached the age of six and then categorized as being normal, irrecoverable or unproductive through physical and psychiatric evaluations. In a clear case of discrimination, those in the first category were sent to institutions run by the Ministry of Education while the remaining were sent to institutions run by the Ministry of Labour. To discourage children from depending on others, staff in the orphanages were instructed not to talk to or hug them, not to answer them when they cried and not to engage them in any games or activities.

The worst was yet to come for these children though. When the honeymoon period for the Romanian economy under Ceausescu ended in 1981 with his government deciding to dig into national reserves to pay off an astronomical foreign debt, orphanages were among the first to suffer. Stringent budget cuts meant shortages of food, clothes and medicines, erratic power cuts, unhygienic environments and undertrained nurses and caretakers, leading to developmental delays, medical oversights and institutional abuse. While several children were said to have contracted HIV due to the use of unsterilized hypodermic needles, caretakers were known to steal food meant for the children, drugging the latter so they wouldn't complain of starvation.

When the Ceausescu regime finally ended in 1989, a conservative estimate pegged the number of orphans across state-run orphanages at no less than 150,000.

The 'World Leader'

Having seen the global reverence for his mentor, Gheorghe Dej, Ceausescu nurtured a personal dream of being considered an influential world leader. It helped that he was already involved in the Sino-Soviet talks. Once in power, he went on to strategically insert himself as mediator into the negotiations between China and the US during and after the Vietnam War. These engagements gave him an opportunity to develop connections with leaders such as the Chinese premier Deng Xiaoping, his Russian counterpart Leonid Brezhnev and the American president Lyndon Johnson. The experience also helped him take a strong political stance when required, without antagonizing allies. Consequently, Romania wasn't ostracized by the Soviet when he openly supported China during the Sino-Soviet split of 1966 or voiced his opinion against the limiting nature of the Warsaw Pact that Romania had been a signatory to. Further, as a hint for the Soviet to step back from imposing its policies on the Eastern Bloc countries, Ceausescu asserted Romania's autonomy on the grounds that all communist parties were equal and none had the right to question the others' policy choices.

Then, in what was seen as a clear violation of the Warsaw Pact, Ceausescu denounced the Soviet invasion of

Czechoslovakia in 1968. Addressing a 100,000-strong audience in Bucharest's Palace Square, he declared that the invasion was a grave error on part of the Soviet, one that could potentially disrupt peace in Europe and cast global aspersions on the ideology of socialism. Although Russia itself wasn't anything more than irked by the defiant stance, with a Soviet diplomat of the time hinting that Brezhnev could have easily squashed Ceausescu but did not find it worth the effort, the Western media and leaders almost immediately sat up and took note of the Romanian leader.

It was just the opening Ceausescu had been seeking to be seen as a principled and important world leader. A flurry of diplomatic exchanges soon followed between Romania and the world as Ceausescu visited the US, Britain, West Germany, France, the Vatican, Italy and India amongst other countries and in turn received their leaders, including Charles de Gaulle of France and Richard Nixon of the US at his offices in Bucharest. Recognizing the possibility of greater appreciation for his diplomacy in the Third World countries, he undertook massive tours through Asia, Latin America and Africa during 1971–73, visiting over 20 countries across the regions, while 1974 was devoted to countries in the Middle East including Libya, Syria, Iraq and Lebanon. At the state-hosted events in each of these countries, Ceausescu enjoyed the fuss created around him and listened to the paeans sung about him with great relish. Thanks to the tours, the number of countries with which Romania established diplomatic relations more than doubled from 67 in 1965 to 138 in 1985.

The Fledgling Dictator

During 1969–71, public protests and rebellions resulted in a change of guard in Czechoslovakia with Gustáv Husák replacing

Alexander Dubček at the helm while Władisław Gomułka's regime in Poland made way for Edward Gierek's and Erich Honecker took over from Walter Ulbricht in East Germany. While the regime changes were seemingly an outcome of a disgruntled public, Ceausescu saw evidence of a Soviet hand in the unfolding events. In his calculated view, all three of the replaced leaders had brought their fate upon themselves by ignoring the weak relationship between the party and people in their countries. This weakness, according to him, not only lead to social disturbances but also put a leader's power at risk. His considered reading of the events led Ceausescu to not only iron out his differences with the Soviet leadership but also improve people-party relations and insure himself against a fate similar to his contemporaries.

It was in this political milieu that Ceausescu visited China and North Korea in 1971 and returned home impressed with the nationalist ideologies embodied in the Chinese Cultural Revolution and the North Korean concept of juche. Whilst there, he took particular note of the personality cult around Mao Tse-tung and Kim Il-sung and their effective use of propaganda to mask what were evidently totalitarian agendas. Ceausescu was also impressed with the spectacle of mass greeting in both countries, with the motorcade of the Romanian delegation being enthusiastically cheered by hordes of well-dressed people holding flags, flowers and welcoming banners. In Beijing, in particular, traditionally dressed dancers had performed under a 20-metre-high portrait of Ceausescu.

While these choreographed political performances fed his narcissism, they also reaffirmed his thoughts about people-party relations and brought about a drastic change in his political ideology. Abandoning his liberalist approach, Ceausescu proclaimed in a July 1971 speech, known as the July Theses, his intention to involve youth in large-scale construction projects as a mark of patriotism, intensify the teaching of the state's political ideology in schools and universities and use radios, televisions, publishing houses, cinemas, theatres and operas for propaganda as well as to rouse nationalist sentiments in the population. Soon, Romania slipped back into the pre-1965 Stalinist era where books, authors, artists and scholars were banned and ostracized if they said anything against the government while the market was flooded with Romanian translations of books on juche. Ceausescu also changed his stance on courting the West albeit without making it obvious to his benefactors. While heavy restrictions were placed on travels to the West and the imbibing of Western culture, he retracted his earlier decision to distance Romania from the Warsaw Pact and went on to sign several infrastructural and defence agreements with the USSR.

The July Theses was followed up with another speech in 1972 where Ceausescu hinted at his wish to blend the workings of the party and the state, resulting in the formation of organizations like the Council for Socialist Education and Culture that blurred the boundaries between what were until then, two separate entities. It was evidently a step towards a larger goal. In 1974, Ceausescu elevated the post of president of the State Council to that of an executive presidency, allowing him to be elected as the de jure President of Romania every five years and giving himself sweeping powers to make national decisions. While his decrees had required the approval of a plenum until then, he was now free to make and dissolve laws at will. He also had the sole power to appoint or remove candidates from important posts, including those of Supreme Court judges and prosecutor generals.

Soon after, Ceausescu set about creating a cult of personality around himself and stepped on the propaganda machine. While the masses were greeted with his face on everything from paintings, sculptures, posters and stamps, his voice was heard in every corner of the country through radios. Furthermore, television reports were mandated to make frequent mentions of his role as the 'architect of modern Romania' and 'guarantor of national independence and unity'. At the same time, while his photographs adorned the walls of classrooms and the first page of textbooks so that his would be the first face children would see before commencing studies, the public was constantly reminded about Ceausescu's role in the 1968 defiance of the USSR, with stories equating him with medieval Romanian princes and Dacian rulers who defied the Roman Empire.

In a bid to gain his favours, regime sympathizers went to various lengths to appease him, with poet Ion Gheorghe, in particular, bordering on the absurd when he equated Ceausescu, his wife Elena and the Romanian fatherland with the Holy Trinity itself. In 1977, after Ceausescu replaced Romania's national anthem that apparently had undertones of 'a problematic adoration of the Soviet', with a more nationalistic anthem, hundreds of songs were written in praise of Ceausescu and Romania, and sung during public events or broadcast across the country. On the other hand, the Romanian Composers' Union provided nationalistic music for the birthdays and anniversary celebrations of Ceausescu and his wife Elena. Following his ascension to the presidency, Ceausescu also introduced the concept of Cântarea României, a bi-yearly eight-month-long cultural festival cum competition that ostensibly celebrated the myriad folk artists in Romania and emphasized the government's deep investment in the nation's cultural and ethnic heritage.

Although music played a vital role in his propaganda, Ceausescu ensured that it was controlled with an iron fist by the state. Not only were undesired lyrics censored, there was also a ban on listening to music in most foreign languages. The Cântarea României also allowed him to control cultural production by diverting the masses away from foreign music and art forms, such as Western pop and rock that the public had grown to enjoy in the initial years of his reign, while also disenfranchising professional musicians and artists of whom he was deeply suspicious.

Despite the elaborate propaganda, opposing voices persisted amongst the masses. While he had been averse to violent methods of silencing rivals in his early years, the ruthless Securitate, amongst the world's most fearsome secret police, now became Ceausescu's go-to organization. Particularly wary of university students, artists, writers, film directors and scientists who protested against his hard-line communist agenda, he ensured that they were frequently targeted for searches, unannounced midnight arrests, threats and torture. Further, the mingling of Securitate informers with the general population in high numbers made it impossible for dissenting voices to go unnoticed. These measures, however, did not seem to satiate Ceausescu who was growing more paranoid with each passing year, what with threats to and assassination attempts on his life. Consequently, he ordered the replacement of telephones and televisions in every household and office across Romania with those that were modified to hold microphones and transmitters, while ashtrays concealing listening devices were placed on every restaurant table. Even typewriters were seen as possible tools of dissent and were required to be registered with government officials.

Soon, the entire nation was living in a constant distrust and fear of communicating with even their loved ones. The iconic gymnast, Nadia Comaneci, who had recently won gold at the Montreal Olympics, too wasn't spared, with the choreographer of the Romanian Olympics team allegedly being one of the many who spied on her activities for Ceausescu. Not only were microphones installed in her home, the Securitate was also deployed to track her down whenever she ran away after a disagreement with her coach. When her coach defected to the US in 1981, her surveillance was tightened at the insistence of Ceausescu who, though obsessed with the medals she won for Romania, did nothing to improve her condition as an official of The Gymnastics Federation drawing a meagre monthly salary of $150.

In 1970, Ceausescu had delivered a speech in which he had said, 'only crazy people would imagine that socialist order could collapse in Romania.' The lines proved to be partly prophetic, with the Romanian leader giving sanction a decade later for the use of political psychiatry—a Stalinist method to curb dissent that involved the isolation and neutralization of those who opposed the regime. Romania soon saw a spurt in the construction of prison-like psychiatric hospitals with barbed wire fences and watchdogs, where perfectly healthy people suspected to be dissidents were admitted for treatment of psychiatric conditions like schizophrenia, senile dementia, extreme personality disorders and political paranoia. Not only were these 'patients' forcefully given antipsychotic medications, they were also compelled to share rooms with real patients in the hope that they would go genuinely crazy. Those who did, were purportedly made to build their own coffins in which, unknown to relatives, they were disposed following forcible drug overdoses.

The American Pet

Ceausescu's ability to remain cordial with Russia despite his non-conformist approach to communism endeared him to the US, who saw in him an important East European ally. He had also surprised the world by becoming the only communist leader to simultaneously maintain relations with Israel and the

Arab nations. Expectedly, his ascent to premiership marked the beginning of a long association between Romania and the US, spanning the presidential terms of Lyndon Johnson, Richard Nixon, Gerald Ford, Jimmy Carter and Ronald Reagan.

After the invasion of Czechoslovakia in 1968, Johnson went out of the way to warn Russia against invading Romania, ensuring that subsequent regimes in the Soviet refrained from interfering in Romania's affairs. In August 1969, Romania was one of the first few countries Nixon visited as president of the US. In his address to the people of Romania, he underlined the importance of the occasion saying, 'This is a historic occasion. While this is not my first visit to your country, it is the first visit of a President of the United States to Romania, the first state visit by an American President to a socialist country or to this region of the continent of Europe.' The visit proved rather beneficial for Romania, with Ceausescu managing to secure promises of US assistance in science and technology, use of nuclear energy for peaceful purposes, and being granted the Most Favoured Nation status upon the conclusion of the Vietnam War. Moreover, in a rare gesture, Nixon presented Ceausescu with a small Romanian flag along with rock fragments from the moon gathered by Neil Armstrong and Buzz Aldrin during their Apollo 11 mission that had concluded just the previous month. The accompanying goodwill message stated—'This flag of your nation was carried to the Moon and back by Apollo 11, and this fragment of the Moon's surface was brought to Earth by the crew of that first manned lunar landing.'

It was not surprising then that Nixon's visit caught the fancy of Romanian commoners and changed their perception of Ceausescu. Back in the political circles in the US, Ceausescu began to be looked upon as a rare leader who could pull off the improbable feat of maintaining good relations with both the Soviet Union and the People's Republic of China. Such was the importance of Ceausescu's diplomatic relations that when he visited the US in 1970, Nixon went out of his way to shine the spotlight on the two-week long visit, inviting the Romanian leader to discuss issues relating to European security, Indochina, the Middle East and communist China.

The US benevolence continued after Ceausescu's return home, with diplomats at the US Embassy being instructed to paint a rosy picture of the Romanian economy that would encourage American bankers and businessmen to invest in the country. What these investors were kept in the dark about was that they were pumping money into a vicious loop—their investment was being used to produce poor-quality factory-made goods that would eventually be sold back to them to help Romania repay its loans. By the time Nixon was ousted from presidency, Romania had earned several undeserved favours and concessions. Furthermore, despite the dichotomy in Ceausescu's home and foreign policies becoming clearer by the day, Nixon's ostensive response to why he patronized the communist Romanian leader was, 'It's true he's a commie, but he's "our" commie.'

Ceausescu was shrewd enough to decipher that as long as he maintained an anti-Soviet stance, the US and its allies would not only support him but also overlook his misgivings. In 1975, Gerald Ford met with Ceausescu in Bucharest and granted Romania the much anticipated Most Favoured Nation status based on freedom of emigration metrics. Although the metrics showed Romania in a favourable light for having allowed hundreds of thousands of Jews to emigrate to Israel, what was not popular knowledge was that the Ceausescu government, as had the Bulgarian and Hungarian governments historically, charged Israel anywhere between $50 to $300 per emigrating Jew. An estimated $60 million was exchanged in cash between Israel and Romania during Ceausescu's regime, with most of the money finding way into the president's personal coffers. Ceausescu later adopted the same strategy when allowing Romanian Germans to emigrate to West Germany. According to a regime defector, Ceausescu often joked that Jews and Germans were Romania's best export goods.

If the US knew about these underhand dealings, it chose to ignore them in order to keep its ally in good humour. In 1978, the US welcomed Ceausescu for the fourth time in eight years. This time, it was under the presidency of Jimmy Carter, who, despite objections of the Congress that doubted Romania's commitment to the emigration problem, lavished praise on the visiting leader and hinted at doubling mutual trade over subsequent years. In 1983, George Bush, then the vice president to Ronald Regan, hailed Ceausescu as 'the good communist', setting the tone for yet another presidential term that preferred to remain blinkered to the Romanian leader's oppressive regime back home.

While the US sought to keep the Soviets in check with Ceausescu's help, Great Britain needed to humour him to overcome its grim economy. With losses from WWII refusing to be salvaged even after 20 years, Britain found itself going through an economic upheaval in the late 1960s and was desperate to find markets to export to. Romania, with a strictly controlled central economy that lacked quality domestic products to aid its industrialization process, was a market waiting to be exploited. Not surprisingly, British exports to Romania doubled between 1968–69 and the period between 1972–75 was marked by diplomats and business leaders criss-crossing the countries, culminating in the 1975 state visit to Bucharest of British prime minister Harold Wilson. The visit resulted in his signing a 10-year economic cooperation agreement with Ceausescu.

The following year, knowing well that Britain was keen on buying cheap Romanian oil, Ceausescu drove a hard bargain for concessions that allowed Romania to not only settle its outstanding debts of close to 40 million pounds at just 3.5 million but also inspired Britain to lend a further 100 million towards export finance. Furthermore, British politicians were consistently generous in their praise of Ceausescu, with Harold Wilson declaring that 'only two or three people in the world possess a vision and understanding of things like that of Nicolae Ceausescu' and his successor James Callaghan adding that Ceausescu had 'achieved a well-deserved reputation as a world statesman'. The erstwhile leader of opposition, Margret Thatcher, too was said to have expressed her admiration for the Romanian leader's personality.

In 1978, Ceausescu went on a much-touted state visit to Britain where he managed to not only secure contracts totalling 300 million pounds for the production of British Aerospace and Rolls Royce engines in Romania but also satiate his personal ego. Indulging his wife's fancy to be treated like a queen, he used his bargaining skills to obtain an invitation to stay at the Buckingham Palace. After an eventful stay there, he also managed to get the queen to confer him with an honorary knighthood. With increasing global awareness of his repressive dictatorship and disastrous socio-economic decisions, the needless British generosity was indeed puzzling.

The Family Man

After Ceausescu's election to the top post in 1965, he ensured that his family was the first to benefit. Soon, his wife Elena rose rapidly in the party ranks from being just another member to being instituted as a member of the Executive Committee in 1973. When her husband became president of Romania in 1974, she joined him as vice president while also becoming a member of the Politburo. At the same time, while Nicu, the couple's youngest son, was made regional party chief in central Romania, their older son Valentin and daughter Zoia found themselves holding important posts in the government. By the end of the year, an estimated 40 members of Ceausescu and Elena's combined families were occupying important posts in the party and state hierarchy.

Part of Ceausescu's propagandist strategy was also to play up Elena on the national and global stage by painting her as a scholar. Although all her whims and expenses were taken care of by the state, Elena was still obliged to work under the communist Constitution. Perhaps because of communism's preference for the sciences or due to the hangover of receiving Margret Thatcher, herself an acclaimed chemist, in Bucharest in 1975, Elena chose for herself the role of a world-famous specialist in polymer chemistry. With her having barely passed fourth grade and ending up as a textile factory worker before meeting Ceausescu, fake degrees were soon generated to bolster her academic standing. She was also made chairperson of Romania's main laboratory for research in chemistry as well as the National Council for Science and Technology. She was subsequently conferred with a PhD in Chemistry followed by her name appearing on several academic papers ghost-written by other Romanian scientists.

Thanks to the patronage of Robert Maxwell, the British media baron who had earlier published her husband's unabashed hagiography titled *Ceausescu: Builder of Modern Romania*, Elena's ghost-written PhD dissertation was published as a book with a foreword by Nobel prize-winning British chemist Dorothy Hodgkin. At the request of the Romanian Embassy, Elena was also made an honorary fellow of the New York Academy of Sciences and London's Royal Society of Chemistry while the Polytechnic of Central London gave her the title of honorary professor.

Having endeared themselves to the public through propaganda, Ceausescu and Elena soon indulged themselves at the state's expense. During his 24-year rule over Romania, even as the ordinary citizen was forced to live in extreme poverty owing to repressive policies, Ceausescu himself managed to own more than 15 luxury palaces across the country, with peacocks roaming in their gardens and rooms filled with priceless marbles, carpets, porcelain, chandeliers, silk and bronze and silverware. His official 150-room residence, the Spring Palace, featured garish mosaics, intricate woodwork, staircases flanked with gilded details, a movie theatre and gold-plated fittings in lavish marble-clad bathrooms.

While Ceausescu would always travel with a fleet of Mercedes cars, Elena would accompany him on all foreign visits and stuff her wardrobes with the most expensive of furs and designer clothes. Despite an abundance of wealth, Elena was obsessed with collecting free gifts and insisted on being gifted expensive articles from countries the couple graced their presence with. When their numerous palaces weren't enough to display these prized possessions, including a cowboy hat presented by Lyndon Johnson, she opened the National Museum of Gifts to the Ceausescus to house them. Moreover, while the couple stayed in only the most lavish historical castles during their travels within Romania, their notoriety emerged during travels abroad, with candid allegations by diplomats of several countries that the couple stole from the presidential suites they were accommodated in. They also purportedly bored holes and dug out walls to ensure the rooms weren't bugged.

The most famous of these was the ostensible warning sounded by the French president to Queen Elizabeth to hide her silver before hosting Ceausescu during his 1978 state visit to Britain. When the Cesusescus finally arrived at the Buckingham Palace, they allegedly held all discussions with their entourage on the palace lawns, suspecting the rooms of being bugged. If these were considered eccentric by the Western media, Ceausescu's excesses touched new heights when Corbu, the labrador pup gifted to him during the visit, was promoted to honorary colonel in the Romanian army. Back in Romania, Comrade Corbu was often driven in a limousine through the streets of Bucharest with a motorcade of his own while the Romanian ambassador in London had official orders to shop for dog biscuits at Sainsbury's every week and dispatch them to Romania in his diplomatic bag.

'Jos Ceausescu'

Although propaganda tried convincing the Romanian citizens that they were living in near utopia, it was becoming exceedingly difficult to ignore empty stomachs and paranoid minds, especially with Ceausescu himself wining and dining with leaders of the West and his wife, collecting degrees and gifts alike by the dozens. It was in such pressing times that Bucharest was struck by a disastrous earthquake in 1977. Instead of plunging into rehabilitation activities, Ceausescu saw in the calamity an opportunity to carry out an elaborate remodelling of the city that he felt was far from being an ideal modern capital.

In no time, the Văcărești Hill in southeast Bucharest was flattened and the sixteenth century monastery that stood on it demolished. Furthermore, the historic Uranus neighbourhood at the heart of the city was bulldozed, tearing down ancient churches, theatres, hospitals, schools, dwellings and sports stadia. In their place sprouted a wide, tree-lined boulevard flanked by rows of concrete government buildings and VIP apartment blocks, evidently inspired from Kim Il-sung's design of Pyongyang. The crown jewel of the scheme was Ceausescu's gift to Bucharest—the world's heaviest building with 1,100 opulent rooms featuring gold leaf ceilings and silver brocade curtains spread over twelve storeys that he ironically named the Palace of the People after having forced over 40,000 people to relocate to make way for the architectural behemoth. Today, the project that had 700 architects and over 20,000 workers toiling to complete it over six years, hosts the Romanian parliament that occupies less than one-fourth of the building. Additionally, over 8,000 villages were razed under Ceausescu's 'rural systemization' plan, giving way to urban industrial centres with purportedly modern infrastructure. For the displaced people though, it meant moving from their homes in picturesque rural lands into tiny concrete apartments and relinquishing their agrarian lifestyles forever.

To add to the surmounting national woes, the extensive network of oil refineries Ceausescu had commissioned to increase exports did not yield desired profits, causing Romania to be saddled with a backbreaking $10 billion in debt in 1981. Deciding to pay off the astronomical debt rather than default, Ceausescu imposed a draconian austerity programme that resulted in acute food and energy shortages across the country. Soon, even as his numerous palaces shone like jewels through the night, ordinary citizens were banned from having more than one 40 watt light bulb in their houses. The power crisis reached its peak in 1984, when streets lights were permanently shut down, homes and factories were prohibited from turning on heating systems even in winters and doctors were forced to perform surgeries only in daylight. Several hundreds of infants and elderly Romanians succumbed to the freezing cold or related illnesses in the years between 1984 and 1989.

The focus on repaying debts also led to Romania exporting both agricultural and industrial produce at the cost of a starving population. As prices soared, imported fruits disappeared from the markets and essentials, such as bread, sugar and cooking oil came, to be rationed, leading to kilometres-long queues becoming common sights across the country. While gasoline too was rationed, citizens were allowed to trade it for more food. Further, the poor quality and prohibitive cost of meat forced Romanians into vegetarianism, with instances of those caught with meat even being sent to prison.

Throughout the period between 1981 and 1989, governments and bankers in the West, particularly the US and Britain, turned a blind eye to the plight of the ordinary Romanian and continued humouring Ceausescu. Consequently, the Romanian people discovered, albeit late, that it was upon them to stop their eccentric leader from dragging the country to its doom. In 1988, protests started getting staged to question his authoritarian rule, prompting Ceausescu to focus on developing counter-measures. The following year, the eviction of a Hungarian pastor from his church-owned house as part of the systemization plan, and his subsequent harassment by the government for speaking up against the draconian laws sparked widespread protests. During one such anti-government demonstration on 16 December, Ceausescu allowed the police and Securitate to open fire on the crowds, resulting in hundreds of injuries and fatalities. The incident, christened the Timisoara massacre, sparked immediate outrage and resulted in several other protests erupting across the country. Taken aback by the sudden turn of the tide, the Romanian leader took to the stage to address the country.

On 21 December 1989, in what was to be his last speech to the nation, Ceausescu addressed a 100,000-strong crowd in a bid to distance himself from the uprising by blaming anti-national fascist agitators for the killings. The angry crowd would have none of it though. Booing him and chanting 'jos Ceausescu', meaning 'down with Ceausescu' and '*moarte criminalului*!'

meaning 'death to the criminal!', they forced him to retreat into the Central Committee Building from where he was addressing them. With the event being broadcast on national television on Ceausecu's orders, the entire country soon broke into riots.

On 22 December, a senior military leader, Vasile Milea, committed suicide, preferring to take his own life rather than that of innocent citizens. However, rumours of it having been an assassination ordered by Ceausescu spread like wildfire through the armed forces, resulting in several loyal officers and Securitate members turning against their president to side with the protestors who had by now surrounded the committee building. Finding themselves cornered, Ceausescu and Elena tried a dramatic rooftop escape by helicopter. However, when the army threatened to take down the helicopter with a surface-to-air missile, their pilot made a landing on a remote country road and abandoned his passengers. The first couple of Romania soon found themselves hitchhiking to the city of Targoviste. Unknown to them though, the driver of the car informed the army about their whereabouts, leading to their unceremonious arrest.

In a televised trial held on 25 December 1989, a kangaroo court found Ceausescu and Elena guilty of genocide, undermining the power of the state, destruction of public property, embezzlement of millions of dollars into secret bank accounts and destabilizing the national economy. Going against the advice of their legal counsel to plead insanity, the duo tried in vain to justify their actions and found themselves being sentenced to death. Immediately after the trial, at 4.00 p.m. on Christmas Day, the Ceausescus were executed by a firing squad at a military base just outside Bucharest, bringing down the curtains on one of the most repressive and cynical dictatorships history has known.

In an interview on 22 December when Ceausescu was still on the run, British prime minister Margaret Thatcher expressed joy at the fall of communism in Romania adding, 'We welcome Romania to the family of free nations'. On 25 December, after Ceausescu's execution, US president George Bush extended full support for the 'reestablishment of a government founded on the democratic will of the Romanian people.' With their complicity in Ceausescu's rise being no secret, one can only wonder at the overnight shift in their political narratives and newfound concern for the Romanian people.

Pol Pot

Theravada Buddhism, which holds Nirvaana or spiritual enlightenment as its highest goal and advocates the ideas of anicca (impermanence) and anatta (not-self), has been the state religion of Cambodia since the thirteenth century when King Jayavarman VII oversaw the mass conversion of the Khmer people to the version of Buddhism considered closest to the teachings of the Buddha. Between then and the mid-1960s, the religion retained its importance in the lives of Cambodians despite numerous changes in guard at the helm of largely monarchic regimes. The religion also survived waves of European influences, including the comings and goings of Catholic missionaries who tried their best to convert the natives. Then, in 1975, the Khmer Rouge came into power in Cambodia, headed by a revolutionary who went by the name Pol Pot. Within no time, nearly

every trace of Theravada Buddhism was wiped off the country's slate, almost every temple and monastery razed to the ground and every Buddhist monk and intellectual done away with.

Cambodia's history was marked by the rise and fall of powerful kingdoms between the ninth and fifteenth centuries. Most notable amongst these was the Khmer or Angkorean Empire that dominated much of Southeast Asia and produced remarkable achievements in architecture, hydrology, and the arts. After the decline of Angkor though, in part due to repeated attacks by the neighbouring Tai invaders, the region experienced periods of instability and shifting regional influence. Yet, it continued to assimilate cultural and religious influences from Malaya and India during peacetime, allowing trade and the arts to flourish.

The nineteenth century however saw frequent conflicts between its neighbouring kingdoms, with Cambodia often becoming a trophy that the winner of the tug of war between Thailand and Vietnam would take home. Offering protection from the warring neighbours, the French made a silent entry into the country in the late 1860s and, with a series of deft political manoeuvres including the forced signing of a document by King Norodom at gun point in 1884, colonized Cambodia by the turn of the century. Soon, rubber plantations cropped up by the dozen to work in which cheap labour from Vietnam, also a part of French Indochina, was engaged. At the same time, the laying of hundreds of kilometres of roads and railway networks across the country, establishment of French-teaching schools run by Catholic fathers and concerted efforts put into restoring the architectural glory of temples in the Angkor Wat complex, earned the colonizers the approval of the Khmer elite. Amongst these elites was the Saloth family.

Saloth Sar

Saloth Sar was born on 25 May 1925, into a prosperous Khmer family in Prek Sbauv, a village 130 kilometres to the north of Phnom Penh. His father, Pen Saloth, owned several acres of farmland where he grew rice and tended to draft cattle while his mother, Sok Nem, stayed at home and took care of the couple's nine children of whom Sar was the eighth. He was named 'Sar' meaning 'pale' or 'white', perhaps because of his skin tone that was lighter than most others in the family.

As was with 98 per cent of the Cambodian population of the time, the Saloth family was staunchly Buddhist and based its conduct around tenets of the religion. Although they lived a humble life, their relative affluence was evident from the size of their village house and its tiled-roofing, both displaying a marked contrast to other houses that were smaller with thatched roofs. Moreover, the family had immediate ties to the royal family of Cambodia. While Sar's cousin, Khum Meak, joined the royal ballet as a dancer in the 1920s and went on to become a consort of King Monivong, even bearing him a son, his older sister Saloth Roeung followed Meak's footsteps and ended up as a royal concubine a decade later. His oldest brother Saloth Suong too worked as a palace clerk and married a ballet dancer.

In 1935, nine-year-old Sar was sent to live with his older siblings in Phnom Penh so he could receive better education. For the next 10 years, he would be a regular visitor to the palace where he was given special treatment, particularly at the women's quarters where his sisters reigned. Now though, his first stop in the capital was at Wat Botum Vaddei, the Buddhist monastery patronized by the royal family where nearly a 100 children between the ages of seven and 12 were sent by their families each year. Here, sporting yellow robes and a shaven head, Sar spent a little over a year learning to read and write the

Khmer language and studying the fundamentals of Buddhism.

The highly disciplined and austere environs of the monastery was a stark contrast to Sar's life in the village. While back in Prek Sbauv he led a carefree life chasing ducks and buffaloes, and swimming in the river with his younger brother Nhep, he lived in the constant fear of being thrashed at the monastery not only for not chanting the sutras without hesitation but also for not walking correctly. The latter meant that he was to always walk slowly, without making any sound with his feet and without swinging his arms. His daily routine involved waking up at 4.00 a.m. with his peers, making obeisance to the Buddha, chanting the sutras, cleaning the temple courtyard, preparing breakfast, accompanying senior monks when they left to beg for alms, preparing and consuming a simple lunch and devoting the rest of the day to learning the scriptures, language and morality. As per monastery rules, no evening snacks or dinner was permitted.

Despite the rigidity of the monastic system, Sar tried his best to grasp the spirit of detachment that the monks constantly advocated. His experience at the Wat would go on to impact him in two contrasting ways in his later life—while he would fondly but falsely reminisce the six years he spent at the Wat, and promote detachment and discipline to his revolutionary group, he would also order the destruction of everything Buddhist.

During 1936–47, Sar led a docile school life at Ecole Miche, a French Catholic primary school for children of the reasonably elite Cambodians. Soft-spoken and mild-mannered, he went through the daily grind without skirmishes with peers or admonishments by teachers. However, academics was his sore point. A mediocre student, he found it difficult to measure up to French standards and failed the primary school-leaving exam twice. Upon finally graduating, he joined a secondary school where he developed a liking for football, basketball and violin even as he continued to struggle with academics. Here, he also formed lasting friendships with Ping Say and Lon Non, oblivious to the future that would pit the latter's brother, Lon Nol, as his archenemy in the early 1970s.

Inhabiting an almost cocoon-like atmosphere in school, Sar and his friends remained shielded from the political upheaval during WWII when, following the German occupation of France in 1940, Japanese troops poured into Cambodia. Encouraged by the change in status quo, Son Ngoc Thahn, founder of the nationalist Khmer-language newspaper *Nagara Vatta*, started publishing anti-colonial material hoping to destabilize the French. His rebellion made the Japanese take note of him and he was soon appointed interim prime minister. Unaffected by these changes, Sar, then 19, was busy helping a travelling theatre stage performances in order to raise money to visit the temples at Angkor Wat. For him, like any other Cambodian, Angkor symbolized the erstwhile glory of the Khmer people and was a testament to what they could achieve if they put their collective minds towards a goal.

In the summer of 1945, the ramifications of WWII finally caught up with Sar when American bombs intended to destroy the Japanese military base in Phnom Penh fell on the Royal Palace grounds instead, killing hundreds of civilians. In October that year, even as Sar prepared to give the secondary school leaving exam, British troops entered Phnom Penh to disarm the Japanese following their surrender, giving France a chance to reclaim its colony. Predictably, Son Ngoc Thahn was arrested and exiled to France. The arrest elevated the status of Thahn in the eyes of a public that saw in him the potential of a common man to trump a monarch to the seat of power. Sar too looked upon Thanh as a heroic figure. However, he himself held no significant political views even as the retreating Japanese sowed the seeds of the idea of complete independence in the collective conscience of Cambodians, leading to the first national elections in September 1946 and the subsequent installation of a democratic government with precarious ties to the monarchy.

Sar also remained unaware of attempts by the Viet Minh, led by Ho Chi Minh, to stir up communist rebellions within Cambodia and the retaliatory massacres of Vietnamese settlers in Phnom Penh. After failing to get into the prestigious Lycee Sihanouk for higher studies in 1948, he reluctantly enrolled as a student of carpentry at the Ecole Technique. Either because carpentry was an easy subject with a teacher who was rather generous with marks or because Sar found it more up his alley compared to other academic subjects, he not only passed the course in 1949 but also bagged a coveted royal scholarship to continue studies at an engineering school in France.

In August that year, Sar, then 24 years old, set sail for Paris along with other scholarship recipients, a mixture of bright and mediocre minds, on the SS *Jamaique*. Amongst them were Mey Mann and Nghet Chhopininto with whom he became good friends during the four-week-long journey, worrying collectively about the cold French weather and their studies but not once indulging in political discussions.

In Paris, Prince Sisowath Somonopong, son of Saloth Roeung's co-concubine, was already studying radio technology at the Ecole Francaise de Radio Electricite. Perhaps influenced by him, Sar enrolled to study the same subject despite it having little to do with his training in carpentry. With Somonopong taking him under his wing, he enjoyed his early days in Paris, joining the Association of Khmer Students (AEK) and occasionally bumping into Mann and Chhopininto during the celebration of Cambodian festivals. However, when Somonopong returned to Cambodia after completing his studies the following year, Sar found himself without a place to stay. At this juncture, in what was to be a life-changing event, he was introduced to Keng Vannsak, an executive member of the AEK. Vannsak not only helped him find accommodation in a room across the road from his own home, he also initiated him into the world of politics.

Twice or thrice a month, a small group of Khmer students assembled at Vannsak's house to discuss the various pro-independence movements gathering steam back home in Cambodia. Keen to contribute to the emancipation of their country, the self-confessed 'progressive group' debated into the night with their utopian ideas. However, when it came to choosing the right approach to gain independence, the group was split into two—while one faction, including Sar, believed in the anti-colonial approach of Son Ngoc Thanh, the other faction, smitten as it was with *The Communist Manifesto,* threw its hat in the Viet Minh ring that promoted armed struggle to liberate Cambodia. In those initial days, Sar remained impervious to the radical communist approach, curiously confessing his admiration for the non-violent path that India and Burma had chosen to gain independence.

Then, in October 1951, King Sihanouk ended Thanh's exile, allowing the latter to return to Phnom Penh. The nationalist leader's absence in France tilted the scales in favour of the communist faction. Soon, select members of the AEK went on to form an underground group called Cercle Marxiste that solicited the help of communists to liberate Cambodia. One of the several six-member cells of the Cercle had both Ping Say and Mey Mann as its members. Another, surprisingly, had Saloth Sar. The communist faction, it seemed, had managed to win over their timid colleague. In reality though, it was just

Sar trying to fit in. Having lost interest in radio engineering and failed the second-year exams, he spent more time with his communist leaning peers, observing and learning from those like Ieng Sary and Rath Samoeun whom he considered intellectually superior to him. During weekly meetings of the Cercle to study texts such as *ABC of Communism*, *On New Democracy* and *The Communist Manifesto*, he remained in the background, trying to discover his own role in the scheme of things. Simultaneously, he was also trying to figure out the purpose of his life. The one idea that resonated with him during the time was that of revolution.

Later that year, Sar, Sary, Samoeun, Mann and several others joined the French Communist Party (PFC) and, in keeping with the organization's pro-Stalinist leanings, were introduced to works by Joseph Stalin including 'Marxism and the National Question'. But the book that impacted Sar the most was the Russian leader's seminal work, *History of the Communist Party (Bolshevik)*, that promoted radical ideas such as criticism of the self and of comrades in order to analyse shortcomings and the need to constantly purge the party of opportunistic elements.

Yet, in early 1952, Sar and his colleagues at the Cercle were nothing but novices struggling to grasp the communist ideology. Their readings of Marxist texts were largely superficial, as was their understanding of how Stalin's approach would apply to the particular case of Cambodia. Indeed, their ultimate motive was not embracing Marxism but to rid their country of the French. Moreover, Cambodia, by the very nature of its national economy, lacked an industrial working class that was as important to a socialist revolution as the peasantry. The question that plagued Sar was how a revolution based on a Soviet or Chinese template could succeed in Cambodia's largely feudal system with a monarch, albeit a colonial puppet, at the helm.

It was at this juncture that he came across Russian anarchist

Petr Kropotkin's 750-page tome, *The Great Revolution*, which focused on the intricacies of the French Revolution that had emerged through an alliance of bourgeois intellectuals and peasants against an oppressive monarch. For Sar, circumstances in current-day Cambodia reflected an uncanny similarity to those surrounding the French Revolution and several of Kropotkin's ideas resonated with him.

Back in Cambodia, Thanh's call to officers in the government, police and military to desert their posts and join an armed revolt for independence was met with enthusiasm from the masses. With the threat of being replaced by a commoner looming large, King Sihanouk decried the sidelining of the royal family, dissolved the democratic government with French sanction, appointed himself prime minister, and set about issuing a series of decrees. Soon, public meetings were banned around the country, Thanh's supporters systematically purged, and villages of deserters burned down. Even as the Americans, who had found in Thanh a potential alternative to the monarchy, waited and watched the evolving situation, the AEK in Paris came out strongly in support of Thanh. In a direct attack on Sihanouk, Vannsak, Sary, Yuon, Mann and other members accused the monarch of being dishonest with his people and adopting a divisive policy. Not surprisingly, the demonstration cost the dissenters their scholarship.

To avoid a similar fate, Sar wrote a provocative essay of his own titled 'Monarchy or Democracy?' using the pseudonym Khmer Deum. In this first known diatribe of his, Sar equated monarchy to an enemy of knowledge, of the people and of religion, and accused the king of seeking to destroy the interests of the people during their moment of weakness. He further charged him with befriending the colonizers and using them to execute what was evidently a royal coup. Despite his juvenile use of language, Sar managed to get across his point that monarchy was 'an unjust doctrine, as infectious as a putrid plague'. Alluding to democracy as 'a precious diamond', he curiously also suggested its implicit ties to Buddhist morality, claiming that the Buddha himself had promoted its virtues.

Even as the student representations stirred up a hornet's nest in Cambodia, leading to a flurry of political rejigging and grassroots revolutionary activity, members of the Cercle Marxiste got together in mid-1952 to plan their path ahead. After nearly a year of weighing their options—supporting Thanh or the Viet Minh—they were back to square one, with just as much ignorance about the ground realities in Cambodia as before. The only difference now was their willingness to acknowledge their ignorance. Consequently, it was decided to send a few representatives to Phnom Penh for a reconnaissance of sorts. Sar volunteered for the task and on 15 December 1952, he set sail back home.

In January 1953, Sar returned to a Cambodia where clashes between government troops and rebels were increasing by the day. With over a 100 rebels having been killed and more than 200 jailed in just one month, and grenades having been dropped into classrooms at the Lycee Sisowath a few days before his arrival, the political situation in Phnom Penh was tense. Back in his village, signs of the diminishing prosperity of farmers were omnipresent, what with the civil war adversely impacting the cultivation of rice, pepper and rubber. Many, including his uncle, had had to sell their land and cattle to stay afloat.

In Phnom Penh, Sar's meetings with Thanh and his associates left him disappointed—the veteran leader, it seemed, was all talk and no action. The discovery left the Cercle with no option but to join forces with the Viet Minh. Consequently, Sar and Rath Samoeun left Phnom Penh in August that year to join the Viet Minh at their Eastern Zone headquarters. There, pledging allegiance to the People's Revolutionary Party of Khmerland (PRPK), established by the Vietnamese, they lived amongst resistance workers in their forest hideouts for nine months, wearing all black outfits and car-tyre sandals.

With the Viet Minh cadres wary of the new members, they were initially given the mundane jobs of cultivating cassava, watering vegetables, feeding chickens and learning Vietnamese communist texts under the supervision of Tou Samouth, deputy commander of the PRPK. When they were finally initiated into the tactics of the fighters, Sar carefully imbibed the Viet Minh strategy that involved infiltrating villages and winning over illiterate peasants one by one until the time was ripe to weed out the old leadership and install a new revolutionary administration. The systematic coaching of sorts not only emphasized the need to mobilize entire villages to hate the enemy (the French) but also specified the recourse if a particular village refused to see things their way—burn it down and scatter the inhabitants.

Then, in early 1954, the Viet Minh routed the French in the Battle of Dien Bien Phu, creating a ruffle worldwide. As part of negotiations at the Geneva Conference that followed, Vietnam was temporarily split into the North and South, ostensibly to facilitate fair elections. Sihanouk, however, rejected a similar division of Cambodia on ideological lines, demanding instead the surrender of the Khmer rebels. Refusing to surrender, Samouth split the PRPK into two in August that year. While the first—a group of nearly 2,000 Khmer rebels, including Samouen—crossed over to North Vietnam to wait for further orders—the second—a 1,000-strong group, including Sar, Mann and Samouth himself—returned to Cambodia through South Vietnam to conduct their future operations from the underground.

In October 1954, Sar returned to a palpable political tug of war in Phnom Penh between the Democratic Party headed by King Sihanouk and the republican faction under Thanh. For the next few years, he lived a double life, taking up a teaching job as a front for his political activities, and even making a name for himself as a progressive and approachable teacher. He lived in a rented house that was one amongst many identical ones in a maze of wooden stilt houses, and had nothing but a mat to sleep on and a pile of books to read. With multiple flimsy bamboo walkways weaving in and out of the cluster, and an absence of street lights in the area that allowed clandestine meetings with colleagues, it was a perfect place to live an undercover life.

A year later, even as Samouth and Sar set about forming a new political party—the Krom Pracheachon (People's Group)—Sihanouk got wind of probable treachery within the Democratic Party. Abdicating the throne in favour of his father, he soon floated his own political party, the Sangkum Reastr Niyum, which won a resounding victory on the back of emotional blackmail, intimidation and electoral fraud in the elections held in autumn of 1955. With the political rout of every single Democratic and Pracheachon candidate, Cambodia transformed overnight into a single-party state led by an autocrat.

The electoral defeat weighed heavily on Sar, what with not a single left-leaning Khmer citizen turning out to vote, fearing Sihanouk's political goons. It made him ponder about the futility of elections that, far from being a fair tool to access power, seemed to be a bigoted struggle whose outcome was dictated by those wielding power.

To add to Sar's frustration, Sihanouk executed two shrewd political moves that found him favour with the otherwise hostile Viet Minh. These were his rejection of a membership to Washington's regional military arm, the Southeast Asian

Treaty Organization, and his ratification of the Non-Aligned Movement that was floated to counterbalance the bipolarization of the world in the wake of the Cold War. With both moves distancing Cambodia from the US, the Vietnamese communists saw merit in aligning with Sihanouk and soon enough, much to Sar's disapproval, the PRPK was instructed to support the new government. With the Pracheachon and the larger group of underground Cambodian communists lacking teeth in what was a relatively new playing field for them, they grudgingly accepted the instructions, spending the next 10 years figuring out their path ahead.

Several things changed for Sar, both in his personal and political life, during these years. Following his loss of face in the elections, his girlfriend Soeung Son Malay left him to marry the second-in-command of Sihanouk's party. Soon after, he met Khieu Ponnary, Ieng Sary's sister-in-law who was six years his senior and a teacher at the Lycee Sisowath. Before the Geneva Conference, Ponnary had been the secret point of contact between the Viet Minh and Phnom Penh, helping send student recruits to the former's guerrilla camps. Perhaps on a rebound from the previous relationship or perhaps due to a genuine recognition of their shared revolutionary ideals, 31-year-old Sar married Ponnary in 1956 in a traditional three-day ceremony conducted by Buddhist monks and attended by several of his friends, including Ping Say and Mey Mann. Those who knew him felt that theirs was an odd match—a fun-loving, good-looking and charming young man marrying a much older woman with a face ridden with smallpox scars and a reputation for being 'prim and proper'. A year into their marriage though, Ponnary was diagnosed with uterine cancer. Although cured of the condition, she would never be able to conceive. With no hope of nurturing a family, both husband and wife plunged back into their respective political activities.

During 1957–63, the PRPK leaders and cadres alike grappled with their unenviable situation. Sihanouk, with his sometimes strategic, sometimes foolhardy political flip flops, was a difficult rival to decipher. With two attempts having been made on his life by what he thought were pro-American elements, the erstwhile king relaxed his anti-communist stance for a while only to reverse it when elections were round the corner. So, although Samouth and his team got an opportunity to rebuild their influence in rural areas and revive dormant cells, they could not get too far with their agenda. In 1961, Sihanouk came down on the communists without warning, labelling them the 'Khmer Rouge', or the 'Red Khmer', and ordering the arrest and execution of 12 Pracheachon members for allegedly collaborating with the Vietnamese. Although the sentence was later commuted to life in prison, no Pracheachon candidate dared to contest the elections that followed.

If Sihanouk's unexpected turnaround was a shock to the communists, things weren't about to get any better for them. In July 1962, Samouth, who had been living undercover disguised as a labourer, was arrested, tortured and killed under the orders of Sihanouk's defence minister Lon Nol. During the next six months, all known communist activists were placed under surveillance and left-wing supporters, be they teachers at institutions or editors of newspapers, found themselves behind bars.

Following Samouth's murder, the Krom Prachecheon was rechristened Kampuchean Worker's Party (KWP) to align itself with the Vietnamese Worker's Party (VWP) and Sar, now in his early forties, was elected its leader. Soon after, he went into hiding in a Viet Cong encampment in the forests bordering Cambodia and South Vietnam. From here, he would operate secretly for the next seven years out of his headquarters code-named 'Office 100'. To maintain a shroud of secrecy around him, Sar used the alias 'Pouk', meaning 'mattress', during these years, the name having been ostensibly chosen to depict his role in softening internal conflicts of the KWP.

Pouk

Being at the helm of the Khmer Rouge was not easy for Pouk. In many ways, he and his colleagues were clueless as to what was to be done next, not very dissimilar from their situation in Paris 10 years earlier. Unlike other communist revolutions, including Ho Chi Minh's in neighbouring Vietnam, they had no intellectual grasp of Marxist concepts or an ideological vision for the future of Cambodia. Despite lacking a clear blueprint for the revolution, Pouk refused to fall back upon the tried-and-tested methods advocated by Marxism and Leninism, preferring instead to trudge along intuitively. In the process, he overlooked the need to study and understand the unique socio-economic context of his countrymen to support the revolution he was hoping for.

In 1963, there were less than 10,000 factory workers in the whole of Cambodia. Even these were denied membership to the party on the suspicion that factories had been infiltrated by enemies, resulting in there being no working class to designate as the proletariat. To resolve this issue, the KWP arbitrarily identified poor, landless peasants as the proletariat and lower-middle-class peasants as the semi-proletariat. Moreover, their own near-zero working class experience meant that party workers lacked empathy towards problems of the newly created proletariat. Consequently, the party slowly stumbled ahead, falling back on Pouk, their leader, to show them the way. Pouk, in turn, mined Buddhist texts and emerged with a concept that turned communism, which determined a person's class based on his or her economic activity, on its head.

Based on a rather naïve understanding of 'consciousness' as discussed in the intensely introspective Theravada Buddhism, Pouk decided that if Cambodia did not have a proletariat, it was the duty of the party to cultivate in the masses what he called the 'proletarian consciousness'. If the masses could be made to *think* like proletarians, they would *become* that, irrespective of their economic status. While the reasoning must have left Marxists around the world stupefied, it found resonance with the Khmers whose lives were inseparable from their Buddhist roots. Consequently, Pouk's approach, however puerile it was, drove several of Cambodia's poorest peasants to join the party. Among the new members were debt-ridden peasants who had migrated to the cities to become coolies and rickshaw drivers, who blamed Sihanouk's policies for their circumstances.

In 1965, nearly 10 years after Vietnam's refusal to support the cause of a Khmer armed struggle against Sihanouk, Pouk undertook an arduous two-month long journey to Hanoi to meet Le Duan, the general secretary of the VWP, hoping to change the status quo. However, Sihanouk's continued soft communist policies and anti-American stance, that now offered permanent sanctuaries for the Viet Cong along the Cambodian border, made him an ally the Vietnamese leaders would rather not alienate. Consequently, Le Duan politely turned Pouk away, urging him to review archived Vietnamese texts to better understand the celebrated relationship between their parties.

The exercise had quite the opposite effect though. Through his readings, Pouk interpreted the actions of the VWP as being historically based on selfish motives, with problems of the Khmer people nowhere in their radar of concern. He would later admit, 'until I read these documents myself, I trusted and believed the Vietnamese, but after reading them I did not trust them anymore.' With suspicions regarding the Vietnamese brewing in his mind, Pouk returned to Office 100 a disillusioned man. Convinced that the seemingly benign communist neighbours were out to swallow his country, he took two key decisions—he changed the name of the party to 'Communist Party of Kampuchea' (CPK) to indicate a severance of ties with the VWP and moved Office 100 from Vietnam to the Cambodian territory of Ratanakiri in the far northeast.

As Pouk tried to get the act of the CPK together from the new headquarters, the Battambang peasant rebellion of 1967 came as a blessing to his cause. Lon Nol's imposition of a rule that mandated the buying and collecting of rice crops only through government channels meant that peasants earned far less than what the illegal trade with the Viet Cong had ensured them. After years of governmental repression and bullying that had left them impoverished, the rule was the proverbial last straw for the peasants. When they took to arms to attack soldiers overseeing the sale of paddy, Lon Nol's men arrested over 200 rebels and executed 19 of them. Soon, over 4,000 terrified peasants fled into the forests to join the anti-Sihanouk communist rebels.

What followed was just the armed struggle Pouk had been hoping to initiate. While peasants attacked military posts with help from communist cadres, the army retaliated by poisoning wells and burning rice stocks. After months of confrontation, when Sihanouk brokered peace and a return to normalcy, rumours of torture and brutal killings by the army had already spread across Cambodia, even reaching the Western media. Some of these described severed heads of rebels being paraded before Lon Nol and the rumoured killings of two of Pouk's undercover men—Khieu Samphan and Hou Yuon—who were said to have been burnt alive by sulphuric acid and crushed by a bulldozer, respectively. Although the authenticity of these could not be verified, they added to the aura of terror in the country, working in favour of the communists.

Bong ti Moi

Pouk spent the rest of 1967 planning for the larger revolution from the confines of Office 100. However, Nol's incessant bombing of Khmer Rouge forest camps forced Pouk, in 1968, to retreat to the extreme north-eastern mountainous area of Naga's Tail where the borders of Cambodia, Laos and Vietnam meet. Here, at his new headquarters code-named K5, he established a silent hierarchy within the communist mandate of collective leadership.

Until then, hierarchy within the Khmer Rouge had been rather fluid. Inspired by their Vietnamese counterparts, cadres addressed leaders as *bong* or brother, to make them feel as respectful towards and comfortable with the leader as they would with an elder brother in the family. The importance of each brother was indicated by the number attached to him, so the title of *bong ti moi* or 'first brother' went to the colleague occupying the most important position at a particular time—if replaced by another colleague, he'd relinquish it for the title of second or third brother or whatever the committee decided. The moniker also served to hide the identity of the bearer of the number, so messages could be safely exchanged between cadres across distances.

Things changed after the shift to K5 though. While Pouk had shared common quarters with colleagues at previous camps, he created separate quarters for himself at K5 that no outsider could access without being escorted by his personal guards. He also appointed personal staff to arrange meetings with other colleagues and CPK members, doing away with walk-in visits.

His authoritative hold on the operations of the Khmer Rouge and the ease with which he managed to negotiate with the Vietnamese and Chinese leaders ensured that he soon became the only and irreplaceable bong ti moi. However, despite his cheerful disposition when amongst colleagues, his paranoia soon turned him into someone quite different from what his family and friends knew him as, perhaps even justifying the Western media's Orwellian-sounding name for him—'Brother Number One'.

During 1968–69, China made open attempts to impose its communist ideology on Cambodia and sent a key Chinese official to visit a region liberated by the Khmer Rouge. Becoming wary of his long-time ally's intentions, Sihanouk made a U-turn in his US policy after having fought to keep the American's at bay through the decade, he gave a silent nod to the US bombing of North Vietnamese army sanctuaries in east Cambodia, surprising the Viet Cong that had had his covert support until now. The result was a windfall for Pouk, with the Chinese becoming more sympathetic to his goals and the irate Vietnamese agreeing to supply small quantities of arms to fuel the Khmer Rouge's armed struggle.

His mission was given a further shot in the arm when, tired of Sihanouk's political vacillation, Lon Nol declared himself president and took over the reins of Cambodia in March 1970. Within months of the coup, he declared war against Vietnamese communists who he believed were 'enemies of the Buddha'. Nol's concurrent abolishing of monarchy and ordering the systematic persecution of the thousands of Vietnamese in the country, communist or not, took both the Chinese and the Vietnamese by surprise. On their suggestion, an irate Sihanouk, who had been off on a visit to Moscow when Nol turned on him, reluctantly joined hands with the Khmer Rouge to form the National United Front of Kampuchea (NUFK). For Pouk, the alliance was a sign of his vision bearing fruit, with Sihanouk's support not only giving Khmer Rouge the legitimacy it coveted but also more teeth to operate across Cambodia and access a large population loyal to its erstwhile king.

At the grassroot level, CPK cadres got into action recruiting as many of these loyalists as possible, rubbing into them the need of an armed struggle to overthrow Lon Nol, an American puppet. With the Americans sending over 50,000 troops into east Cambodia in search of the elusive Viet Cong headquarters at around the same time, it was not long before the average Cambodian saw reason in the cadre's proposition. The Vietnamese too were more than eager now to increase arms supply to the Khmer Rouge while Sihanouk, who had been sentenced to death in absentia by Nol, conceded more power to communists in the NUFK than he would otherwise have. The time was ripe for Pouk to make some drastic changes in the CPK strategy in preparation for the future.

In mid-1970, Pouk shifted headquarters from K5 to the forests adjoining Kampong Speu, just over 50 miles from the hotbed of action in Phnom Penh. Before leaving for the plains, he called a meeting of the Central Committee comprising a handful of loyalists, including Ieng Sary, Ping Say, Son Sen and So Phim, to discuss party issues and inform the group that he would no longer answer to the name 'Pouk'. His new name would be 'Pol Pot' meaning 'the original Khmer'.

Pol Pot

In July 1970, seeing Cambodia gradually slip into communist hands, Nixon authorized the use of B-52 bombs against the guerrillas, driving thousands of villagers into cities where they jostled for space and scrambled for food. In the milieu of fright and misery that followed, CPK cadres gathered every embittered, angry and demoralized Cambodian they could identify and initiated them into the communist agenda. By the end of the year, the Khmer Rouge boasted 12,000 soldiers.

With his goal closer than ever, Pol now set about enforcing stricter discipline within the CPK from his new base code-named K1, essentially a cluster of barely furnished stilt houses. Laying down more stringent norms for those wishing to join the party, he ensured that students and middle and high-income peasants were no longer welcome into the party fold; only the poorest made the cut. He then designed training sessions for new recruits that emphasized on abstinence from drinking, gambling and extramarital affairs, and banned the use of respectful feudal terms to address comrades. What was also underscored was the need for a blind faith in the *angkar*, or organization (the CPK).

In early 1971, Pol shifted base yet again to a larger cluster at S71 in Kampong Thom, his home province. Over the last nine years, partly due to paranoia and partly owing to his being an intensely private person, Pol had created a shell around himself that not even his closest aides could penetrate without permission. He had also largely remained confined to his headquarters, save for a few trips to China and Vietnam, making him an enigma to the masses. Now, at Kampong Thom, Pol was a ghost who operated from the shadows—no one, including his own family, knew the real identity of the person they looked upon as their leader. Moreover, with Ponnary's schizophrenia making her see and hear traitors all around her, Pol's own paranoia redoubled. Consequently, the exact location of his office within S71 was kept a secret, zone commanders wishing to meet him were required to leave their guards and arms outside, and food or medicines meant for Pol had to be tested before being served.

Despite his personal demons, Pol remained steadfast in his

pursuit of the revolution and was unanimously chosen as head of both the party and and its military unit during the September 1971 party meeting. Under his leadership, almost a third of Cambodia was living in communist controlled provinces by the end of 1972. However, life as they knew it had taken a dramatic turn.

Towards creating an equal society, all Cambodians were required to abandon any sign of their economic, religious, cultural or social status and wear only what the poorest peasants wore—black clothes with a red and white chequered *krama* around their necks, and car-tyre sandals. Under Pol's directive to collectivize farming, richer peasants were made to part with excess land that was then distributed amongst their poorer counterparts, ensuring that every family had exactly the same area of farm land irrespective of the number of mouths to be fed. For the CPK, the definition of equality meant 'zero for you and zero for me'. Consequently, affluent families were forced to sell their furniture so they too could live the Spartan lives of their peasant counterparts.

The rules were no less strict for Pol and his subordinates. While the Stalinist practice of criticism and self-criticism was already in place in the party, mandatory sessions to rote-learn texts of the CPK was also introduced, as was the concept of manual labour that required members to grow their own food, catch their own fish and clean their own latrines. Pol himself devoted time to writing texts on topics related to proletarian principles and fighting individualism, the latter being an important driving force behind most of his directives. Members were soon forced to relinquish both material and spiritual ties in order to demolish the 'individual' in them and replace it with absolute adherence to collectivism.

Despite these changes, the Khmer people continued to sympathize with the communist cause, perhaps lacking an alternative to Nol's oppressive rule. Moreover, rural communist belts prospered during the first few years, with rubber and paddy production increasing substantially. With the angkar controlling the money made from their illegal exports, infrastructure in 'liberated' villages improved vastly as did life of the common man. In contrast, the cities, poorly managed under Nol's control, were bursting at their seams with refugees.

In 1973, even as Khmer rebels rejected an offer to negotiate a ceasefire, Vietnam signed a peace accord with the US, flaming Pol's antagonism and suspicion towards his unreliable neighbours. Even as he pushed forward his agenda for an armed struggle in Cambodia, he changed headquarters twice—first from S71 to K30 and then from K30 to a village in the eastern foothills of the Cardamom Mountains barely 30 miles north of Phnom Penh. By 1974, the Khmer Rouge military had surged to nearly 40,000 soldiers and over a 100,000 guerrillas. With arms constantly being smuggled into communist zones through Chinese sanction, the army was more than well equipped to take on Nol's troops. In preparation of launching an offensive, Pol ordered the laying of floating mines across the Mekong River to cut off US supply of rice and ammunition to Nol's army through South Vietnam. In early 1975, his army surrounded the capital from the north, east and west and as the siege continued, the Phnom Penh airport and runway were pounded with rockets to stop US airlifts that were Nol's last hope for support.

In April that year, staring at certain defeat, Lon Nol escaped to Hawaii while several of the capital's affluent families, including those of French, American and Japanese diplomats, made a beeline to exit the city. Those who stayed back, willingly or unwillingly, were to soon face their worst nightmare when Khmer Rouge soldiers finally took Phnom

Penh. In retribution for the merciless bombing of peasants in the countryside, hundreds of government officials, politicians and army officers, including Lon Non, the escapee president's brother and Sar's childhood friend, were rounded up by the Committee for Wiping Out Enemies and executed in public. Moreover, with most soldiers being the poorest of peasants who had never set foot in a city, let alone seen suited men, dolled-up women, fridges, television sets and wrist watches, their curiosity wreaked havoc as they crashed vehicles, slashed tyres to pull out rubber for sandals and barged into shops to admire and pillage their intriguing offerings.

After the initial euphoria of seizing Phnom Penh wore off came the decree for residents to evacuate the capital and other major cities. Khmer Rouge soldiers were soon going from house to house 'requesting' residents to leave the city immediately for 'just a few days'. Although rural immigrants were only too glad to return to their village homes, a hurried departure was not what they had anticipated. For city dwellers, including patients in hospitals who had nowhere else to go, the directive was nothing short of traumatic. In the capital alone, over two million migrants and 600,000 city dwellers were forced onto the streets in the sweltering April heat. Over the next several days, they would walk hundreds of miles to reach either their villages or the co-operative zones carved out by the CPK. Amongst the evacuees were Sar's siblings Loth Suong, Nhep, Chhay and Saloth Roeung and his friend May Mann. Of these, Chhay, his favourite brother, was one of the over 20,000 who collapsed en route and died.

On 23 April 1975, Pol Pot entered Phnom Penh nearly 12 years after slinking out of the city into the jungles on the Vietnamese border. If this was a triumphant moment for him, he did not show it. In fact, dressed in hallmark black clothes and car-tyre sandals, it would have been difficult to identify him amongst the thousands of Khmer Rouge soldiers pouring into the city, had it not been for the convoy surrounding him. In a stark contrast to the recklessness of his foot soldiers, Pol's takeover of the capital was a silent one, with no formal announcement of the liberation of Cambodia or any address to the citizens. Even as the exodus to the villages continued, he set up the offices of the CPK, first at the Phnom Penh railway station and later at the Silver Pagoda in the Royal Palace, and put into motion plans that would make Cambodia a communist utopia.

Amongst the first few decisions taken by Pol as head of liberated Cambodia was the renaming of the country to 'Democratic Kampuchea', and redesigning its flag to depict the temples of Angkor Wat. At a meeting of the Standing Committee, it was decided to allow Sihanouk to continue as the puppet head of state from exile in Beijing. Plans were then devised to lay land mines along all national borders, patrol maritime boundaries, cut off telegraph and telephone lines across the country, and curb international mail, effectively isolating Kampuchea from the rest of the world. Finally, Pol outlined his strategy to achieve a 'total revolution', with his mantra for development being, 'If we run fast enough, Vietnam will not be able to catch us.'

For Pol, 'total revolution' meant every last Cambodian going back to the countryside and becoming a peasant. Consequently, whether in villages or in co-operative zones, the newly resettled and impoverished urban folk had to build their own wooden huts and toil hand-in-hand with poor peasants in rubber plantations and paddy fields under the constant supervision of Khmer Rouge cadres. Several of them, irrespective of their intellectual ability, were sent to build roads, bridges and irrigation canals.

With Theravada Buddhism never placing value on acquisition or consumption of wealth, the Khmer were historically a satisfied, laid-back people who worked just enough to meet their requirements. Now, under the new regime, they found themselves working ceaselessly for a cause that did not know the word 'enough'. In return, they were given clothing and a large pot of water with a little rice that passed for rice porridge, but no payment. Pol's radical directive to end the system of paying wages sprouted from the belief that the buying and selling of goods was both corruptive and wasteful, and soon led to the abolition of currency in Cambodia. What also got abolished in the process was the exercising of free will by the people.

With the Khmer Rouge already having enforced strict discipline in communist controlled provinces before the fall of Phnom Penh, the new directives reduced the Cambodians to being modern slaves. Citizens were now divided into three groups to decide their place in the new hierarchy. The poorest of peasants were the most privileged with eligibility for party memberships, high-level political and military posts, and access to full rations. The next group received less rations and was eligible for lower-ranking administrative positions. The last group, comprising mainly of former city dwellers, was the least privileged with no political rights. While the first group could get away with small transgressions, the actions of the last were always suspect and would get them severely punished or even executed.

Within no time, the party percolated every layer of life in Cambodia, not sparing even something as personal as marriage. While the party often ended up as the matchmaker, with people forbidden from choosing their own life partners, the family's sole purpose was to beget children who could be separated and placed in Khmer Rouge camps upon turning seven. In what was morbidly comical, children were taught to address their parents as 'uncle' and 'aunty' while other grown-ups were to be addressed as 'mother' and 'father' to discourage formation of unnecessary emotional bonds. To create a uniform society, racial classifications of Khmer, Vietnamese, Cham and Chinese were discarded in favour of the unifying term 'Kampuchean', even as the speaking of languages other than 'Kampuchean' were banned across the country.

With the putrid mix of terror and frustration engulfing Cambodia during this time, Pol's attack on Buddhism came as a final blow to public morale. Although religion did not have a place in communism, nowhere in the world was its annihilation as severe as in Democratic Kampuchea. For Theravada Buddhism in particular, it was as though its own teachings had come back to haunt it. Deeply impacted by the religion's philosophical concepts of detachment and erasure of individual identity, Pol had come to believe that a new Kampuchea could never be built on the foundation of the past. According to him, it was necessary to eliminate the feudal and reactionary institution of Buddhism in order to create a new, progressive identity for the country. The problem was not Buddhism itself but what it stood for and symbolized. Consequently, monks were decried as being 'leeches living off the blood of people' and either executed or defrocked, idols and images of the Buddha were desecrated, and temples and monasteries were converted into granaries, pig houses and prisons. At places, monks were made to work in the fields and forced to violate their strict dietary laws by overeating and consuming alcohol.

Thus, Cambodian citizens soon lost their identity, not just symbolically but literally. Uprooted from their homes, forced into modern-day slavery and deprived of the comforting arms of religion around them, they went about their lives almost zombie-like, living under the constant surveillance of Khmer

Rouge cadres. If caught saying or doing things they ought not to, the cadres would warn them at first. If the 'offence' was repeated, they'd be taken into the fields and killed with pickaxes or cudgels irrespective of their age. The clothes of those executed would be removed and handed over to others to wear, while their corpses would be buried in the fields in the belief that they would fertilize the soil.

Satisfied with the implementation of his ideal so far, Pol turned his attention to cultivating allies in 1975. In June that year, he travelled to Hanoi once again to extend Le Duan a hand of friendship, even as thousands of Vietnamese who had been living in the country for generations were being asked to leave Cambodia for good. With his hallmark smile and easy disposition, he convinced Duan that the persecution of Vietnamese was not a state-sanctioned act. He then visited Mao in China who, keen on balancing the Soviet-Vietnam alliance in the region, offered generous aid to get infrastructure in the war-ravaged country back into shape, including the construction of military and naval bases, industrial processing units, and oil refineries that had been destroyed by American bombers. Pol's final stopover was in Pyongyang, North Korea, where Kim Il-sung assured him of assistance in agriculture and generation of hydroelectricity.

Back in Cambodia, while Pol's speeches emphasized the need to 'grow at least 3 tons of paddy per hectare', naïve directives such as replacing expensive chemical fertilizers with natural manure resulted in a contrary outcome. Not only were harvests impacted, peasants had to put in more work hours for lesser rations. Moreover, Cambodian cities were gradually converted into pseudo villages with parks and gardens being devoted to growing fruiting trees, concrete basketball courts being covered with layers of soil so they could be used for cultivation, and cattle and pigs being allowed to roam free on the streets.

Even as the Cambodians grappled with their unenviable situation, they were clueless as to the true identity of the angkar that controlled their lives. At the same time, the world outside assumed that the country was being run by Sihanouk from his safe haven in Beijing. Things changed, however, when Sihanouk stepped down from his responsibilities in 1976. With the country requiring a face to show the world, Pol came out of the shadows to be formally installed as prime minister, surprising not only the Western world but Cambodians settled abroad and friends and family back in the villages who found it difficult to reconcile the charming personality of Saloth Sar, always soft spoken and with a ready smile, with that of Pol Pot, a brutal leader.

The revelation that Cambodia was now under communist rule proved advantageous, at least initially. With Sihanouk out of the picture, communist regimes across the world, especially immediate neighbours such as Thailand, Malaysia and Burma, seemed eager to collaborate with Cambodia. Accordingly, Pol changed his isolationist stance and organized propaganda to emphasize the country's non-existent progressive policies, hoping to paint an amenable enough picture of the country to invite foreign investments. The exhilaration that came with the trickling in of investments, however, was marred by a series of unclaimed bomb blasts in Siem Reap in mid-1976. Indiscretions and indulgences of the CPK cadres soon started to surface with scandals surrounding the love life of colleagues and unexplained incidences of rebellion being more than an embarrassment for the Kampuchean leader.

Even as a blame game ensued between party members, Pol addressed the Central Committee in December that year, airing suspicions about Vietnamese hands behind attempts to destabilize the CPK. In the meantime, S21, a school converted into a prison and torture centre, started filling up with alleged traitors and would soon see the deaths of over 20,000 suspects after coerced confessions of one crime or the other. In the villages, even as Khmer Rouge cadres continued executing people for arbitrary reasons, those amongst the cadres who were found to be overworking peasants or labourers were in turn suspected of sabotaging the CPK's utopian vision and subsequently deported to S21. Once a person had been done away with, whether in the villages or at S21, his entire family was sought out and killed.

By mid-1977, killings had become commonplace across the country, be they of peasants for trivial mistakes, cadres for anti-communist behaviour or CPK officials suspected of being Vietnamese moles. Not surprisingly, those who had once seen the Khmer Rouge as a better alternative to Sihanouk and Lon Nol were now questioning their own choice. However, rather than address the growing discontentment, Pol chose to focus on annihilating Kampuchea's hostile and covertly expansionist neighbour in what was an invitation to his own nemesis. On 30 April, the second anniversary of the liberation of Phnom Penh, the Khmer Rouge army crossed into Vietnamese territory on Pol's orders, razing villages to the ground and killing their inhabitants, burning down schools and pagodas, and allegedly raping and disembowelling women.

In retaliation, Vietnam bombed villages along the Cambodian border, sealed off its maritime border to choke supplies to the Khmer Rouge and, in December that year, sent 50,000 troops into Cambodian territory. Alarmed at the development, both China and the US extended covert support to the CPK to ward off the threat of a takeover. At the same time, realizing that defeating Vietnam required more than military support, Pol set off on a campaign to get more countries across the world to appreciate Kampuchea's ethos.

To the relief of Cambodians, Pol also relaxed several extreme directives. People could now cook at home, feed their families better, wear coloured clothes, take a day off work every 10 days and even marry across the three hierarchical groups. By summer that year, the distinction between the groups was completely done away with, granting political rights to every citizen. In Phnom Penh, schools were reopened and intellectuals relegated to manual labour in the villages were brought back and offered government jobs. However, the targeting of anyone with ties to Vietnam continued without check. By mid-1978, hundreds of thousands of people accused of bearing 'Vietnamese minds in Khmer bodies' were executed across the country. By late 1978, Pol was drumming up patriotic fervour in his speeches, calling for every Kampuchean to kill at least 30 Vietnamese.

Towards the end of December that year, a vexed Vietnam sent over a 100,000-strong troop across the border into east Cambodia. With little resistance from a surprised and disorganized Khmer army, the attack progressed rapidly towards the capital. Even so, Pol went about his daily routine with his signature smile, organizing the mass evacuation of CPK officials from Phnom Penh rather than organizing a concerted defence. Then, days before the fall of Phnom Penh in January 1979, he fled the capital in his Chevrolet, assuring everyone that the phase would last but a few days. When he subsequently flew from Siem Reap to hide in the jungles bordering Thailand, he left behind him a leaderless country and an army waiting for orders that would never come.

Grandfather 87

Pol Pot's rule on Cambodia lasted exactly three years, eight months and three weeks. His disastrous stint as a despot revealed that Pol, in 1978, was as much a novice as Sar in 1952 and Pouk in 1963—a novice who thought he could run a country based on intuition, create an equal society by dragging down the masses to the lowest common denominator and take a country into a glorious future by obliterating its past.

After the surprising walkover he presented the Vietnamese with, he spent the next 19 years trying to win back what he had so easily let go of, continuing to helm the Khmer Rouge from his headquarters code-named Office 87 at Anlong Veng. Believing that he would be able to wrest Cambodia back from the Vietnamese, he held regular sessions with soldiers and officers of his army to both teach and devise military strategies. There was no talk, however, of politics and ideology. As before when he was a teacher in Phnom Penh, he was warm with his students, mixing humour with discipline, earning him the sobriquet 'Grandfather 87'. Down below in the villages and cities though, the name 'Pol Pot' still evoked fear—a fear that would constantly revisit them every time a hidden landmine laid by the Khmer Rouge exploded somewhere, maiming or killing someone.

During 1979–1989, Pol's efforts towards dislodging the puppet government installed by the Vietnamese was sustained by the clandestine support of China and presidents Jimmy Carter and Ronald Reagan of the US. Then, with the withdrawal of Vietnam from Cambodian politics following the collapse of the USSR, the country was handed over to the UN Transitional Authority of Cambodia in 1991, to hold free elections.

The elections of 1993 returned power to the royal family, with Sihanouk's son Norodom Ranariddh taking charge. By then, many of Pol's close colleagues had left him to look after their own interests. In 1996, Ieng Sary defected to the Cambodian government and shirked off any responsibility in the atrocities committed by the Khmer Rouge, placing the blame entirely on Pol. The betrayal left Pol embittered and yet again distrustful of the handful of colleagues who were still by his side. In 1997, suspicious about Son Sen's absence at a key meeting, he ordered him dead. In what was the trademark Khmer Rouge style, Pol's security chief allegedly drove to Sen's house after dark and shot him and his wife dead before killing 13 other family members including children.

At the age of 72, Pol clearly hadn't yet let go of his misgivings. Following the incident, his sole remaining loyalist, Ta Mok, turned against him. Sensing trouble, Pol took Khieu Samphan hostage and planned an escape with Mea Son, his new wife nearly 40 years his junior, their 12-year-old daughter Sith and three loyal soldiers. However, Mok's men captured the group and placed Pol under house arrest. During a show trial conducted a month later, he was formally sentenced to life in prison.

On 15 April 1998, 23 years since he walked into 'liberated' Phnom Penh, Pol Pot died in his sleep—some say of heart failure, some say of suicide or poisoning. Whatever the reason, it was a rather peaceful exit from this world for a despot who had given sanction to the killing of over a million Cambodians in just three years. Ironically, he was cremated as per Buddhist rites, albeit over a pile of tyres and rubbish.

Idi Amin

When you are a capitalist imperialist, as Vladimir Lenin would have liked to brand the British colonizers, and discover something as exquisite as the 'pearl of Africa', you would want to milk it dry. In the process, you would have to clench your fists, and, as the cliché goes, grin and bear with everything that's thrown at you...even if that something is a 6'4" tall, 20 stone weighing illiterate yet audacious north Ugandan who answers to the name Idi Amin.

It was in 1890, 28 years after the first European explorer John Hanning Speke arrived in the region north of latitude 1°S, that the region we now know as Uganda was accorded to the rule of the British. Sitting snug between Sudan in the north, Tanzania in the south, Kenya in the east and Congo in the west, the region, comprising the Bunyoro and Baganda provinces, was small but important for the British. Back then, it was indeed nature's paradise with a rich variety of ecosystems ranging from the tall volcanic mountains of the eastern and western frontiers, including the 16,762 feet high Ruwenzori Range, popularly believed to be Ptolemy's Mountains of the Moon, to the densely forested swamps of the Albert Nile to rainforests hosting a variety of flora and fauna and the vast expanse of Lake Victoria that in turn fed the Victoria Nile.

Having arrived here in 1877, the first Christian missionaries had already been witnessing the slow rise to power of the smaller southern kingdom of Baganda, under the rule of its aggressive *kabaka*s (kings), over the larger Bunyoro kingdom of the north. Now, the Imperial British East Africa Company that had agreed to administer the region on behalf of the government, capitalized on the flux in tribal equations and took the Baganda kingdom under its wings. When the company ran out of funds to manage the province, Baganda found itself being declared a protectorate of the British government. In the next few years, the protectorate was annexed to include Bunyoro, Ankole, Busoga, Toro and other states that lay to the north and east of the Nile, with the signing of agreements that recognized the local kabakas as rulers as far as they remained loyal to the British government.

By 1914 when WWII broke out, the colonizers had managed to divide the country through differential treatment—while Bantu speaking people of the south were empowered through economic reforms and by encouraging education, the Nilotic speakers of the north and northwest, including the brutal warrior tribes of Acholi, Lango and Kakwa, were recruited for almost all positions in the army, police and paramilitary forces. Not surprisingly, this tug of war between economic and military power was key in shaping the politics of Uganda much after the colonizers hurriedly left the country in the aftermath of WWII.

In more ways than one, post-colonial Uganda was evidence of the victory of the military over economic power and education. When Milton Obote, belonging to the Lango tribe, became prime minister of the country in 1962, his choice for the coveted post of 'Deputy Commander' was an ambitious Kakwa youth, Idi Amin, who would go on to etch his name in the history of Africa for all the wrong reasons.

The Beginning

Not much is known about Idi Amin's childhood; there are only conjectures. Some accounts say he was born in 1925, some say in 1928. Some say Amin's mother Assa or Aisha Atte separated from his father and brought him up single-handedly, supporting herself and her child by selling love potions and charms; others say he spent quite a few years of his childhood with his father, who taught him to be a good Muslim. Some say his mother abandoned him, leaving him to fend for himself by selling snacks and doing casual labour, yet others say he lived with his mother right until her death in 1969.

What is known though is that Amin's father Andreas Nyabire was a member of the Kakwa clan that populated a small region west of the Albert Nile. After joining the army of Sultan Ali Kenyi, a prominent chieftain who had sworn allegiance to the British government, Andreas converted from Roman Catholicism to Islam and adopted the name Amin Dada. In the early 1900s, he joined the colonial police, but was moved into the British army's King's African Rifles (KAR) once WWI broke out. Although life as a soldier was hard, Amin Dada enjoyed the financial perks that allowed him to take four wives like most wealthy Muslims of the time. Aisha Atte was his second wife, who, much after he was honourably discharged from the army, bore him a son on the auspicious day of Idd. He named his child Idi, which, in Swahili, means 'one born during the Idd (or Eid) festival.'

The new parents separated soon after, allegedly because Amin Dada suspected that the child was born out of wedlock, the real father being the Baganda chieftain Daudi Chwa. However, some accounts talk about how the older Amin spent four years with the toddler after the separation during which he admitted Idi into the Arua Muslim School and monitored his progress. In 1937, Idi went to live with his mother and her new husband in Semuto, where he allegedly sold *mandazi* (African doughnuts) to supplement his mother's earnings. Later, he was sent to live with his maternal uncle in Bombo, where he attended the Garaya Islamic School between 1941 and 1944. There, he earned recognition for memorizing and flawlessly reciting Quranic verses. While Amin did go to religious school, he never had a formal school education and remained illiterate all his life. However, being an aggressive young lad with a decidedly large build, he emerged a natural leader among his peers. He also had a certain sense of humour that won people over, helping him form a strong bond with the south-Sudanese Nubian community that his mother had belonged to.

In 1945, after finishing religious education, Idi moved to Kampala where he is believed to have worked as a bell boy at the Imperial Hotel. Already sufficiently enamoured by the mystique and traditions of the army that had a constant presence in the region, he managed to impress a visiting officer of the British military who offered him a job with the KAR in 1946.

The Rise and Rise

The job that Idi Amin, then 21, was offered with the KAR was that of a chef's assistant. Right from his early days in the army, he took great pride in his regiment, always turning out in an impeccable uniform, boots polished to a shine, and obeying all orders. Back in the barracks, he cracked jokes and kept his peers and seniors in good humour. He also excelled in sports and went on to become the national heavyweight boxing champion. His colonial bosses took notice of him and he was soon shifted to the armed forces.

In the next few years, Amin was deployed to various regions within British Africa to quell rebellions and negotiate deals with the natives and insurgent militia. Notable among these was the Mau Mau rebellion in the Aberdare Mountains, where Kenyan nationalist guerrillas were fighting to end British rule. During these assignments, Amin did not refrain from showing off his violent and ferocious streak. Indeed, for his British employers, he was a curious mix of humour and terror that was waiting to be exploited. Instead of censuring his extreme brutality, they sent him for further training and promoted him to the rank of sergeant despite his near-zero literacy and palpable difficulties with English. Amin took his promotions seriously and quickly rose within the ranks to become an *effendi* in 1959, the highest rank a native soldier could achieve. He also won the Sword of Honour in recognition of his leadership potential.

It was around this time that the British government started feeling the pinch of the economic disaster that WWII had brought in its wake. No longer able to sustain its rule, the empire had already started withdrawing from several of its colonies worldwide and similar action in Africa seemed impending. With an urgent need to promote a larger number of senior officers in preparation for Ugandan independence, the British army chose to commission Amin as a lieutenant despite his penchant for violence. Amin thus became one of only two non-British commissioned officers in the pre-independence KAR that later became the Ugandan army.

First Blood

Among the many missions that Amin was assigned to as lieutenant was one against the Turkana, Karimojong and Pokot tribes in north-eastern Kenya in early 1962. Considered to be a 'wild land' that bustled with gun-toting, cattle-stealing tribesmen, the mission was to disarm the natives by blocking access to their watering holes, forcing the tribesmen to trade their weapons for water. While the mission was an overall success, Amin's platoon in particular had been unable to achieve its target and had returned empty-handed. Humiliated, he redeployed his soldiers to reverse the results and this time around, the platoon returned with the desired bounty.

It was only after a few days that the truth of what had transpired came to light. A group of Turkana elders complained that Amin's soldiers had unleashed their fury on the tribe, torturing and massacring several of their men in the pretext of disarming them. Allegations included the forced castration of eight Karimojong tribesmen. An inquisition found the allegations to be true, with officials unearthing a mass grave and post-mortem investigations verifying that the men had been tortured before being killed.

If the British army had stuck to its strict code of conduct, Amin would have been court-martialled for his actions. However, the colonizers were working towards Ugandan independence and any extreme action taken against one of the only two Ugandan officers in their ranks could have resulted in political embarrassment. In a telephonic conversation between the British governors of Kenya and Uganda, it was decided to sweep the incident under the carpet. Once independence had been declared though, the Ugandan governor discussed the issue with newly elected prime minister Milton Obote, suggesting Amin's immediate termination from service and possible imprisonment. Obote, however, disagreed and recommended nothing more than a severe reprimand.

Perhaps the decision was based on a political strategy, perhaps it was a show of leniency to a fellow north-Ugandan. Whatever it might have been, little did Obote know of the turn of events that lay in store for him. As for Amin himself, this purposeful turning of a blind eye to his brutal actions seemed to have given him the proverbial 'license to kill'.

Partners in Crime

Milton Obote's stint as prime minister of free Uganda wasn't an easy one. With the Baganda constantly rebelling, demanding a separate kingdom of their own, he had had to patch together a coalition government in order to become prime minister. However, members of the coalition owed allegiance more to their local ethnic supporters than to Obote and constantly pressured him to correct what was seen as an imbalance in the political power of key factions. Hoping to appease the Baganda, Obote carved out the position of 'President' and appointed their kabaka to the largely ceremonial post. The conciliation lasted for but a few months. As hostility in Baganda grew, so did the frustration of Obote's ministers, who threatened to topple the government.

It was 1966 and the stage was set for political unrest in Uganda. Ordering the arrest of five rebelling ministers, Obote went on to amend the Constitution to vest all important rights and powers on the president, eliminating in the process, the position of prime minister. He then swore himself in as president under heavy military protection. Outraged by Obote's actions, Baganda leaders demanded the removal of his government from their province. It was then that Obote summoned Amin, whom he had already promoted to deputy commander of the army and air forces.

A year earlier, Obote had sent Amin on a military operation along the Congo border in the West Nile province. In a bid to support Congolese rebels who wanted to topple the Joseph Kasavubu-led government, his instruction to Amin was to equip the rebels with arms and ammunition in exchange for gold, coffee and ivory. Although Obote's plan backfired, leading to other political manipulations, he was impressed with Amin's success in the mission that is said to have resulted in a misappropriated stash worth $350,000. It was the beginning of a lucrative association between the two north-Ugandans to smuggle ivory and gold from Congo. So, when the time came to crack down on the rebelling Baganda, Obote did not have to look far to find the right person for the job.

When Obote's orders came along, Amin's troops laid siege to the Kampala Palace of the kabaka of Baganda, with Amin himself ostensibly attacking the palace with a 122 mm gun mounted on his jeep, using it to knock down several chunks of the palace walls. Although the kabaka managed to escape to England, Amin and his soldiers ransacked the palace, gunning down anyone who came in their way. They also looted the kabaka's other palaces at Masaka and Bamunanika, leaving in their wake hundreds of dead Baganda tribesmen. While some accounts claim the number to be 1,500, others claim it to be close to 4,000. Whatever the actual toll, all corroborate rumours of army trucks rolling out of the city with blood dripping from their tailboards as they transported dead bodies under the shroud of canvases.

After the siege of Kampala, which in a way legitimized political violence in Uganda, Obote turned to Amin whenever he had to deal with rivals. By 1968, the autonomy of the Baganda kingdom had been destroyed completely, with its parliament building becoming the new headquarters of the Ugandan armed forces and the kabaka's palace being turned into a military garrison. Uganda under Obote was very close to becoming a military dictatorship. However, the country's tryst with a dictator was still a few years away.

Seeds of Doubt

As deputy commander, Amin had endeared himself to his soldiers, winning over their loyalty. The fact that he, like many of them, hailed from the north and had risen in rank to attain his current post was an inspiration to many. Amin took care of them, joked and drank with them. With the rise in his position in the army and the amassing of ill-gained wealth, he also started to display a liking for the good things in life. He enjoyed watching the latest movie productions at the local cinema hall and listening to brass bands playing at the Gaba beach. Amin also gleaned early in his career, the necessity to remain popular amongst his people. In public, he maintained a charming and cheerful countenance, forging bonds with the masses by simple gestures like joining in with the dancers during state functions. It was also around this time that Amin took in three wives in succession—Malyamu, Kay and Nora. Although things seemed to be looking up for Amin, suspicion on both sides had started to sour the relationship between him and Obote by the beginning of 1969.

An engineer by education and politician by choice, Obote had relied upon Amin thus far to oversee the militarization of Uganda. Although the latter had been nothing but loyal, his growing popularity, however, began to unsettle Obote. To reduce reliance on the army, create an alternative support base for himself and increase personal security, he now created two groups that would answer to none but the office of the president. These were the Special Forces that catered to paramilitary operations and the General Service Unit, an underplayed name for the Secret Police. Comprising largely men from his own Lango clan, the two organizations quickly proliferated to almost a 1,000 security and intelligence agents spread across Uganda and its overseas embassies. In 1967, Obote additionally established the Military Police Force to tackle indiscipline and lawlessness within the army ranks.

The last move set Amin's alarm bells ringing. Although the Military Police Force was headed by loyalists, he wasn't happy with his men having to answer for their deeds. Afraid that Obote was out to replace him, he aggressively supplanted his own men into posts previously occupied by recruits from the Lango tribe. Within a year, the number of Sudanese speaking Nubians in the Ugandan army rose to 74 per cent of the recruits.

Even as power at the centre was slowly but surely being split into two, much to Obote's consternation, an anonymous shooter took aim at Obote as he was leaving a party meeting in Kampala in 1969. Although he escaped with minor injuries, the assassination attempt left Obote shaken. Having managed to create strong enemies during his seven years in power, it wasn't surprising that someone wanted him dead. However, in a situation where there was no one to point fingers at, Amin attracted attention by remaining silent. Instead of deploying troops to hunt down the shooter, the deputy commander was nowhere to be seen the entire evening of the shooting. He complicated the situation further when Obote's close aide Major David Oyite-Ojok arrived at his door the next day to brief him on the incident. Rather than meeting Ojok, Amin escaped through the back door, making his way to the closest military base.

Amin lay low for the next month, even as Uganda was put under a state of emergency while Obote recuperated. During this time, an investigation found and arrested the shooter, unravelling in the process, a plot by the Baganda politician

Benedicto Kiwanuka to seize power. Although the arrest cleared suspicions surrounding Amin, Brigadier Okoya confronted him at a meeting of high-ranking military commanders, asking for an explanation to his disappearance post the assassination attempt. The temerity of a junior officer to question him irked Amin. Soon after, Okoya and his wife were found murdered at their home in Gulu.

Although there was no evidence of Amin's hand in the incident, rumours aplenty floated around town. The death of Okoya further unsettled Obote. Yet he chose not to arrest Amin, deciding instead to bide his time. He found a chance to strike back in September 1970 when President Gamal Abdel Nasser of Egypt passed away. Sending Amin to attend the funeral, Obote reorganized the security forces by installing two of his own men to head the army and air force, demoting Amin to the ceremonial post of Chief of Defence Forces and removing all his loyalists from positions of power. However, Amin was not one to take the change lying low. Having got wind of Obote's intentions, he returned unannounced to Uganda just in time to overturn Obote's orders.

Coup d'état

At a time when the relationship between Uganda's two most powerful men was already strained, came the revelation from the auditor general that large amounts of money had disappeared from the military budget. Evidence suggested that Amin had used it to fund the south-Sudanese Anya Anya rebels, supplying them with illicit arms and ammunition for their fight against the Arab-led Sudanese government that had Obote's support. In early 1971, rumours emerged of Amin's intention to assassinate Obote and take over the reins of the country. Already on the edge after the first attempt on his life, Obote, then in Singapore for a Commonwealth conference, called the army barracks at Jinja with a message to arrest Amin. The phone call proved to be costly for Obote.

Obote's call to the barracks on 24 January was intercepted by Amin loyalist Sergeant Major Musa, who soon mobilized a group of Nubian soldiers to start a coup against the president even as he went in search of his leader who was believed to be duck hunting at Lake Kigo. In the fight that ensued within the army ranks, Amin's men overpowered Obote loyalists. When Amin returned to Kampala the next morning, his soldiers had already surrounded the parliament. Soon, the radio station, airport, railway station, post office and banks were stormed, and telephone and telefax lines were cut.

That afternoon, a radio broadcast listed 18 grievances that the people of Uganda purportedly had with the Obote government that had left them 'angry, worried and unhappy'. This was followed by the announcement that soldiers of the Uganda Armed Forces had decided to hand over power to 'their fellow soldier' Major-General Idi Amin Dada, 'entrusting him to lead the beloved country of Uganda to peace and goodwill among all.'

Hearing the news, crowds took to the streets to hail Amin as their saviour. As celebrations ensued, they danced, sang and drank to their new leader. While the jubilation in the army and among the Nubians was genuine because they cared for Amin, most others across Uganda rejoiced not because they loved Amin but because they hated Obote. The Baganda, for instance, joined in the carnival because of Obote's rout; he had become their sworn enemy since the attack on and expulsion of their kabaka. Even Ugandan women, who blamed Obote for many of their woes, thanked Amin for delivering the country from the former's terrorist regime. The rest of the world too received the news with elation, believing that nothing could be worse than the nine years of mismanagement and corruption under Obote. Newspapers in Britain declared Amin a friend of the country and a welcome contrast to other African leaders; Israel called him 'a special African friend'.

Flying back home from Singapore, Obote grudgingly accepted defeat and flew to Tanzania where he would live in exile for the next nine years, watching from the wings as the beast he had nurtured went on a rampage.

Reign of Terror

The 25 January 1971 radio broadcast ended with Amin humbly accepting the responsibility given to him and assuring the public that his would be a caretaker government that would soon ensure free and fair elections. He invited exiles to return to the country and ordered the release of political prisoners who had been held on unfounded charges. He exhorted the people of Uganda to return to work as usual. But the definition of 'usual' had already changed, as the nation would soon discover.

If Amin had already developed a taste for the good life after his appointment as deputy commander, he developed a taste for power soon after the coup. Forgetting his promise to hold free and fair elections, he dissolved the parliament within a week and declared himself president and commander-in-chief of the armed forces, obliterating the roles of the chief of army and air forces. He then renamed the Government House 'the Command Post' and declared that his military government would remain in power for the next five years. Soon, loyalists, including Nubian cooks, hairdressers and drivers who lacked both education and experience in administering a country, were appointed to all top posts in the government and army. This done, Amin set about systematically taking down his adversaries.

During his early days in the British army, Amin was just the type of African his colonial bosses liked—uneducated, uncouth and willing to obey orders. But now, the same uneducated and uncouth soldier was set to give orders and get them executed to satisfaction. In the weeks that followed, several decrees were passed that gave absolute power to Amin's military administration along with immunity for all the hell he was planning to rain down on his enemies. These included the Detention Decree and the Suspension of Political Activities Decree that openly weighed against Obote loyalists. In under a month of these being passed, over 2,000 army officers and men belonging to the Acholi and Lango tribes were killed on Amin's orders, with code words being used to communicate the treatment to be meted out to the unsuspecting victims. 'Give him the V.I.P. treatment' or 'go with him to where he sleeps' were euphemisms to kill someone, while 'give him some tea' meant the person was to be whipped and dismembered.

Amin also established two organizations with seemingly innocuous names—the Public Safety Unit and the State Research Bureau—housed on a bougainvillea-draped street next to the President's Lodge in Kampala and connected to it by an underground tunnel. Their roles, however, were far from benign. With the former being an intelligence-gathering agency and the latter a secret police of sorts, the two organizations specialized in infiltration, assassination and the extraction of information through torture and were responsible for a majority of the 300,000 deaths during Amin's regime. So bizarre were the workings of these organizations that when the bureau was not sure whom to kill next, it simply chose people whose name started with an 'O', an indicator of Acholi or Lango origins.

Soon after, a series of orchestrated political killings led to scores of men just 'disappearing' from the face of the earth. Amongst these were Obote's brother-in-law and his family, and Benedicto Kiwanuka, who had by then become chief justice. Dragged out of the High Court by soldiers, the latter was never seen again. Other people to disappear included the vice chancellor of the University of Makerere, cabinet ministers, diplomats, surgeons, lawyers, bankers and prominent Catholic and Anglican churchmen. After their disappearance, their houses and cars were appropriated by Amin's men for personal use. Although only Amin's dissenters were targeted for torture and murder at first, his men, drunk on power and an unmonitored freedom, soon started to choose victims at random—farmers, students, shopkeepers, clerks—sometimes for money or property, sometimes for women. Buses were randomly stopped and looted, their occupants beaten mercilessly if they tried to oppose; foreign journalists who tried to send home the gory details of Amin's workings were targeted and killed.

Amin's soldiers particularly favoured torturing and slow-killing to delivering a decisive death blow. Brigadier Hussein Suleiman, who had been chosen by Obote to replace Amin as the army chief of staff before the coup, was imprisoned and slowly bludgeoned to death over several days. Senior officers belonging to rival tribes, who arrived at the Mackindye prison purportedly for training in internal security, found themselves imprisoned and killed slowly and mercilessly with bayonets over several days. It was common for the limbs of inmates to be smashed with sledgehammers and wrenches before they bled out. For some of Amin's men, the morbid killings became a source of amusement. They'd promise to release prisoners if they hammered their cellmates to death but once the gruesome task had been accomplished, they were made the target of some other gullible prisoner. Not for nothing was Mackindye nicknamed—House of Death. With bodies piling up in prisons and with neither the space nor the patience for burials, dumping them at the Namanve Forest just out of Kampala became a norm. In Jinja, the crocodile-infested Nile was the chosen place. Consequently, as hundreds of workers shuttled across the Owen

Falls Dam daily, what greeted them was the sight of half-eaten floating corpses.

No one was spared the consequences of Amin's displeasure, not even his family. Kay, who divorced him in 1972, was found dead and dismembered in the boot of a car a year later. She had allegedly been seeing someone and had recently tried to abort a child. Her supposed lover also mysteriously disappeared. Although there was no proof of Amin playing a part in the gruesome killings, it could not be completely ruled out. In 1974, Amin fell in love with 19-year-old go-go dancer Sarah Kyolaba, whom he decided to take in as his fifth wife. Sarah already had a boyfriend, Jesse, though. When Jesse openly registered his displeasure over Amin's wooing of his girlfriend, he was picked up by the State Research Bureau, stuffed into the boot of a car and driven off, never to be seen again. In the lavish two-million-pound ceremony that followed next year, Sarah was wedded to Amin, a man old enough to be her father.

When he wasn't ordering killings, Amin was looking for ways and means to appropriate as much wealth as he could, both for himself and for sustaining the army. With a large number of soldiers dead due to ethnic purging, there was an urgent need to recruit more men. Another immediate requirement was the improvement of military infrastructure and supplies. Consequently, military spending went through the roof, causing inflation to increase to 700 per cent. The Ugandan shilling became virtually worthless, basic monthly wages dropped to \$30 and everyday needs, including staples and clothes, became inaccessible for most. While a pound of sugar and butter cost \$5 and \$9 respectively, a bar of soap cost two weeks' wages for the layman. Shoes cost \$185 a pair, and trousers \$100.

Instead of tackling the situation, Amin thought it simpler to print more currency, doubling the money supply between 1976 and 1978. Granting the contract to print two million shillings worth of 100 shilling notes, Amin is said to have told the British printer to print an extra million for himself as payment. Having flooded the country with new notes, Amin and his high-ranking cronies continued taking special flights to London and Paris to spend on luxury goods and holidays. His foot soldiers, on the other hand, started to devise ingenious methods to gain wealth. One such method was to kill random citizens and then charge their families thousands of dollars in exchange for handing over the bodies for a decent burial.

'Every hundred years, God appoints one person in the world to be very powerful, so the words of the Prophet can be followed. When I dream, then things are put into practice...' These were the words of Amin's speech during the inaugural meeting of the Uganda Development Bank, formed in 1972. The five-year development plan subsequently laid out by his team emphasized on not only increasing agricultural exports but also on the 'Ugandization' of trade and industry. However, none of these were implemented as originally intended. In a bid to 'give Uganda back to the ethnic Ugandans' as counselled by none other than God, Amin expelled the 80,000-strong Asian community from the country, giving them all of 90 days to evacuate. Most of these were third-generation descendants of workers brought from the Indian subcontinent to build the railway. Although the move was hailed by natives, who had until then grudged the Asians their education and business acumen, Uganda soon came to a standstill. Despite comprising a small minority of the population at 9.5 million, the Indians and Pakistanis controlled nearly 90 per cent of the country's trade and commerce including shops, businesses, hospitals, hotels, schools and other enterprises. They also constituted nearly 80 per cent of doctors, teachers and lawyers in Uganda.

Some of the key sectors to be adversely affected by the expulsion were tourism, poultry, railways, telecommunication and, of course, agriculture. Soon, the production of key export crops—coffee, cotton and sugar—as also construction, fell by 51 per cent while activity in the mines and quarries went down 82 per cent. After the Asians left, Amin's men expropriated their houses, cars and businesses even as Uganda fell into a downward spiral. With the economy now controlled by army officers who had no experience in running businesses, local enterprises and stores soon ran into the ground from mismanagement and abuse of power.

Meanwhile, farmers, who formed the backbone of Uganda's primarily agricultural economy, abandoned cash crops like cotton and coffee, and began concentrating on food crops to feed their families. This, coupled with the expulsion of the Asians who were key contributors in the collection and ginning of cotton, led to the collapse of the otherwise well-organized cotton sector. The country also experienced a sudden shortage in sugar apparently because of production difficulties caused by the failure of machines that had traditionally been serviced by Asians. To add to the farmers' woes, Amin centralized coffee exports, forcing farmers to accept bogus promissory notes in return for their produce that would then be sold for weapons and cash. Disgruntled, the farmers resorted to smuggling coffee into neighbouring countries, preferring to cross the corpse-ridden, crocodile-infested Nile to barter their produce for basic consumer goods. Soon, a parallel black market or *magendo* emerged in almost all sectors in Uganda.

Born to Face the Camera

Even as Amin went about the systematic butchering of his people with a total disregard for human rights, there was hardly a whimper from the rest of the world. Although it was difficult to get word of the ongoing rampage out of Uganda with mail censorship and phone tapping becoming the norm, gruesome details did make it out via surreptitious radio broadcasts that sent out messages in codes and through the odd exiles who managed to escape out of the country. However, no one seemed to be interested. Amin had become the favourite of the media across the world, thanks to his carefully cultivated charming ways and his penchant for humour. In some ways, he had also ignited the Western world's curiosity about this unapologetically inarticulate and outlandish black leader who was very different from his more sophisticated peers.

Amin always appeared in front of the media in full military splendour, wearing a crisp uniform that was weighed down by the sheer number of medals tacked on to it. During his eight years at the helm, he would confer several titles upon himself including 'His Excellency the Life President of Uganda', 'Al Hajji', 'Field Marshal', 'DSO', 'MC' and 'Lord of All the Beasts of the Earth and Fishes of the Seas'. During his inauguration as president, he had his body carried around by 'white men' and proclaimed himself as the 'Conqueror of the British Empire in Africa'. In 1976, ordering the Makeree University to award him a doctorate of law for 'having done too much in so short a time,' he added the title of 'Doctor' Idi Amin Dada to the list. He also gave himself the Victorious Cross, allegedly for having crossed Lake Victoria but more obviously to cock a snook at the British who valued their Victoria Cross. Such grandstanding only added to the intrigue of international media, with his so-called 'buffoonery' becoming the favourite subject of comedians, satirists and tabloids.

Despite the British royalty and commoners recognizing his presidency, Amin took special delight in taking jabs at them at every given opportunity, purportedly as vengeance for the colonial subjugation he and his countrymen had earlier faced. On one occasion, he quipped in the *Voice of Uganda* that the queen should mark the silver anniversary of her coronation by sending her 25-year-old knickers to President Kaunda of Zambia who had criticized Amin at the Commonwealth Conference in London. At another, he proposed marriage to Princess Anne as a way of mending relations between Uganda and Britain. Even as he nationalized all British property in Uganda, he started the 'Save Britain Fund' to 'help' its former colonizer tide over an economic depression and promised to send the queen a cargo ship full of bananas as a thank you for 'the good days of the colonial administration'. On the side-lines, he gave the media the fodder it was looking for, with statements like, 'I am the greatest politician in the world; I've shaken the British so bad, I deserve a degree in philosophy.'

In what was no longer bizarre and unexpected, Amin not only took a liking for all things Scottish, including the kilt and bagpipes, after a grand state reception in his honour by Scotland, but also offered to become their king. His fascination with the bagpipe went on to inspire in him a love for the accordion. Not only did he take up playing the instrument as a serious passion, he also made sure his colleagues, subordinates and guests danced to its screechy tunes till they dropped during state celebrations and parties. He also loved song writing and tried to convince the African leaders at the Kampala summit of the Organization of African Unity (OAU) to launch his song as the African anthem.

In 1974, Amin allowed French director Barbet Schroeder to come to Uganda to make the documentary film *General Idi Amin Dada: A Self Portrait.* True to its name, the hour-long film aired in Uganda showcased only the best of Amin, following him as he supervised the Ugandan paratrooper school, played the accordion in a jazz band, went boating through a wildlife park, staged a mock assault on a hill, lectured his cabinet on hard work, cautioned doctors not to drink too much and talked about his plans to attack Israel. One sequence showed him racing younger associates across his swimming pool and, of course, winning. Although Amin had authorized the creation of an extra half hour of footage for the world to view, he was later disappointed with some of that content and asked for it to be cut. When Schroeder refused, Amin rounded up 200 French citizens living in Uganda, threatening to imprison them unless the cuts were made.

The Fall

For a man with a rather holy name who was raised a Muslim, Idi Amin was never quite religious. True, he used his religion to enjoy the perks it offered, taking in as many as five wives (the fifth one only after the fourth had died) and siring more than 50 children. Although he also talked about God every now and then, especially about how God came in his dreams and gave him directions, he did not use religion to persecute citizens. In fact, the Church had welcomed the coup that brought Amin to power, with the Church Missionary Society even giving him its seal of approval. When he did order the killing of churchmen, it was because they had either crossed him or sided with Obote, not because they were Christian. The same rule had applied to Muslims too; at least four prominent Muslim leaders had been murdered by Amin's men by 1973.

So, when Amin turned to Islam, it was more for monetary gain, rather than to woo the country's tiny Muslim population. This was apparent in his decision to commission the construction of Africa's largest mosque on Kampala Hill; it was more for the bounty he hoped Saudi Arabia would give him in foreign aid than out of love for his religion. With all funds intended for the mosque being embezzled by Amin and his men, it was only as late as 2008, 30 years after it was commissioned, that the mosque was finally completed. The monetary angle was also apparent when Amin attended the summit meeting of the heads of Muslim states in 1973 where he convinced Colonel Muammar Gaddafi of Libya that Uganda had a Muslim population of 70 per cent when in reality, the number was around 15 per cent.

In some ways, Amin had found a like-minded friend in Gaddafi, who had proclaimed himself the 'King of Kings' and advocated an indiscriminate use of military power in Libya. The two leaders soon formed a sort of camaraderie—a camaraderie that eventually resulted in Amin switching allegiance from Britain and Israel to the Libyans and Palestinians. The switch proved counterproductive for Amin. Not only did he start selectively persecuting, and hence alienating, Christians under Gaddafi's influence, he also rubbed Israel the wrong way until the latter could no longer afford to sit back and watch.

Until then, the Israelis had been Amin's close military advisors. While they had had vested interests in Uganda since the early 1960s, owing to its shared border with Sudan, the interest only deepened when Amin started helping the south-Sudanese with arms to fight their Arab government. In return, Israel invested heavily in infrastructure projects across Uganda while also providing the country with military instructors and tactical support. It is alleged that Israel had a big hand in the success of Amin's coup against Obote, with the Israelis convincing both Britain and the US to supply Amin with the required arms and equipment.

The friction between the two countries started when, in 1973, Amin decided on a whim to bomb Tanzania and asked Israel for a squadron of Phantom jets to carry out the mission. Israel, already seething after Amin's surprise public praise of Hitler and Germany for having burnt six-million Jews, refused to oblige. An irate Amin immediately turned anti-Israel, severing diplomatic ties with the country and expelling several

Jews from Uganda. He then turned to Gaddafi for both military support and cash, although the latter was spent in buying himself three magnificent villas outside of the Libyan capital of Tripoli. For his 1975 wedding with Sarah Kyolaba, he invited Palestinian leader Yasser Arafat to be his best man and much later, in a public announcement, he advised the then Israeli prime minister, Golda Meir, to 'tuck up her knickers' and run to Washington. For someone who, during his days as the deputy commander, had danced with the wife of the then Israeli prime minister Levi Eshkol, this was a marked departure in allegiance.

Then, on 3 July 1976, Palestinian terrorists hijacked an Air France plane carrying 300 passengers from Tel Aviv to Paris. With Amin's approval, the hijackers flew the aircraft to Uganda's Entebbe airport where passengers were to be held hostage until 53 terrorists imprisoned in Israel and other European countries were released. A deadline of 48 hours was set for the same. Although Amin did not have a direct hand in it, he revelled in the international attention the event attracted. However, in a remarkably daring night raid on 4 July, Israeli commandos managed to rescue all but one hostage, leaving all seven kidnappers and 20 Ugandan soldiers dead.

The hostage who did not make it out was 73-year-old Dora Bloch, who had to be taken to the hospital after choking on her food. When Amin came to know of the Israeli raid, he was beside himself with anger. Soon, Dora Bloch was hauled out of bed by the State Research Bureau and dragged to a waiting car. Her body was later discovered in a wasteland outside Kampala. Although Amin once again threatened to attack Israel, he soon forgot about it, attending to the more urgent matter of further ethnic purging; at least 5,000 Ugandans were killed during 1977–78 after multiple attempts were made on his life.

What Amin did not forget about, though, was his intention to attack Tanzania. The country had irked him ever since it allowed Obote to take refuge, even helping him organize a failed coup against Amin in 1972. He had since then taken to insulting Tanzanian president Julius Nyerere, calling him an old woman and prostitute one day and shooting off conciliatory messages the next, with declarations like 'I love you very much. If you were a woman, I'd consider marrying you.' In 1978, it became necessary to divert public attention from a plunging economy. So, with help from Libya and the Palestinian Liberation Organization, Amin invaded Tanzania with 3,000 troops on the pretext of annexing Kagera Salient. However, Tanzania, with the support of a large number of Ugandan exiles and rebels, responded by sending 45,000 troops for the battle, causing Amin's largely mercenary army to flee.

In 1970, Amin had famously proclaimed that he feared no one but God. However, when the Tanzanians finally took Kampala on 11 April 1979, Amin's true nature came to the forefront. Fearing what the rival army and Ugandan exiles would do to him, he fled with his large family to Libya where he lived in exile for a few years before moving to the Red Sea port of Jeddah, Saudi Arabia. The Saudis, sympathizing with a fellow Muslim, provided Amin asylum conditional to him retiring permanently from politics.

The End

Idi Amin was a Frankenstein's monster created by the British Empire in Africa and subsequently fed and nurtured by Obote, Israel, the US and the media alike. In a nation of roughly 10 million in 1970, an estimated 300,000 were killed on his orders during his eight-year-long regime even as the rest of the world watched from the wings. When he took charge of Uganda, Amin seemed to have filled a strange need in black Africans for a leader who could snub the white colonizers; to many, he symbolized the revival of black nationalism and fellow anti-colonial African leaders preferred to ignore his atrocious ways rather than confront him. But while the behaviour of his sympathetic peers was understandable, what was not was that of the Western world.

The way Amin was allowed to live a lavish life until as late as 2003 when he died at the age of 73 is testament to the fact that Britain and Israel, as also the US, were never really bothered about him or the Ugandans. The US, which started importing coffee from Uganda in 1970 had already become an important trading partner by 1977, buying as much as 34 per cent of the Ugandan crop worth $250 million at the time. Although direct purchase from Uganda stopped the following year when the US announced an embargo, US traders continued to source the coffee via Djibouti and Mombasa. In 1974, a US firm sold its Gulf Stream G-II executive jet and a Lockheed Hercules C-130 cargo plane to Amin and, in exchange for the business, gifted him a Cadillac Eldorado limousine. During 1974–77, Israel too continued covert trade with Uganda despite breaking diplomatic relations, establishing aviation companies as fronts for Mossad-backed projects. In 1977, the US, along with the UK and Israel, trained several dozens of Amin's State Research Bureau agents as helicopter pilots or communication specialists and supplied them with arms, spy equipment and communication gear. Britain also unofficially allowed Amin to make his 'whiskey runs', flights that landed in London with Ugandan tea and coffee and took off with liquor, food and luxury items to appease Amin's henchmen and rivals alike, well into 1979. The three countries had entered Uganda with selfish motives and once these were either fulfilled or determined to be futile, they ejected from there, preferring to forget the entire affair as a bad dream.

And so it appears that the protests against human rights

violations under the Amin regime were for the camera; anger towards the despotic leader was a farce. Under international law, any nation, including Saudi Arabia, had the right to prosecute Amin, but none did, prompting the frustrated special counsel for prosecutions at the Human Rights Watch, Reed Brody, to famously remark, 'If you kill one person, you go to jail; if you kill 20, you go to an institution for the insane; if you kill 20,000, you get political asylum.'

Amin never returned to Uganda to answer for his crimes. Uncharacteristic of him, he kept a low profile during his exile in Jeddah. But low profile didn't necessarily mean low key. Until his death, Amin lived a lavish life in a spacious villa with cars, drivers, cooks, maids and a handsome monthly allowance. Many of his children went to universities in the UK and US. Having exchanged his military uniform for a modest white Arab robe, he spent his days in the local club, getting massages, watching television and eating his favourite foods.

Afterword

Cut to the present day, the world continues to have its share of dictatorships. From enduring ones like those in North Korea, China, Russia and Belarus to relatively volatile ones like the military rules in several African nations and, more recently, Myanmar. However, dictatorship has steadily shed its twentieth century garb, opting for a more ordinary avatar. So there exist today, several more nations (some sources indicate as many as 50) that are ruled with iron fists and reduced freedoms. These might not be textbook dictatorships but are sure to get there if left unchecked.

While their predecessors revelled in their larger-than-life personas, harboured world-altering ambitions and used violence—no-holds-barred—most modern-day dictators choose to be the proverbial wolves in sheep's clothing, hiding their agendas behind seemingly democratic language. They are suave politicians who employ image consultants to 'look right' and and political consultants to 'speak right'. Some pretend to be humble servants of the people, some trash-talk their opponents and the public alike, some schmooze with the wealthy and elite, some cultivate popular support through flattery. Using a mix of consent, deal-making and coercion to gain and remain in power, they introduce one repressive law after the other even as they pander to the masses through hollow promises and fool them into compliance.

The in-your-face tyranny of earlier dictatorships has also

been replaced by subtler forms characterized by consensual surveillance where information about every citizen is digitized in the pretext of improving service efficiency. Realizing the value of fighting a known demon rather than an unknown one, they have also developed better tolerance for dissent, with public endorsements for freedom of speech ensuring that dissenting voices, both offline and in social media, live in an illusion of power even as they are covertly marked as potentially problematic. How these problematic citizens are dealt with, too, is quite different—rather than use of extreme violence or physical torture, modern dictatorships resort to psychological harassment including intimidation, creation of fabricated charges and deployment of financial investigative agencies to launch legitimate but politically motivated cases against them.

Digital media has broadened the scope of not only vendetta but also propaganda, with information rather than terror being deployed to reshape beliefs. While artificial intelligence is used to generate deep fakes to discredit rivals or rewrite history, algorithmic manipulation ensures that only certain kinds of news and information reach the masses. Meanwhile, content bombardment overwhelms a gullible public into believing in half-truths and falsities alike, and political alignment with influencers contributes to the blurring of lines between news and opinion. What's more, modern-day dictators need only to subtly instigate followers against particular social media posts for the posters to find themselves being diligently trolled and cancelled into retraction and resignation.

Which brings me back to the question I raised in the introduction—why do citizens allow oppressive rulers to come into power? While it may be tempting to place the blame squarely on the needy masses, I am prepared to risk pointing fingers at the classes. If recent elections in several key nations are anything to go by, it was the latter—a mix of business people and the intelligentsia, including professionals, journalists, writers, artists, academics, lawyers, teachers and professors—that got swayed by the intelligent-sounding rhetoric of those who eventually got elected. Although a minority in terms of numbers, these are the people who wield the power of money, knowledge and language to influence election outcomes. However they have constantly failed the masses in most countries. The intelligentsia, in particular, have shown no commitment to act on the words that spill from their mouths, despite being responsible, in different ways, to safeguard the ethics of political discourse. In many cases, they have been inhabiting cocoons, shielding themselves from grassroot realities, only to be jerked out of their intellectual stupor when the unexpected happens.

In his essay 'The Intelligentsia in the Age of Trump', German-Australian philosopher and writer Raimond Gaita bemoans the shocking ignorance and indifference of the intelligentsia when it comes to their obligation toward truth and truthfulness. That it was written in 2017 when Donald Trump was first elected to the White House reiterates the political inertia of the so-called intellectuals—they obviously repeated their folly to ensure him a second term last year. Although Gaita's essay focuses on Trump, the pertinence of his discourse to quasi-democracies worldwide, should ideally not be lost on an intelligent reader. Perhaps it is time for some soul-searching and to step out of safe spaces to confront the dire and dangerous political realities that confront us. Else, there will come a day when, as Guatemalan poet Otto René Castillo describes '...the apolitical intellectuals / of my country / will be interrogated / by the simplest of our people. They will be asked / about what they did / when their fatherland / was being slowly extinguished / like a sweet fire, / small and alone.'

Bibliography

Stalin

Davies, S.R., Popular Opinion in Stalin's Russia: Terror, Propaganda and Dissent, 1934–1941, Cambridge University Press, UK, 1997.

Deutcher, I., Stalin: A Political Biography, Penguin, Harmondsworth, 1949.

Đilas, Milovan, Conversations with Stalin, Harcourt Brace Jovanovich, New York, 1962.

Khlevniuk, O.V. and Nora Seligman Favorov, Stalin: New Biography of a Dictator, Yale University Press, 2016.

Montefiore, Simon Sebag, Young Stalin, Weidenfeld & Nicolson, 2020.

Pisch, A., The Personality Cult of Stalin in Soviet Posters, 1929–1953: Archetypes, Inventions and Fabrications, Anu Press, 2016.

Rappaport, H., Josef Stalin: A Biographical Companion, Abc-Clio, 1999.

Souvarine, B, Stalin: A Critical Survey of Bolshevism, C.L.R. James (trans.), Longmans, Green & Co., 1939.

Stalin, J.V., Works, 1, Foreign Languages Publishing House, Moscow, 1954.

Stalin, J.V., Works, 2, Foreign Languages Publishing House, Moscow, 1954.

Suny, R.G., Stalin: Passage to Revolution, Princeton University Press, UK, 2020.

Tse-tung, M., Selected Works of Mao Tse-tung: Volume 7, Marxists.org, 2014, https://tinyurl.com/prux49xn. *Accessed on 5 December 2025.*

Zenkovsky, S.A., 'The Emancipation of the Serfs in Retrospect', The Russian Review, Vol. 20, No. 4, 1961, pp. 280–293.

Hitler

Arendt, H., 'Ideology and Terror: A Novel Form of Government', The Review of Politics, Vol. 15, No. 3, 1953, pp. 303–327.

Bouverie, T. Appeasing Hitler: Chamberlain, Churchill and the Road to War, Random House, UK, 2019.

Hitler, A. and J. Murphy, Mein Kampf, Hurst and Blackett, 1925, 1942.

Hitler, A. and W. Maser, Hitler's Letters and Notes, Bantam Books, US, 1976.

Hitler, A., M. Bormann and F. Genoud, The Testament of Adolf Hitler: The Hitler-Bormann Documents, February-April 1945, 2nd ed., Cassell, London, 1961.

Jewish Virtual Library, https://tinyurl.com/4hx5bn3t. *Accessed on 5 December 2025.*

Katz, J. 'On Jewish social history: Epochal and supra-epochal Historiography', Jewish History, Vol. 7, No. 1, 1993, pp. 89–97.

Kershaw, I., The 'Hitler Myth': Image and Reality in the Third Reich, Clarendon Press, UK, 2001.

Kubizek, A. and G. Brooks, The Young Hitler I Knew: The Memoirs of Hitler's Childhood Friend, Frontline, 2011.

Sweeney, K.P., 'We Will Never Speak of It: Evidence of Hitler's Direct Responsibility for the Premeditation and Implementation of the Nazi Final Solution', Constructing the Past, Vol. 13, No. 1, 2012, p. 7, https://tinyurl.com/5fp9zym8. Accessed on 5 December 2025.

TIME, 'Adolf Hitler: Man of the Year', 2 January 1938, TIME, https://tinyurl.com/msta5776. Accessed on 5 December 2025.

Weikart, R. 'The Role of Darwinism in Nazi Racial Thought', German Studies Review, Vol. 36, No. 3, 2013, pp. 537–556.

Khomeini

'Ayatollah Ruhollah Khomeini, Address to the nation, April 1, 1979', National Security Archive, https://tinyurl.com/3kwr8jxj. *Accessed on 5 December 2025.*

Fazlhashemi, M., 'Imāmiyya Shī'a (The Twelvers)', Handbook of Islamic Sects and Movements, M.A. Upal and C.M. Cusack (eds.), Brill, pp. 181–202, 2021.

Ibrahimn, Y.M., 'INSIDE IRAN'S CULTURAL REVOLUTION' [Review of INSIDE IRAN'S CULTURAL REVOLUTION], The New York Times, 14 October 1979, p. 9, https://tinyurl.com/mra4u867. *Accessed on 5 December 2025.*

Jahanpour, F., 'Iran after Khomeini', The World Today, Vol. 45, No. 8/9, 1989, pp. 150–153.

McQuaid, T., Sacred Dictators: A Wholly Unholy Relationship between Dictatorships and Religious Leaders, Theses and Dissertations, University of New Orleans, 2018, https://tinyurl.com/2z2n3f6p. *Accessed on 5 December 2025.*

Sadjadpour, K., Reading Khamenei: The World View of Iran's Most Powerful Leader, Carnegie Endowment for International Peace, USA, 2009.

Satrapi, M., Persepolis, Vintage Books, UK, 2008.

Shevlin, N., 'Velayat-E Faqih in the Constitution of Iran' [Review of Velayat-E Faqih in the Constitution of Iran], JOURNAL of CONSTITUTIONAL LAW, Vol. 1, No. 2, 1998, pp. 358–382.

Soltanzadeh, M. and M.R. Othman, 'The Iran-Iraq war and the role of Ayatollah Khomeini', SEJARAH: Journal of the Department of History, Vol. 22, 2 December 2013.

Vaez, H., 'Post-Revolutionary Politics in Iran: Continuity and Change' [Review Article], British Journal of Middle Eastern Studies, Vol. 31, No. 2, November 2004, pp. 235–241.

Duvalier

'DUVALIER TAKES LIFE PRESIDENCY; Haitian Leader Tells Crowd He Is an Exceptional Man—Army Men Renew Oath', The New York Times, 2 April 1964, https://tinyurl.com/j2y9w3hu. *Accessed on 5 December 2025.*

Belleau, J.P., 'The Stranger-King of the Caribbean: François Duvalier,

State Politics, and the Othering of Brutality', The Journal of Latin American and Caribbean Anthropology, Vol. 24, No. 4, 2019, pp. 935-957.

Charlier-Doucet, R., 'Anthropologie, politique et engagement social: L'expérience du Bureau d'ethnologie d'Haïti', Gradhiva: Revue d'anthropologie et d'histoire des arts, Vol. 1, 2005, pp. 109–125.

Chochotte, M., The History of Peasants, Tonton Makouts, and the Rise and Fall of the Duvalier Dictatorship in Haiti, Doctoral Dissertation, University of Michigan, 2017.

Drumhiller, N.K. and C. Skvorc, 'A Psychological and Political Analysis of a 20th Century "Doctator": Dr. François Duvalier, President-for-Life of Haiti', Global Security & Intelligence Studies, Vol. 3, No. 1, 2018.

Fabien, J. 'Le Poids Du «Macoutisme» Dans Les Conflits Armés Et Violences Collectives À Cité Soleil/The Weight Of "Macoutism" In Armed Conflicts And Collective Violence In Cité Soleil', 2021, https://tinyurl.com/mvuxv632. *Accessed on 5 December 2025.*

Ferguson, J., Papa Doc, Baby Doc: Haiti and the Duvaliers, B. Blackwell, UK, 1987.

Greene, G., The Comedians, Random House, UK, 2010.

Henley, J., 'Haiti: a long descent to hell', The Guardian, 14 January 2010, https://tinyurl.com/3z7htcv6. *Accessed on 5 December 2025.*

Lundahl, M., 'Papa Doc: Innovator in the Predatory State', POLITICS OR MARKETS? Essays on Haitian Underdevelopment, Routledge, 1992, pp. 255–289.

Remy, A., 'The Duvalier Phenomenon', Caribbean Studies, Vol. 14, No. 2, 1974. pp. 38–65.

TIME, 'Haiti: A Warning to Renegades', *TIME*, 27 November 1964, https://tinyurl.com/ynswypkh. Accessed on 5 December 2025.

TIME, 'Haiti: The Birthday Blowout', *TIME*, 28 April 1967, https://tinyurl.com/43a6cbe2. Accessed on 5 December 2025.

Trouillot, Michel-Rolph, Haiti, State against Nation: The Origins and Legacy of Duvalierism, Monthly Review Press, 1990.

Kim Il-sung

Chua-Eoan, H. 'The Last Hard-Liner: Kim Il Sung (1912-1994)', *TIME*, 18 July 1994, https://tinyurl.com/4m84u5u4. Accessed on 5 December 2025.

David-West, A. 'The Literary Ideas of Kim Il Sung and Kim Jong Il: An Introduction to North Korean Meta-Authorial Perspectives', *Cultural Logic: A Journal of Marxist Theory & Practice*, Vol. 16.

Il Sung, Kim, *Reminisces: With the Century 1*, Foreign Languages Publishing House, North Korea, 1992.

Il Sung, Kim, *On Juche in Our Revolution 1*. Foreign Languages Publishing House, North Korea, 1975.

Kristof, N.D., 'Death Doesn't End Rule of Kim Il Sung, "Eternal President"', *The New York Times*, 7 September 1998, https://tinyurl.com/mr2h23ta. Accessed on 5 December 2025.

Kristof, N.D., 'All Nature Mourns Late Leader, North Korea Says', *The New York Times*, 8 July 1999, https://tinyurl.com/ujysvrkt. Accessed on 5 December 2025.

Lee, G., 'The political philosophy of Juche', *Stanford Journal of East Asian Affairs*, Vol. 3, No. 1, 2003, pp. 105–112.

Lutz, T., 'Cult of Personality: North Korea under Kim Il-Sung', Paper 10, *Senior Capstone Theses*, 2015.

Powell, B., 'North Korea's Next Kim: Dad's Favorite, Kim Jong Un', *TIME*, 1 June 2009, https://tinyurl.com/2breh4fu. Accessed on 5 December 2025.

Ramzy, A., 'Kim Jong Il's Life: Myth, Mystery and Mayhem', *TIME*, 19 December 2011, https://tinyurl.com/42wz9nfj. Accessed on 5 December 2025.

Szalontai, B. '"You Have No Political Line of Your Own": Kim Il Sung and the Soviets, 1953-1964', *Cold War International History Project Bulletin*, Vol. 14, No. 15, 2004, pp. 87–103.

TIME Photo and C. Campbell, 'The Despotic Dynasty: A Family Tree of North Korea's Kim Clan', *TIME*, 24 February 2017, https://tinyurl.com/dbpftfs8. Accessed on 5 December 2025.

Foreign Languages Publishing House, *Kim Il Sung: Prodigy of Human Thinking*, 1979, North Korea, https://tinyurl.com/mdpzbwsa. Accessed on 5 December 2025.

Ceausescu

Bandi, I., Ş. Bosomitu, S. Bottoni and L. Jinga, Memory of Nations: Democratic Transition Guide [The Romanian Experience], CEVRO, Czechia, 2017.

Binder, D. () 'The Cult of Ceausescu', The New York Times Magazine, 30 November 1986, p. 32, https://tinyurl.com/2m3jdzeb. *Accessed on 5 December 2025.*

Danta, D., 'Ceausescu's Bucharest', Geographical Review, Vol. 83, No. 2, 1993, pp. 170–182.

Dumbauld, B., 'Spectacular Politics and Everyday Performance: Tracing Music from Ceauşescu's Romania to Multicultural America', Doctoral Dissertation, CUNY Academic Works, 2017, https://tinyurl.com/yc786f4z. *Accessed on 5 December 2025.*

Gorun, H. and I.L. Branescu, 'The Paradox of Nicolae Ceausescu's Foreign Policy and Several Reasons for the Deterioration of the International Image of His', European Scientific Journal, Vol. 14, No. 29, 2018, pp. 75–83.

Kamm, H., 'Cold Days are Back in Rumania'. The New York Times, 4 January 1987, p. 3, https://tinyurl.com/534dfx2k. *Accessed on 5 December 2025.*

Ceauşescu, Nicolae, Nicolae Ceauşescu, Builder of Modern Romania and International Statesman, Pergamon, 1983.

Percival, M., 'Britain's "Political Romance" with Romania in the 1970s', Contemporary European History, Vol. 4, No. 1, 1995, pp. 67–87.

Petrescu, D., Explaining the Romanian Revolution of 1989, Editura Enciclopedică, 2010.

Petkov, P. and M. Simmons, 'Romania 1989: Ceauşescu goes down in blood', The Guardian, 23 December 1989, https://tinyurl.com/ybwvdhpy. Accessed on 5 December 2025.

Volceanov, G., 'The Paradoxes of Romania, n Pop / Rock / Folk in Communist Romania' [Review of The Paradoxes of Romanian Pop / Rock / Folk in Communist Romania], European Academic Research, Vol. 1, No. 5, 2013, pp. 746–754.

Pol Pot

Chandler, D.P., Brother Number One: A Political Biography Of Pol Pot, Taylor & Francis, UK, 2018.

De Vries, M. and M. Weerdesteijn, 'The Life Course of Pol Pot: How his Early Life Influenced the Crimes he Committed', Amsterdam Law Forum, Vol. 10, No. 2, 2018, p. 3.

De Nike, H.J., J. Quigley, K.J. Robinson, H., Jarvis, and N. Cross (eds.), Genocide in Cambodia: Documents from the Trial of Pol Pot and Ieng Sary, University of Pennsylvania Press, 2000.

Democratic Kampuchea is Moving Forward, Department of Press and Information of the Ministry of Foreign Affairs, Cambodia, 1977.

Kamm, H., 'THE AGONY OF CAMBODIA', The New York Times, 19 November 1978, https://tinyurl.com/bdejdj3e. *Accessed on 5 December 2025.*

Kiernan, B., The Pol Pot regime: Race, Power, and Genocide in Cambodia under the Khmer Rouge, 1975-79, Yale University Press, 2008.

Pot, P., [Speech] 'At the banquet given in honour of the delegation of the Communist party of China and the government of the People's Republic of China', Internet Archive, 2014, https://tinyurl.com/yuawzxen. *Accessed on 5 December 2025.*

Roth, H., 'Pseudotransformational Leadership, Leadership Styles, and Emotional Intelligence: A Comparative Case Study of Lon Nol and Pol Pot', Theses and Dissertations, Mississippi State University, https://tinyurl.com/ytm8huem. *Accessed on 5 December 2025.*

Short, P., Pol Pot: The History of a Nightmare, John Murray, 2005.

The Guardian, 'Khmer Rouge take over Cambodia', 18 April 1975, https://tinyurl.com/2968t4ud. *Accessed on 5 December 2025.*

Idi Amin

Amin, J. and M. Akulia, Idi Amin, Hero Or Villain? His Son Jaffar Amin and Other People, Millennium Global Publishers, 2010.

Decker, A.C., In Idi Amin's Shadow: Women, Gender, and Militarism in Uganda, Ohio University Press, Greece, 2014.

Glentworth, G. and I. Hancock, 'Obote and Amin: Change and Continuity in Modern Uganda Politics', African Affairs, Vol. 72, No. 288, 1973, pp. 237–255.

'In Defense of Idi Amin', Umoja Sasa, Vol. 2, No. 3, 1977, pp. 6–10.

Keatley, P., 'Obituary: Idi Amin' [Review of Obituary: Idi Amin], The Guardian, 18 August 2003, https://tinyurl.com/2hctb6xu. *Accessed on 5 December 2025.*

Leopold, M., 'Sex, violence and history in the lives of Idi Amin: Postcolonial masculinity as masquerade', Journal of Postcolonial Writing, Vol. 45, No. 3, 2009, pp. 321–330.

Munnion, C., 'The African who kicked out the Asians, who said Hitler was right, who has made his country a state sinister', The New York Times Archives, 12 November 1972, https://tinyurl.com/yy3hsv76. *Accessed on 5 December 2025.*

Nayenga, P.F.B., 'Myths and Realities of Idi Amin Dada's Uganda', African Studies Review, Vol. 22, No. 2, 1979, pp. 127–138.

Oded, A., 'Israeli-Ugandan Relations in the Time of Idi Amin', Jewish Political Studies Review, Vol. 18, No. 3/4, 2006, pp. 65–79.

Pirouet, M.L., 'Religion in Uganda under Amin', Journal of Religion in Africa, Vol. 11, No. 1, 1980, pp. 13–29.

Short, P., 'Amin's Uganda', Transition, No. 40, 1971, pp. 48–55.

Singh, M., Culture of the Sepulchre: Idi Amin's Monster Regime, Penguin Books Limited, India, 2012.

TIME, 'Amin: The Wild Man of Africa', TIME, 7 March 1977, https://tinyurl.com/y26m9hhd. *Accessed on 5 December 2025.*

Index